Fighting Visibility

STUDIES IN SPORTS MEDIA

Edited by Victoria E. Johnson and Travis Vogan

A list of books in the series appears at the end of this book.

Fighting Visibility

Sports Media and Female Athletes in the UFC

JENNIFER McCLEAREN

UNIVERSITY OF
ILLINOIS PRESS
Urbana, Chicago, and Springfield

Library of Congress Cataloging-in-Publication Data
Names: McClearen, Jennifer, author.
Title: Fighting visibility : sports media and female athletes in the
    UFC / Jennifer McClearen.
Other titles: Sports media and female athletes in the Ultimate
    Fighting Championship
Description: Urbana, Chicago : University of Illinois Press, 2021.
    | Series: Studies in sports media | Includes bibliographical
    references and index.
Identifiers: LCCN 2020037057 (PRINT) | LCCN 2020037058
    (EBOOK) | ISBN 9780252043734 (Cloth : acid-free paper) |
    ISBN 9780252085727 (Paperback : acid-free paper) | ISBN
    9780252052637 (eBook)
Subjects: LCSH: Mass media and sports. | Women in mass media.
    | Mass media and women. | Women martial artists. | Mixed
    martial arts. | UFC (Mixed martial arts event) | Feminism
    and sports. | Discrimination in sports. | Women in popular
    culture—20th century.
Classification: LCC GV742 .M26 2021 (print) | LCC GV742 (ebook) |
    DDC 306.4/83—dc23
LC record available at https://lccn.loc.gov/2020037057
LC ebook record available at https://lccn.loc.gov/2020037058

For Janet Duros McClearen
August 10, 1948–July 27, 2012

Contents

Acknowledgments

Research in the humanities is often stereotyped as an individual pursuit that one toils at alone in cavernous libraries, but that assumption couldn't be further from my experience. I am brimming with gratitude for the wonderful people and institutions that have made this project a collaborative endeavor. It takes a village to raise a book, and my village includes the countless friends, family members, colleagues, and training partners who have supported, encouraged, consoled, challenged, and motivated me the past six years while writing this book and beyond. *Fighting Visibility* is a better book because of each of you.

Thank-you to the Brattleboro School of Budo for opening up the world of martial arts to me and to Megan Featherstone for asking me "why don't you just write about martial arts" at a pivotal point in my academic career. This specific project on the UFC began as a curiosity when some training partners at Ballard Jiu Jitsu first introduced me to the spectacle of mixed-martial arts (MMA). Thank-you to Ballard Jiu Jitsu, Seattle Jiu Jitsu, and Integração Jiu Jitsu Austin for keeping me grounded in my training and in my MMA spectator's education. You've been a constant source of stress relief and fun even as you challenge me to think more critically about martial arts and MMA in particular. I wrote the book's conclusion, "Coda: On Love and Violence," for you and our broader community of martial artists because you have taught me about trust, respect, and consent through something others often mischaracterize as violence.

Many thanks to everyone who contributed to this project while I was at the University of Washington. To Ralina Joseph, LeiLani Nishime, Susan Harewood, Lauren Berliner, and Jennifer Bean, thank you for your guidance and keen feminist eyes when the ideas on these pages first began to materialize. Ralina, you are the type of scholar, teacher, and mentor I aspire to be every day. Thank you for the privilege of being part of your aca-family. Thank you to the Simpson Center for the Humanities, the Peter Clarke and Susan Evans Research Fund, the Janice and William Ames Endowment and the University of Washington Department of Communication for providing research funding for this project. I am also indebted to the faculty and students at the 2014 Annenberg Summer Institute on Difference in Media and Culture (especially Herman Gray and Sarah Banet-Weiser) who planted the seeds for the critical interventions this book would eventually make. Thanks to Sara Ahmed, Larry Gross, Kim Toffoletti, Holly Thorpe, and Jessica Francombe-Web as well as several anonymous reviewers, who each gave crucial feedback on early versions of *Fighting Visibility*. Thank-you to the members of the Communication and Difference Research Group at the University of Washington—Anjuli Vats, Kris Mroczek, Kai Kohlsdorf, Liz Cortez, Tanya Oshi, Victoria Thomas, Ralina Joseph, LeiLani Nishime, Carmen Gonzales, and Andrea Otanez—for making the academy more transparent. To alma khasawnih, Adaurennaya Chidinma Onyewuenyi, Michael Aguirre, Anna Van Windekens, and Andrea Delgado, thank you for sharing your hopes, dreams, and fears with me during our "Bump it Out" writing group. My last year at the University of Washington was my favorite because of your friendship and comradery.

I am grateful for all the people who have helped evolve this project while I have been in the Moody College of Communication at the University of Texas at Austin. Thanks to the faculty and students in the Department of Radio-Television-Film and the Center for Sports Communication and Media for embracing me and my work, among them Mary Beltrán, Mike Butterworth, Kathy Fuller-Seeley, Noah Isenberg, Madhavi Mallapragada, Curran Nault, Alisa Perren, Tom Schatz, Suzanne Scott, Adrien Sebro, Craig Watkins, and Jay Bernhardt. To my brilliant undergraduate and graduate students: thank you for discussing various aspects of this book with me in classes and continually pushing my thinking in new directions. I couldn't ask for a better place to call my aca-home; thank you for making me a part of your village. To Victoria Johnson, Travis Vogan, Daniel Nasset, Samantha Sheppard, Deborah Oliver, Tad Ringo, Laura Portwood-Stacer, and Michelle Martinez: thank you all for stewarding this book at various stages with the enthusiasm and care you each gave it. To Mia Fischer and Evan Brody, thank you for sitting on countless panels with me as I developed this project and for being my favorite conference buddies. Your work energizes me, and it's inspiring to have such generous and smart people in my corner. Thank-you to the Faculty Success Program at the National Center for Faculty Development and Diversity for your support as I wrapped up this project and to the Office of the Vice Provost for Diversity and the Moody College of Communication at UT Austin for funding my participation.

I have been lucky to have excellent research assistants during this project who have made a tremendous impact on the work. Che Capili and Zack Perine, thank you for providing insight and ideas as you transcribed interviews and collected articles. Jeff Luebbe, you have been my numbers guy and my MMA historian throughout this project as well as my friend and training partner. Thank you for your diligent work collecting pay data from the athletic commissions and analyzing it for the appendices. Your insights and skill have been invaluable. Thanks to Sam Miller for sharing your walking encyclopedia of knowledge on the UFC. My favorite research assistants have been the furry ones, Molay and Bodhi McClosmond, who ensure I take regular snuggle breaks.

I'm in enormous debt to Amy Kaplan for letting me use her beautiful photographs inside the book. Also thank you to Willie Petersen and Rose Namajunas for the image that captures the book so well on the front cover.

To the fighters who contributed to this project both through interviews and insights off the record, thank you for your time and bravery. Julie Kedzie, Leslie Smith, and Angela Hill, you are renaissance women whose intelligence and fighting prowess (in the ring and out) continually inspired me as I wrote. Thank you.

To Kate Osmond: you have been my partner in crime and main cheerleader throughout so many adventures, including this one. You moved first to Seattle and then to Austin so I could pursue my dream job. On top of that, you encourage me to reach further and do more, even when it means sacrifice on your end. You've been my main editor and have read countless versions of everything I've ever written. No one has nor ever will read *Fighting Visibility* as often as you have. Your keen eye, knowledge of the UFC, and feminist and cultural studies acumen has been essential to this project. Yes, I probably could have written a book without you, but it would have been nowhere near as good without having you as my critical sounding board. I owe you at least one trip to Las Vegas.

Finally, to Janet Duros McClearen: thank you for being the most influential teacher in all my years of education. Your divine patience and confidence in me never permitted anyone to tell your dyslexic child that she wasn't smart enough. In fact, your calm and composed demeanor would quickly transform to momma bear if anyone tried. I recently reread Madeleine L'Engel's *A Wrinkle in Time*, one of the books you read to me as a child because I didn't learn to read for myself until I was ten. The father of the heroine of that book also told her she was "not dumb." Instead, he said, "Your development has to go at its own pace. It just doesn't happen to be at the usual pace." I remember you repeating this refrain to me over and over again when I became frustrated with schoolwork. "You just have to go at your own pace. Keep trying." Your belief in me eventually instilled in me belief in myself. I went from hating reading and writing to falling in love with it and spending my days immersed in the idea world, just as you did. As my teacher, you allowed me to follow my interests and spend days researching anything that sparked my fancy rather than dictating what I would learn each day. I didn't know it then, but that is precisely why I have chosen the academy as my career home. I spend my days in the idea world researching and teaching the things that compel me. I wholeheartedly believe that without you, I would never have become a scholar. Thank you. I dedicate *Fighting Visibility* in memory of you.

Fighting Visibility

Introduction

Visibility and Difference in the UFC

For nearly twenty years the Ultimate Fighting Championship (UFC) swore it would never include women into its notoriously hypermasculine sports media empire. The fight promotion began in 1993 as a contest to determine which martial artist would rise above the rest in a tournament of elite fighters from various martial disciplines. The spectacle later developed into a global competitive sport that combined once distinct martial arts—including jiu jitsu, karate, kickboxing, judo, and wrestling, among others—into one. The more concisely named mixed-martial arts (MMA) encourages its athletes to be skillful at fighting on the ground with joint locks and chokes, at fighting on the feet with punches, elbows, and kicks, and at wrestling between the feet and the ground to maintain positions of control over one's opponent. The move to include female fighters in MMA's largest promotion in 2013 came as a surprise to fans and pundits alike, since the sport that U.S. Senator John McCain once called "human cockfighting" seemed like an unlikely candidate to join the long-presumed untenable business of women's sports.[1]

Curiously, women's MMA has witnessed an explosion of popularity since the UFC's initial foray into including female athletes, as evidenced by the meteoric rise of Ronda Rousey. Rousey became the UFC's highest paid athlete—male or female—just two years after signing with the promotion. Even after Rousey's stardom waned following her loss to Holly Holm in late 2015, women's MMA has remained a lucrative endeavor for the UFC brand. The three UFC cards on

UFC fighter Ashlee Evans-Smith grappling. Photo by Amy Kaplan.

Fox Sports 1 headlined by women in early 2017 averaged 21 percent higher rat-ings than cards headlined by men (Lole 2017).[2] In June 2017, the UFC celebrated the success of its three women's divisions by adding its fourth weight class in as many years. All the while, the UFC has incorporated diverse female fighters into its brand in sometimes unexpected ways considering its notoriety as a spectacle of masculinity.

This book examines the promotion's inclusion of female fighters across its vast array of digital and legacy media ventures including live fights, the UFC's reality TV show, television specials, Web series, and social media. As the UFC increases its promotion of women across these various channels, the UFC brand becomes a compelling site to interrogate how discourses about women's sports are shifting because the UFC's communication strategies are beginning to signal a long-awaited level of visibility for female athletes in combat sports. Sports-women remain drastically underrepresented and comprise a meager 5 to 10 percent of all sports media coverage (Bruce, Hovden, and Markula 2010), and academics and activists have long suggested increased visibility as a key strategy for ameliorating gender inequality in sports. Many presume more visibility will lead to more girls aspiring to be professional athletes because "if she can see it, she can be it." The embrace of women in the UFC suggests forward momentum for female athletes since they now have greater representation within combat

UFC fighter Ashlee Evans-Smith boxing. Photo by Amy Kaplan.

sports than ever before. What is more, the UFC's promotional strategies initially address what feminist sports media scholars and women's sports fans have eagerly anticipated: more diverse media representations across the spectrum of identities that comprise contemporary sports media.

The incorporation of diverse female fighters is noteworthy within the sports media industry and built on a proliferating trend in media culture: diversify representations to appeal to previously disregarded segments of the media market. Feminist, critical race, queer, and cultural studies scholars have begun to problematize the growing interest in representing diversity across a range of popular media (Warner 2017; Kohnen 2015; Ouellette 2016; Pham 2015; H. Gray 2013b; Beltrán 2010; Himberg 2018; Fischer 2019; Griffin 2016). Following these intellectual genealogies, this book focuses on women in sports media to consider how these diversity trends are beginning to take a specific shape in women's athletics and to what ends. Despite the seemingly progressive nature of the UFC's embrace of female fighters, this book peels back the artifice of representation to critique the exploitative practices that now make the image of the diverse female fighter not just possible but also lucrative for the fight promotion. I examine how UFC uses representations of gendered difference, which intersects with race, ethnicity, sexual identity, and nationality, to grow the brand by leveraging an inexpensive and expendable labor force. I argue that visibility in the UFC can actually be detrimental to female fighters because media exposure offers promises of success, fame, and fortune that it cannot deliver for most athletes within the current structure of the promotion. Instead, the under-fulfilled promises of representation motivate unpaid and underpaid fighter labor that ultimately benefits the UFC to a much greater degree than it does the fighters themselves. All the while, a focus on the inherent cultural value of visibility and difference in the brand detracts from the plight of many of its athletes. While male fighters face similar issues, the UFC's labor practices disproportionately impact female fighters due to structural factors within the promotion and broader gendered ideologies of visibility. *Fighting Visibility* urges scholars, activists, and fans to dig below the surface of the image to ask who benefits from representing sportswomen and who is harmed by sports media labor practices in late capitalism. This book offers a cautionary tale for the future of women's sports by questioning the presumption that visibility is a panacea for gender inequity in sports.

Female Fighters: From Invisible to Visible

The UFC held its first event in 1993 as a tournament to pit various male martial artists against one another in a test of martial disciplines. The promoters arranged the competition around one central question: which martial art and artist would prove superior to all others when facing opponents with a different fighting style?[3] Part of the original vision of UFC 1 (November 11, 1993) included creating a forum for testing fighting prowess and hypermasculine ferocity—a forum that would be hindered by too many rules preventing these men from using everything within their power to win. Thus, the first UFC competition proceeded with very few rules or regulations. MMA has evolved since the UFC's origins in order to establish a safer competition and mainstream sport; but the emphasis on the domination of masculine fighting prowess remained firmly implanted. Women had competed in MMA since the sport began, but it took a cultural shift for the promotion to view women as "marketable" fighters and for the women's divisions to grow to what they are today.

The evolution of women's MMA from obscurity to visibility in the UFC was more than twenty years in the making because the promotion adamantly refused to include female athletes. The UFC cited gendered concerns that its fan base would be reluctant to watch women punch, kick, wrestle, and grapple with one another and that female MMA fighters were categorically unathletic enough to ensure an entertaining spectacle for the fans. Effectively, women were unmarketable to the fan base. The UFC's official stance on women's MMA reflected the overt sexism that many MMA promoters encountered when trying to book and advertise women's fights. Jeff Dudek, a women's MMA promoter, discussed the challenges of sponsoring women's competitions from the early 1990s to the mid-2000s: "I was shocked by the resistance I got. People called [women's MMA] a gimmick or a freak show or said it would be boring because women were fighting. Venues wouldn't book us. . . . Out of 10 phone calls, I'd get two to consider it and the other eight would hang up on me" (quoted in Hunt 2012). Sponsors and promoters believed women's fights would not sell; the massive crowd exodus when promoters scheduled women's fights last on a card seemed to prove them right.

The MMA community's assumptions about the lack of interest in female fighters mirrored persistent trends in sports media more broadly. For example, women's sports received only 1.3 percent of the coverage on ESPN's SportsCenter in 2009 (Cooky, Messner, and Hextrum 2013) and 3.6 percent of *ESPN Magazine* covers (Cooky and Lavoi 2012) and the research shows little improvement over time (Cooky, Messner, and Hextrum 2013; Cooky, Messner, and Musto 2015). Much of the underrepresentation of female athletes in sports media has stemmed from long-standing notions about who watches sports (i.e., men) and what representations those demographics prefer to see (i.e., women as objects of desire instead of powerful athletes) (Cooky and Lavoi 2012; Cooky, Messner, and Hextrum 2013). These beliefs joined the all too prevalent refrain that women's sporting bodies are not as interesting to watch as men's. The enduring myths about women's lack of athleticism has ensured that the intertwined businesses of sports leagues, television networks, sponsors, and advertising agencies have largely neglected women's sports.

Although other organizations in the United States dabbled in promoting women's fights, Jeff Osborne's promotion, Hook-n-Shoot, has been recognized as one of the first serious attempts at promoting women's MMA in the States in the early 2000s (Green and Svinth 2010). Osborne was a UFC commentator and former professional wrestler who first sponsored a women's fight in 2001. Loretta Hunt (2012) of *Sports Illustrated* notes that later that year Osborne noticed his wife and daughter watching a DVD copy of a Japanese all-women's promotion called Remix.[4] The Japanese promotion fascinated U.S.-based Osborne because his five-year-old daughter showed interest in watching women fight. He realized that powerful female fighters could be role models for his young daughter. Osborne began planning the first U.S. card to consist of only women, calling it Revolution. He faced numerous obstacles promoting the card because sponsors believed no one would watch an event exclusively featuring women. The stigma against women's fighting proved strong. Revolution received only local NBC and Fox affiliate attention, and Hook-n-Shoot ended up losing $8,800 on the event. Despite the financial flop, Osborne said, "Sometimes it's better to make history than money. This was that kind of show. It's one of my greatest achievements" (quoted in Hunt 2012).

Tides began to turn in the late 2000s, when promotions like Fatal Femme produced women's cards and EliteXC and Bellator MMA featured women alongside men's bouts. (Hunt 2012). EliteXC aired the first women's fight on a major cable television network in 2007, when Gina Carano defeated Julie Kedzie on Showtime. Carano became the "face of women's MMA" for several years, when the impressive fighter and attractive fitness model sustained a successful fighting record and posed for magazines like *Maxim* ("Dana White" 2017). Carano's success in striking the balance of athleticism and attractiveness speaks to the beauty imperative that so many sportswomen face (Kane and Maxwell 2011; Kane 1988). As a result, promoters began to realize that the objectification of pretty female fighters was a potential marketing tactic for women's MMA (Weaving 2014, 2015; Jennings 2014).

The emphasis on Carano's attractiveness and femininity proved to MMA promotions that there was at least one way to market female fighters: by focusing on their appeal to a male gaze. This meant that the visibility of White, able-bodied, traditionally feminine, and attractive sportswomen could be profitable.[5] At the same time, nonnormative femininities, sexualities, abilities, races, ethnicities, and other differences continued to be more invisible in sports. Consider, for example, the most famous women's MMA fight prior to the inclusion of women in the UFC: Carano vs. Cyborg (August 15, 2009). During the height of her popularity in MMA, Carano fought Cris "Cyborg" Justino for the Strikeforce women's featherweight championship title. The fight was significant for a few reasons. First, it was the first time a major television network featured a women's bout as the headlining event. The Showtime fight between Carano and Justino inaugurated the Strikeforce women's featherweight championship. Second, the press leading up to the event proved that women's MMA had an uphill battle. Strikeforce billed the fight as "beauty versus the beast," referencing Carano's good looks and Justino's more "masculine" appearance. Justino knocked Carano out in the first round of the fight, which led to questions about her gender identity and steroid use. Evidently, to be the "face of women's MMA," female fighters had to conform to narrowly defined feminine ideals.

Carano left MMA and went on to star in action films like *Haywire* (2011), *The Fast and the Furious 6* (2013), and *Deadpool* (2016) while Justino has had an impressive MMA career despite continuing to be demonized by MMA fans and by prominent UFC personalities for her physical appearance (A. Dawson 2019).

Cris "Cyborg" Justino. Photo by Amy Kaplan.

For example, consider the unequal treatment of Justino's steroid infraction compared to her male counterparts. Justino tested positive for steroid use in 2011 and for an unidentified banned substance in 2016. The former resulted in a one-year suspension from MMA. The latter was simply a failure on her part to submit the proper paperwork and was later reconciled without a suspension. The U.S. Anti-Doping Agency (USADA) randomly tested Justino eleven times in 2016 and thirteen times in 2017 and all of them came back clean (Botter 2017). While other male MMA fighters have tested positive for steroids (including Vitor Belfort, Chael Sonnen, Alistair Overeem, Nate Marquardt, and Anderson Silva), perhaps no other UFC athlete has been more scrutinized for a steroid infraction than Justino (Kurchak 2016). Fans and pundits on social media frequently argue that Justino's muscular appearance and dominant fight record must benefit from steroids. While she has clearly transgressed, the penalty in the court of public opinion has been greater for her than her male counterparts because of her appearance and dominance in the ring. Justino's treatment in MMA media shows us that discourses of women's athleticism and appearance also limit their power to an acceptable range that must be mitigated through conventional notions of femininity.

The pretty and powerful imperative for female athletes was undoubtedly a factor in the UFC's later decision to include women as a "six-month experiment" that built a division around Ronda Rousey. That imperative meant that untalented pretty women weren't marketable and neither were unattractive talented women; instead, sportswomen had to fulfill both sides of the equation to be visible in sports media (Bruce 2016). When Rousey entered MMA, promoters took notice because she was a striking and charismatic fighter at the top of her game. In 2011, Rousey made an impressive debut in Strikeforce and went on to beat Miesha Tate for the women's bantamweight championship title in 2012. The UFC's president Dana White famously changed his mind about including women in the UFC after emphatically stating that women would "never" be in the UFC in 2011 ("Dana White" 2011). He describes his decision to give women's MMA a chance based on Rousey's impressive rise:

> [Rousey] has the whole package . . . I've never been interested in women's MMA. First there weren't enough girls to create an entire women's division. When I talk about a superstar or standout, people talk about Gina Carano and talk about all these others. I'm telling you: this girl, she's nasty. She might be beautiful on the outside, she's a Diaz brother on the inside. She's a real fighter and she's very talented. She has the credentials, the pedigree, everything. And she has the 'it' factor. I think she's going to be a big superstar. (Quoted in Gordon 2012)

Notice White's insistence that the "whole package" included being "beautiful on the outside" and a tenacious and confrontational fighter like UFC fighters and brothers Nick and Nate Diaz on the inside. Rousey's decisive win record certainly propelled White's decision. When she signed to the UFC, Rousey had

Rousey vs. Carmouche at UFC 157. UFC Fight Pass.

Rousey's armbar submission win at UFC 157. UFC Fight Pass.

accumulated six professional MMA wins and zero losses, with five of her victories coming from an arm-bar submission within the first minute of the fight—a virtually unprecedented form of dominance in the sport. For women's MMA to take off, Rousey shouldered the burden through her spectacular fighting prowess and charismatic star power.

Dana White has stated on numerous occasions that Rousey single handedly changed his mind about promoting female fighters in the first place and has since recanted his original stance that female athletes could not draw audiences (Rousey and Ortiz 2015; Martin 2015a). The White, blond, charismatic, and conventionally attractive Rousey became a *Sports Illustrated Swimsuit Issue* cover model and was MMA's most visible star through 2015, to the surprise of the UFC and many of its fans. Rousey's superstardom has extended beyond MMA to include movie roles in *The Fast and the Furious 7* (2015), *Entourage* (2015), and *The Expendables 3* (2014) and a stint in the professional wrestling promotion WWE (World Wrestling Entertainment). Her dominant record early on, her movie-star good looks, and her charisma certainly went a long way in propelling the women's divisions in the UFC. Rousey's ability to fit into the marketable mold of femininity, attractiveness, and physical power fueled the growth of women's MMA and the popularity of the UFC.

Despite the popular rhetoric that Rousey was the lone athlete to propel women forward in the UFC, Chimamanda Ngozi Adichie (2009) asserts that there's a "danger in the single story" or in focusing on one narrative to the detriment of all others. In the more than thirty-five years of research on women in sports media, the themes of sexualization, objectification, invisibility, under-representation, and ambivalence have each featured prominently in the books and articles published about women in sports media indicating that market-ability is often reliant on narrow formulas for female athletes (Antunovic and Whiteside 2018; Toffoletti 2016; Bruce 2016). These critiques maintain their relevance, but at the same time the image of the sportswoman is becoming much more complex and contradictory (Heywood 2018; Thorpe, Toffoletti, and Bruce 2017) and cannot be read as unilaterally invisible or unfairly represented; rather, representations of women in sports media circulate within numerous hierarchies and contours. Sports leagues and sponsors are beginning to real-ize that their audience is no longer confined to the demographic of a straight, White male, age eighteen to thirty-four. For example, various teams have be-gun marketing to gay and lesbian fan groups by featuring "pride nights" and selling rainbow merchandise at official team stores, including teams in the NBA, WNBA, NWSL, MLS, and MLB (Ennis 2019a; Macur 2014; Ennis 2019b; Buzinski 2018).[6] In March 2019, the Golden State Warriors NBA team, along with their sponsor Chase Bank, celebrated Women's Empowerment Month by featuring various female athletes and women leaders during games, sponsor-ing an all-girls basketball camp, and showing short films celebrating women in the community, including WNBA star Breanna Stewart (Golden State War-riors 2019). Sports leagues and their sponsors are expanding their conception of sports fans from a mass audience to a kaleidoscope of niche identities who may gravitate to a range of different representations of athletes (Johnson 2016; Osborne and Coombs 2015; Toffoletti 2017). The adage that sports media only ever markets to the straight male gaze is a totalizing assessment of the media landscape that instead requires more nuanced analysis.

While Rousey's story of conventional attractiveness and athleticism selling a women's sport had been told before, another story stemming from that no-torious night in 2013 when women's MMA exploded fascinates me. The *Other* woman in the first women's UFC fight is perhaps the more intriguing story. The UFC signed Rousey to the promotion first, but they carefully selected Liz Carmouche to face her at UFC 157 (February 23, 2013). Carmouche won this honor by galvanizing her Twitter and Facebook followers to inundate the UFC with requests to book her for the first women's fight. Carmouche affectionately calls her fans the "lizbos"—a combination of the words "Liz" and the colloquial "lezbos" to signal her out-lesbian identity and her virtual relationship with a dedicated group of fans. Carmouche's labor making herself visible online paid off, because the UFC took notice of the buzz around the talented fighter with a compelling story and selected her as Rousey's first opponent. The UFC's

Liz Carmouche on Larry King. YouTube, Larry King, UFC President Dana White and fighter Liz Carmouche.

promotional machine went to work narrating Carmouche as a former marine who had been closeted during the "don't ask, don't tell" period (1993–2011) that prevented visible queer identities in the U.S. military. Dana White even asserted that the UFC was reaching out to LGBTQ groups to promote her as its first openly queer fighter. Even though Carmouche never received as much fanfare as Rousey, the out lesbian and former U.S. marine became the first female fighter to set foot in the Octagon, crash through the UFC's glass ceiling, and signal a moment when branded difference became a marketing strategy to promote women in the sport.[7]

Carmouche's selection for the first women's UFC fight highlights a moment in media culture when difference of all varieties has gained new exposure in legacy and new media. At the same time, Carmouche's engagement with her fans via social media demonstrates how an ever-expanding array of media platforms circulates diverse content at rapid rates. These two features of modern society—a highly networked system of media content and the increasing visibility of difference—have not occurred in a vacuum. Users now have a greater ability to locate and consume content that reflects their individual identities through the proliferation of digital technologies even if broader society marginalizes those identities (like Carmouche's lizbos). Likewise, sports media brands such as the UFC, and media industries writ large, have begun to make difference more visible on multiple platforms in order to appeal to the ever-diversifying demographics of the United States as well as global audiences. Images of diverse fighters in the UFC now travel at astonishing rates in the cavernous world of the global UFC mediasphere. Media technologies ensure that brands can produce a plethora of media content with relative ease and draw upon a culture of digital media participation, or "participatory culture," to share that content on a global scale. The ability of Carmouche or the UFC to use numerous social media and digital platforms to market her to niche audiences is important to how we theorize women's visibility in sports. Diverse female fighters have indeed become marketable, but it's not exclusively because they can fulfill the pretty and powerful imperative.

The UFC's six-month experiment in promoting women's fights was a gamble that paid off for the promotion. During an interview on the podcast *The Fight Life*, Dana White said he agreed "100%" that women's MMA had become as popular if not more popular than men's MMA.

> It's tough to find a sport where the women are financially taken care of the way that the men are and that's definitely the case here. In this business, it's all about who's the attraction, who sells pay-per-views, and who puts bodies in the arena. . . . One of these things that happens in sports like the WNBA or women's golf—"they hit from shorter tees"—or "they don't hit as hard at tennis," and all this stuff. Nobody says that about fights! Fights are fights, man. And when you have two women who are technically sound, and they're putting on an absolute war, it's fun . . . these girls who fight in the UFC would murder 90 percent of the men walking around in the streets. ("Dana White on Conor McGregor" 2016)

White identifies the ways that the UFC has radically changed its view on women's MMA since 2013. The promotion no longer assumes that women's fights cannot sell pay-per-views or that female fighters cannot put on an impressive show. Instead, women now have unparalleled visibility in combat sports because they have proven themselves marketable.

Visibility: Politics vs. Economies

This book considers the cultural and industry forces that now make diverse female athletes marketable in the UFC. These forces are redefining representational practices into neoliberal labor models and it is critical to determine how these practices impact sportswomen becoming more visible. This requires a shift in the typical conversations we have about visibility in women's sports. I decentralize the well-documented representational issues facing female athletes not to suggest that the UFC is beyond this type of criticism, that this valuable scholarship is suddenly irrelevant, or that we should now ignore the sexist history of the sport. These critiques are prevalent in feminist scholarship on sports because female athletes are disproportionately invisible and ignored in the sporting world compared to their male counterparts. Instead, I background these documented trends around visibility in women's sports because they originate from a paradigm that can no longer fully explain the representation of women in sports media.

The dominant paradigm researching women in sports media has focused on female athletes as invisible or represented in problematic ways, or what media studies scholars call the politics of visibility. This refers to how we, as scholars, activists, fans, and journalists, typically use our work to advocate for more visibility and more diverse representations of sportswomen because we view these politics as important for increasing women's rights in society writ large. Since the civil rights and women's movements of the 1960s and '70s, much academic and popular attention has focused on the politics of visibility as a means of political engagement and societal change. In the politics of visibility paradigm, who is seen, who is not, and how they are represented are all wrapped up in broader cultural and political structures (Hall 1997). This paradigm assumes that identities that are visible have a degree of power through media and society whereas those invisible remain disenfranchised and lack opportunity. As a result, in sports media we demand that female athletes are visible and represented in ways that celebrate women as serious and compelling athletes because they deserve the political power that comes through visibility. We echo MMA promoter Jeff Osborne's statement that "it's more important to make history than money." This paradigm is not irrelevant, but it cannot completely account for the logics used to market women in sports. What happens when making history leads to making millions of dollars for promoters? We are now witnessing a cultural moment when gender and other differences are visible *and* profitable across a whole host of digital and legacy media platforms causing a reconfiguration of what visibility means and can do for female athletes.

This book backgrounds the politics of visibility common in writing on women's sports in order to map the contours of other logics around the visibility of female athletes. I instead urge us to consider how neoliberal ideologies are now elevating the visibility of female athletes and to what ends. Contemporary media and brand cultures now incorporate diverse identities into what Sarah Banet-Wesier (2018; 2015) theorizes as "economies of visibility." Economies of visibility describe a moment in twenty-first-century media that is witnessing a surging recognition of gender, race, and other identity categories through representational practices and neoliberal market logics. Banet-Weiser (2015) argues "economies of visibility do not describe a political process, but rather assume that visibility itself has been absorbed into the economy" (55). In other words, visibility is now a brand logic that interpolates consumers instead of a political practice seeking to rectify social injustice. Herman Gray (2013b) asserts further that the politics of visibility may have reached a limit in terms of what it can offer for social change. He says "culturally, in this conjuncture, struggles for media representation, visibility, and recognition no longer index collective histories and political struggles but the triumph of the market where difference affirms the celebration of diversity as lifestyle politics, market choice, and the promise of individual freedom to maximize market options" (771). In other words, media culture has traded identity politics, complete with collective histories and struggles for equity, for economies of visibility that assume that the mere presence of difference in the media is the end goal. We as a society tend to believe that the ability to see women in sports media heralds revolutionary social change without adequately considering the consequences of that change.

This shift from the politics to the economies of visibility begs a critical question for women's sports: how do these market logics impact female athletes now and how might they shift women's sports in the future? In order to begin answering these questions, I focus on representations of female fighters in the UFC to what can sometimes be considered "meaningful" and other times "plastic" (both discussed in the next section). As Heywood and Dworkin (2003) suggest, "while mainstream images of the female athlete can function in multiple ways, both positive and negative, some academic discourse tends to negate the positive role that cultural images can play in daily life" (5). I focus on what the UFC is doing "right" in terms of representing women in order to investigate who the meaningful or "positive" visibility of female athletes in the UFC benefits and what remains enshrouded when shining a light on diverse female athletes. Admittedly, it's important to be clear that male fighters still vastly outnumber female fighters in the UFC, so the promotion is still a long way from producing demographic parity. Given the current trajectory of the UFC, even if it represents women meaningfully and steadily increases the number of women in MMA, the structural inequalities might actually increase.

The long push for increasing the presence of sportswomen in the media has worked under a politics of visibility model, that is, one that connected the representation of marginalized identities in media to the struggles against sexism, racism, and homophobia. Yet, much of media culture no longer understands visibility as an entry point into these broader discussions of difference and power but rather an endpoint that "look[s] to representational parity as the most salient benchmark of diversity in the entertainment business" (Gray 2016, 242). The UFC depicts the presence of female athletes on screen as revolutionary because they are visible and often marketed in ways that resonate with women and girls. However, I examine how this celebratory discourse attributes inequalities to other factors by focusing on individual fighters' shortcomings, or hides them from view amidst the celebration of "breaking barriers." Instead of asking "are women present in the UFC" or "are these representations fair," I take a cue from Donna Haraway (1997) to ask "How is visibility possible? For whom, by whom, and of whom? What remains invisible, to whom, and why?" (202).

Branded Difference

I use "branded difference" to describe the marketing and branding strategies the UFC utilizes to make diverse fighters shine in the promotion. I further theorize the term as a discourse that presumes that the visibility of difference (including gender, race, sexuality, ethnicity, and nationality) in the UFC will lead to success in the ring and a stable livelihood. This presumption inspires fighters to work for the promotion even though there is limited return on the literal blood, sweat, and tears that visibility requires while the UFC remains the primary benefactor of that labor. At the same time, branded difference celebrates the presence and meaningful representation of diverse female fighters in the promotion while serving as a distraction that deflects attention from the ways visibility can hurt those same fighters. As a result, the exposure that branded difference in the UFC facilitates is a culturally and economically problematic brand strategy rather than a unilateral victory for women.

The definition of difference in the UFC brand demonstrates the ways the promotion's branding strategies divert attention from labor inequalities. To explain this, I must first discuss the tension between a politicized meaning of difference concerned with equity and a popular understanding of the term that concentrates on individualized differences between people. I ground the word "difference" in critical race and feminist scholarship and use it to signify how gender, race, sexual, and other minoritized identities are representationally fraught and face structural barriers to equity in society (Joseph 2017). This means that particular discourses about gender, race, sexuality, and other identities impact the experiences of fighters in different ways. Consider the following example that represents a composite of fighters working in the UFC and whose individual stories I discuss. A straight White male fighter grew up having his sporting interests supported by friends and family, and MMA promotions sought him out as a fighter because he is a formula that has sold before. The sport was created for men just like him, which makes his job easier and the pay for his labor higher. In contrast, a queer Black female fighter was never encouraged to pursue martial arts by friends or family, she has never seen a Black woman in her MMA gym, and she was barred from even competing in the most prestigious MMA promotion prior to 2013 because they were uninterested in women's fights. Now that she is signed to the promotion, they are unsure how to market her to fans because they have never had a queer Black woman become a successful fighter before. Even if the promotion decides that there is a market of fans to be created for her, they must figure out a formula that will work. In the meantime, she is paid less than her male counterpart because he is already considered marketable and she must prove herself equal. A definition of difference concerned with identity, power, and privilege can locate the layers operating in discourses of gender, race, and other differences that impact female fighter all at once—a concept that Kimberlé Crenshaw (1991) coined as "intersectionality." This definition of difference assesses how multiple structures in sports, ranging from experience as a child in sports, to life at the gym, to marketability, to the pretty imperative, to fighter pay, to fan support all tend to privilege the straight White male fighter over the queer Black female fighter and explain the disparities she faces in doing her job.

In contrast to a critical race and feminist understanding of difference, the UFC's brand identity depicts *all* fighters as possessing some form of difference. This definition equates the queer Black female fighter's experience of "being different" with the straight White man's. In this logic, he is different because he is dyslexic and struggled in school, while she is different because her gender, race, and sexuality are uncommon in the promotion. Both fighters' differences are recognized and understood as creating challenges in life, which makes them seem inclusive on the surface. By the same token, the UFC maintains that everyone experiences adversity and setbacks, which equalizes the experiences of both athletes. Many of the narratives the UFC weaves appear progressive at face value because they focus on the trials and tribulations located in a superficial definition of difference—that is, everyone possesses difference in some way—and a limited understanding of social and economic hurdles facing particular groups of people. Just because two fighters have encountered adversity in life, it does not mean that their careers as fighters are impacted in the same way. In this logic of difference, everyone receives equal treatment, while unequal pay is simply tied to differences in marketability or personal drive on the part of the fighter. The "we are all different"—or "we are all fighters" as discussed in chapter 1—definition of diversity is written into the very fabric of the UFC brand and circulates across its many media platforms in brand culture.

Branded difference finds kindred spirits in Mary Beltrán's articulation of "meaningful diversity" and Kristen Warner's concept of "plastic representation." Beltrán (2010) describes "meaningful diversity" as a media text that includes fully realized minoritized characters, writers who are knowledgeable of perspectives of nonwhite characters, and diversity as naturally occurring in the setting of the show instead of tokenized. Applying these criteria to the representation of gender, race, and sexuality in the UFC could yield an argument that the promotion's branding of difference often progresses meaningful diversity because it creates representations of diverse female fighters that shows them as fully realized women, presents them as possessing a range of ethnic, racial, national, and sexual identities, and shows them as natural members of the UFC rather than tokens. That said, because the UFC is inconsistent with its marketing and branding of diverse female fighters, scholars and MMA pundits often critique the promotion's focus on emphasized femininity—a passive, attractive, White femininity that contrasts an active, dominating, and muscular White masculinity—to market its sportswomen without also considering the moments when the UFC presents female athletes in meaningful ways.[8]

Kristen Warner (2017) questions the neoliberal impulse to include diverse bodies on screen without providing the depth and nuance that meaningful diversity offers. She uses plasticity as a metaphor to critically examine the present push for a quantifiable number of Black identities in media and the simultaneous assumption that the mere presence of Black actors breeds societal progress. We may see more minoritized identities on our television sets and on the silver screen, but Warner cautions that this representational practice is "a combination of synthetic elements put together and shaped to look like meaningful imagery, but which can only approximate depth and substance because ultimately it is hollow and cannot survive close scrutiny" (35). Her critique lies in the idea that media executives can simply count the number of Black actors on screen without attending to the stories told about Black identities. Warner's analysis extends beyond creating a binary opposition with stereotypes, or "negative" representations, on one side with "positive" representations on the other. Even "positive" images can be plastic if there isn't a sincere attempt to add nuance and depth that stem from real lived experiences of Black people, which can be achieved by a diverse writer's room. Consequently, "plastic representation uses the wonder that comes from seeing characters on screen who serve as visual identifiers for specific demographics in order to flatten the expectation to desire anything more" (35). Warner finds these representations hollow and devoid of substance when they simply measure the presence and absence of Black characters in film and television.

Warner shows how media executives sometimes inorganically plug-and-play Black actors as a means of achieving some sort of assumed parity; while Beltrán imagines how meaningful diversity can take shape in media culture. Following these scholars, I position branded difference as an extension of these ideas that describes the strategic efforts by the UFC to lure audiences and fighters through either meaningful or plastic representations of a variety of identities while masking the inequalities produced when difference glistens in brand culture. To *brand* difference then, means to integrate a "we are all fighters" ethos as part of the promotion's identity and determining certain aspects of difference as sellable. Branded difference could sometimes be plastic and hollow and other times can represent female athletes in meaningful ways because the stories about them sometimes speak truth to women's experiences in the sport and recognize forms of gender discrimination. Chapters 2 and 3, for example, examine how the UFC deploys imagery of women's empowerment and the American Dream tailored for White women and queer women of color. One might conclude that these representations are meaningful because they represent diverse women within the context of the sport and create narratives specifically for them and their identities. However, these representations are also plastic stand-ins for progress for women in sports media because they maintain, erroneously, that female fighters have the same opportunities as male fighters regardless of their difference and fail to consider the labor issues facing all fighters. Because of the logic that presumes if difference is present in media, then equality follows, the celebrations of representation mattering pull attention from less visible inequalities. Thus, this book is concerned not only with plastic or meaningful images of difference, but with the material effect (and affect) of those representations on diverse female athletes in brand culture.

At a basic level, brands sell things in a capitalist economy, but brand culture is a far more intricate marriage of consumerism, identity, meaning, and belonging. Corporations, for example, spend millions of dollars to develop a brand that conveys strategically crafted messages about who they are, what they offer the consumer, and why that consumer should invest in their product or service. Yet, defining branding as just the selling of commodities is reductionist. Brands circulate particular images, ideas, or feelings about themselves in order to acquire the attention of consumers and build memorable associations with that brand—this process isn't simply to persuade consumption but to generate nonmaterial value as well. Jonathan Gray (2010) cautions that scholars are often too quick to judge branding as simply commodification in a capitalistic system instead of also seeing brands as having other purposes and significances. Brands are not only a means for a company or individual to accumulate wealth, but they are also meaningful aspects of people's identities and social and cultural lives (Aronczyk and Powers 2010; Klein 2009; Wernick 1991). Nyimpini Mabunda, a marketing manager at Smirnoff Vodka, says "Consumers define themselves through brands they use. The branded clothes they wear, the cars they drive, the drinks they consume, the university they attended, favorite spots to hang out, and so on" (quoted in Barakat 2014). Brand attachments are the "building blocks" of identity because identity is engrossed in consumerism in the era of late capitalism (Banet-Weiser 2012). A fan's favorite sports team or athlete becomes incorporated into who they are and what symbols they choose to represent their identities. Branding in the late twentieth and early twenty-first century has widened across various sectors of society so that nations now develop highly constructed brands (Aronczyk 2013), individuals can create brands for themselves because of the ease of access to social media and digital communication platforms (Banet-Weiser, 2012), and public personalities like professional athletes construct their branded personas. As a marketing professional recently told me, "everything is brandable, and branding is everything."

Branded difference is a contextualized brand strategy that draws upon economies of visibility to fold fighters into the logics of the market, as values, as commodities, as inspirations, as sites of identification, and as benchmarks for progress. The result is a proliferation of sometimes meaningful and sometimes plastic representations of female fighters. The central aim of this book is to examine how this branding process works for female fighters, what remains invisible, and what are the consequences of visibility within the specific context of the UFC. I take seriously Herman Gray's (2016) call to "identify sites, discourses, and practices of producing difference . . . that [operate] as a logic of production" (249), since more sports media brands are beginning to reorder themselves "around diversity and multiculturalism as markers of consumer brands, lifestyle choices, and postracial cultural appreciation" just as other media brands have before them (248). I also draw upon the academic tradition of cultural studies to "radically contextualize" the visibility of difference within a specific sports media brand in a particular moment in time (Grossberg 2015; Hall and Massey 2010). This means that I examine the cultural, political, and economic conditions that make the visibility of female fighters in the UFC attractive within the brand amid all its specificities.

At face value, branded difference is a promotional strategy enmeshed within contemporary culture; yet, it is also an ideological process that works to illuminate certain aspects of difference while hiding others in the shadows. Cultural theorists Sarah Banet-Weiser (2018), Gilles Deleuze, and Angela McRobbie have discussed how "luminosities" such as branded difference function ideologically. Deleuze (1988) describes visibilities or luminosities, depending on the French translation, as not "forms of objects" that become discernible in light, but rather as created by the light itself allowing it to exist "only as a flash, sparkle, or shimmer" (45). In other words, Deleuze sees the central power of visibility as stemming from *the action* of shining the light not from the status of *being* in the light. McRobbie (2009) extends this metaphor by using it to show how media representations of women depict them as being in possession of "the light," that is, possessing equality in society. She says, however, that the power that these women seem to have is actually "created by the light itself" because the light is a "theatrical effect" created by a "moving spotlight" that holds the power to dramatize some things and disguise others (54). Branded difference becomes the spotlight and theatrical effect that chooses how and when diverse sportswomen are luminous and for what purpose.

When considering the fact that the UFC, a patriarchal White-helmed promotion, decides when and where they shine the light on fighters, the fact that difference is luminous loses any radical potential for women in sports. Richard Dyer (1997) pushes his critique of the light in media culture further by demonstrating that Western culture's fascination with light in the arts, in photography, and in film have always associated light with goodness, transparency, knowledge, and Whiteness. Dyer reasons that this functions to bolster Whiteness since "light shows through white subjects more than through black, so that they appear indeed illuminated and enlightened" (110). For example, as I discuss in chapter 3, the UFC can celebrate Nicco Montaño as the "first Native UFC champion" while downplaying the fact that they stripped her of her title after a series of fighting-related health issues prevented her from competing for nearly two years after she won the flyweight championship.[9] As an independent UFC contractor, she also had limited health insurance to cover her medical expenses. The UFC has, however, allowed other White male champions to miss weight on multiple occasions (Guillen 2018; Lee 2019). Montaño's difference as a Native woman is luminous, while the unequal treatment of her remains overshadowed.

Contract Labor in the UFC

My focus here on the relationship between representation and labor practices lays bare the consequences of the increased visibility of difference in popular culture that sets this book apart in sports media studies. Feminist sports media scholars, in particular, have long hoped that increased meaningful diversity would open more opportunities for women in sports, and much of our scholarly endeavors have critiqued a lack of adequate representation in some form or fashion. I show that visibility works to the detriment of female athletes when considering the labor of visibility placed on the athletes themselves and that the majority of fighters fail to benefit economically from the exposure. Instead, the UFC's labor practices produce significant income inequality and poor working conditions for its professional athletes compared to some other major professional sports in the United States. The chapters cover these labor issues further, but for now, it's important to establish a few ways the UFC's labor model is problematic for fighters.

The UFC's financial model pays most fighters only a small proportion of the promotion's overall revenue. While the issue of fighter pay is difficult to analyze because the UFC is currently not publicly traded and the company is under no obligation to make financial data available for the public or its fighters, the gap between fighter compensation and organizational revenue is worth evaluating from the information that is obtainable.[10] In 2016, Zuffa, the UFC's parent company, sold the promotion to the media group Endeavor (formerly William Morris Endeavor and WME-IMG) for $4 billion, proving that the fight business is lucrative (Rovel and Okamoto 2016). The UFC is now valued as high as $7 billion; yet, documents from various UFC legal proceedings reveal that roughly 10 to 20 percent of that revenue goes toward fighter payouts and other compensation (Gift 2019; Reinsmith 2018a). To compare, players in the big four—the NFL, NBA, MLB, and NHL—receive around 50 percent of league revenue each year as negotiated by thriving players' unions (Gift 2019). A key difference between sports leagues that offer a greater share of the revenue to their athletes and promotions like the UFC is that the big four must disclose their financial information to their players associations, while UFC fighters have no collective voice representing them at the bargaining table (see chapter 5).[11]

The gap between the financial information the UFC does disclose and what the majority of fighters make in the promotion gives enough reason to believe that fighters are disadvantaged in the relationship as independent contractors who must pay a great deal of expenses themselves. Since the UFC doesn't supply comprehensive data on fighter pay, one avenue to obtain a snapshot of how male and female fighters fare financially as independent contractors in the promotion is to examine specific UFC events that take place in states where the governing athletic commissions require them to disclose how much they pay fighters. While not comprehensive, this snapshot of fighter pay suggests that after fighters pay all the costs associated with fight preparation and competing, the vast majority make very little in the UFC, with White women and women of color the most disadvantaged groups. Certain state commissions require MMA and boxing promotions to publicly disclose how much a fighter makes for a bout, which provides a glimpse into fighter pay but not the whole picture. For example, from 2015 to 2018, fifty-five UFC events took place in states that required the UFC to disclose fighter pay to the commissions, including Arizona, California, Florida, Georgia, Massachusetts, Nevada, Oklahoma, Ohio, Oregon, Virginia, and Wisconsin. These commissions report "show" money, which is given to a fighter for participating in the fight, and "win" money if that fighter defeats their opponent. The commissions also report on bonuses for Fight of the Night and Performance of the Night and pay from the UFC's official apparel sponsor Reebok. These fifty-five events from 2015 to 2018 yielded an average gross payout for all athletes of $98,000 (all pay numbers are rounded to the nearest thousand) with roughly twenty-two athletes fighting per event.

These payout averages might not appear to be concerning, since they are higher than the yearly gross income of many Americans, and athletes might fight in more than one event per year. However, that number is misleading for a few reasons. First, there is a pay gap between the average payouts for men and women at those fifty-five events: men made $99,000 on average, White women earned $89,000, and women of color made $83,000 (see appendix B for a breakdown of these payouts). The fact that in 2018 men fought a median of twice a year and women a median of once per year further suggests that most men have twice the chance to earn a payout as women in a given year.[12]

Second, and more strikingly, there is a drastic difference in payouts between a fighter who headlines an event and a UFC newcomer; yet, when those numbers are averaged together, UFC stars skew the overall payment average much higher. The UFC operates under a star model that allows for a small proportion of their fighter roster to make large amounts of money. For example, championship challenger Holly Holm earned $300,000 in show money at UFC 239 (July 6, 2019) for her loss to Amanda Nunes, while UFC newcomer Pannie Kianzad made $12,000 for her loss to Julia Avila. When taking into account the median payouts disclosed by commissions for the 2015–18 events, the numbers show a more accurate picture of what most of the fighters keep from those fifty-five events: approximately $44,000 for male athletes and $30,000 for female athletes.[13] These numbers translate to female fighters making 68 percent of a male athlete's salary at those events. This snapshot, however, may skew fighter pay higher than reality overall because Nevada and California are more popular venues than, for example, Oklahoma and Georgia.[14] The UFC often schedules marquee fights in Las Vegas and various California cities and pays a greater sum to fighters overall than in other locations. For example, between 2015 and 2018, the average total UFC payouts in Nevada and California were $2.476 million, while in the other states that publicly report payouts the average was $1.8 million. (See appendix A for a breakdown of payouts per event in states that confirm fighter pay.)

A third reason UFC payout totals are misleading stems from how the UFC classifies fighters as workers. UFC fighters are independent contractors, which means they bear the burden of much of the associated costs for training and

Cris "Cyborg" Justino vs. Amanda "Lioness" Nunes. Photo by Amy Kaplan.

competing in the promotion. From their winnings, fighters pay approximately 15 percent to their managers and 10 percent to their trainers, which reduces the 2015–18 disclosed pay median the fighter keeps to an estimated $33,000 for men and $23,000 for women per fight before taxes. Fighters must pay up to 37 percent in taxes in the United States because independent contractors bear a higher tax burden than salaried employees.[15] In addition to the percentages allocated to trainers and managers, many other variable costs associated with training for a professional fight must be taken into account because athletes spend months of fight preparation, require nutritional support for cutting weight, and incur healthcare expenses (Harris 2017). Additionally, several fighters I spoke with pointed out that although the UFC pays for the flight and lodging of one of their trainers, or "corner" for the event, they typically work with three or four coaches who specialize in different arts and often pay for additional corners for the fights themselves. If a fighter has major surgery or an injury that occurs outside of the contracted period for the fight (typically a couple of months before the fight and the fight itself), then the UFC has no financial obligation to support them or their healthcare costs. The athletes I spoke with confirmed that fighters are financially responsible for the medical testing that state commissions require in order to clear them to compete in a sanctioned MMA event; the required testing typically costs up to $1,500 or even more. Fighters must pay for their own routine medical care, and many also use massage, acupuncture, and cryo-therapy for recovery, cross-train to improve athletic performance, and employ nutritionists.

In addition to diverting much of the associated costs of MMA competition to the fighters themselves, UFC contracts further stipulate a number of clauses that secure the income of the promotion while disadvantaging the majority of fighters from sharing in that revenue (Snowden 2013). Contracts in which UFC fighters consent to the use of their name and likeness for apparel, DVDs, or video games deny fighters royalty rights for the sale of these products. These types of secondary profit are a major source of income negotiated by players in profes-sional sports leagues. The UFC also has the right to terminate contracts after a fighter loses, without recourse, while the fighter has no reciprocal clause to ensure the UFC fulfills its obligations (Snowden 2013). The UFC has thwarted any major attempts for fighters to unionize and ameliorate these contractual disparities. Fighters must secure sponsorships to train, often work outside of MMA to feed and house themselves, and face pressure to use social media to build their fol-lowing and the UFC's brand. All the while the athletes assume much of the risk and responsibility for their livelihoods and the risk to their bodies.

The UFC's labor model of hiring independent contractors mirrors the grow-ing number of other industries that now rely on contractual work wherein the worker assumes the risk and responsibility for steady income, health, and pro-motion. Contracted labor—like driving for Uber, freelance writing for Upwork, or walking dogs with Rover—is an increasingly common method for hiring part-time workers without the associated costs of healthcare, retirement benefits, or paid vacations, resulting in a gig economy. For example, there are graduate students hired to work 19.5 hours a week so universities can avoid paying the requisite health insurance required if an employee works at least 20 hours. By cutting the student's weekly hours by 30 minutes, departments save those ex-penses, leaving the students to bear the burden of health insurance premiums or go without. Universities, just like other organizations, benefit from a part-time labor pool because they have a ready supply willing to participate and no unions or weak unions with which to contend. Numerous employment sectors have developed part-time and contingent labor at the expense of full-time po-sitions in order to support their operations at a lower cost. Currently, a quarter of the U.S. labor force now works as freelancers or strings together a series of part-time jobs, with those in the millennial generation making up most of these laborers (Hartman 2018).

In sports, professional boxers and wrestlers face working conditions similar to UFC fighters since they are also independent contractors. They also receive smaller shares of the revenue than athletes in the big four. Comparable boxing promotions tend to pay a greater share of their revenue to their athletes than the UFC (Nash 2016), while the WWE operates using a very similar model to the UFC (Sager 2019). Since there are very few fight promotions and professional wrestling organizations that rival the UFC and WWE, both organizations have been able to draw the most talented athletes without also having to fairly compensate or provide benefits for them. As Naomi Klein (2009) concludes about labor in the present moment, "one thing is certain: offering employment—the steady kind, with benefits, holiday pay, and measure of security and maybe even union representation—has fallen out of economic fashion" (231). In the UFC, the promotion has adopted a contract labor model that limits the financial risks for the company by making individual fighters expendable and responsible for most of their own healthcare.

While branded difference facilitates the increased visibility of women in MMA, I interrogate how the brand strategy creates a mirage of possibilities that both attracts an inexpensive and expendable labor force and casts shadows on the labor of that visibility by shining the light elsewhere. Branded difference works by affirming representation matters and producing media texts that celebrate the accomplishments of diverse female fighters. All the while, the strategy obscures the UFC's labor practices behind a familiar meritocratic narrative: a fighter overcoming all obstacles through individual hard work and determination. The UFC inserts meritocracy rhetoric into branded difference as a rationale to justify why they compensate most fighters poorly: fighters in the lower payout tiers aren't working hard enough for the opportunities that the UFC is providing (see chapter 3). This allows the UFC to continue to market themselves to diverse audiences and fighters while not compensating those fighters fairly. Although branded difference serves as window dressing to obscure inequalities in neoliberal brand culture, it is important to highlight that the UFC deploys the strategy with varying degrees of effectiveness in often contradictory ways.

On Ambivalence and Hierarchies of Visibility

Branded difference in the UFC is complex and contradictory rather than unified and singular. Even though this brand strategy carries significant weight in the promotion, the UFC also behaves in inconsistent ways when it comes to diversity and inclusion, which further reflects how discourses of difference are convoluted and often contradictory in twenty-first-century media. Our current social, cultural, political moment is characterized by tensions between the growing visibility of difference and White heteropatriarchy's perceived loss of power. This means that Dana White can speak at the Republican National Convention in support of Donald Trump, a U.S. president now notorious for his xenophobia and racism, while also signing a sponsorship deal with a Mexican beer brand that celebrates prominent Latinx immigrants and UFC fighters with immigration stories in its marketing. This means that the UFC can make a series of short films celebrating the UFC's twenty-fifth anniversary and include a tribute to the promotion's relationship with Donald Trump, an admitted harasser of women, while producing another film that celebrates the ways women have "broken barriers" in the promotion. Large sports media brands are not monolithic, nor are they always consistent with their politics for a couple of reasons. First, a range of individuals and teams make decisions about what they produce for sports media resulting in conservative and progressive content all housed under the same brand. Second, sports media brands seek to provide a variety of content to reach niche audiences rather than a mass one, which allows the same brand to produce multiple and often contradictory discourses. Nike, for example, donates to the Republican Party to support business policies that benefit the company while also creating ads that celebrate former NFL quarterback Colin Kaepernick, who was criticized by many Republicans for his protest of police brutality against Black Americans during NFL games (Papenfuss 2018). Nike isn't unified in its political and cultural affiliations, and neither is the UFC.

Discourses of feminisms, sexism, empowerment, misogyny, homophobia, heteronormativity, inclusivity, homonationalism, and racism all circulate ambivalently under the umbrella of UFC media. For example, the UFC positions female fighters as a symbol of women's empowerment in one instance while parading Octagon Girls—models clad in bikinis—at live events and fan expositions in another. The UFC employs these women as objects-to-be-looked-at as they circle around the Octagon. While in Rio de Janeiro for a Ronda Rousey fight, I found the public display of men's gawking to be particularly offensive. Each time one of the Octagon Girls entered the stage, the tenor of the room changed from deep-barreled cheers for fighters to a chorus of whistling for the woman in skimpy clothing. The UFC is a complex sports media brand that encourages fans to objectify women in one breath and celebrates female fighters and women's empowerment in another. When Rousey entered the Rio arena before her fight, no one whistled at her (see chapter 2). The room was instead electric with anticipation and reverence for her, her star power, and her athletic prowess even though the fans preferred male Brazilian fighters for every other fight that night. Never before had I witnessed such a thrilling fervor for a woman athlete, and the experience left me considering the UFC's efforts to promote her. Focusing on how the organization had leveraged her sex appeal or paraded Octagon Girls misses the other significances rising from her representation, including the UFC's interest in drawing women fans through empowerment rhetoric. What might we learn if we also focus on when, how, and why sports media brands succeed at promoting women? The sexual objectification of the Octagon Girls does not refute the simultaneous presence of a women's empowerment discourse; rather, it exposes the ambivalence of the UFC brand and the uneven experience of women in the sport.

Likewise, the fact that the UFC featured an out-lesbian athlete in the first women's UFC fight doesn't suggest that she received an equal amount of media exposure as some of the UFC's male stars, as a White, blonde, heterosexy woman, nor that homophobia and racism are tempered in the sport. Rather, the promotion vacillates between celebrating and disparaging many forms of difference in often contradictory ways. There have never been any openly gay male fighters in the promotion, which speaks to the broader culture of homophobia in male sporting spaces. Likewise, the UFC has an uneven record in its ability to gesture toward inclusion despite the trend toward accepting lesbian athletes in the brand. For example, the UFC has a history of fighters and staff spewing homophobic rhetoric. Dana White offended multiple communities the UFC now promotes through branded difference when he used an antigay slur, called a woman reporter a "bitch," and referred to another fighter as "retarded" on a vlog. After public pressure in the MMA community to apologize for his homophobic statements, White was contrite: "At the end of the day, the worst thing for me is that I don't want anybody thinking that it's cool to say that word especially now that I know the word 'faggot' is as powerful as the n-word. I don't want these kids out there watching me and thinking it's cool. I don't want that" ("UFC's White" 2009). White, Ronda Rousey, and other MMA personalities later adamantly rejected the inclusion of Fallon Fox, a transgender MMA fighter, in the UFC, further showing that LGBTQ "inclusion" just refers to lesbians (McClearen 2015a; Fischer and McClearen 2020).[16]

Homophobia, sexism, and racism are ever present in the UFC, and a woman like Liz Carmouche doesn't receive the same promotional backing as a woman like Ronda Rousey or as male athletes competing for championship belts. Nevertheless, examples like Liz Carmouche show us that sportswomen no longer face a binary of visibility that sorts them simply as visible/invisible or included/excluded; rather, the vast array of digital and legacy media content that circulates around them facilitates exposure at some level or another. For example, in their research on feminist sports journalism surrounding athlete activism and the U.S. Women's National Soccer Team (USWNT) and the WNBA, Cooky and Antunovic (2020) argue that while mainstream sports outlets like *Sports Illustrated* and ESPN still privilege narratives of men's activism in sports, various other media distribute feminist content about female athletes protesting social injustice. They further point out that media outlets that write more stories about sportswomen tend to fall outside the realm of what is commonly considered sports media and instead exist in other publications such as the *Nation*, the *New York Times*, *Slate,* and *Teen Vogue*. I'd further contend that Cooky and Antunovic's research reveals that women aren't *invisible* in sports media; instead, they exist within a hierarchical structure of visibility that makes content harder to find for a more mainstream sporting audience not necessarily seeking stories about female athletes. Yet, those who do seek out coverage of women's sports, or who are broadly interested in women's activism in a variety of sectors, can find that content through other journalistic channels or through following their favorite women's sports teams, athletes, and media outlets online. In a similar way, the presence of an out-lesbian in the first women's UFC fight became partially possible through Liz Carmouche's additional labor on social media. Within the economies of visibility there are still *hierarchies of visibility* that privilege hegemonic masculinity and essentialized femininity—the dominant gendered order that elevates men above women, heteronormativity over queerness, and Whiteness over all other races, and sets rigid boundaries for masculine and feminine attractiveness. Hierarchies of visibility in women's sports give greater exposure

UFC fighter Angela Lee at a UFC event. Photo by Amy Kaplan.

to traditionally beautiful, straight, White, women even as women of color and lesbians are recognizable as having their own degrees of visibility.

When surveying the various types of UFC-produced media, it is clear that media produced for mainstream or mass audiences favor emphasized femininity, while short videos produced for the UFC Website or YouTube are more likely to feature extended content on women who fall outside representations considered traditionally marketable and are instead perceived as niche. Consider the differences between a promotional video created for two straight, White, conventionally attractive women, Ronda Rousey and Holly Holm titled *Revolution* versus one created for an out-lesbian fighter from Brazil dubbed *Jessica Andrade Emerges*. The UFC outsourced *Revolution* to Digital Domain, a media production company that makes movie trailers for Hollywood, including the trailer for the blockbuster film *Avatar*. The promo is cast with actors who tell a cinematic story of both women as they fought through adversity to compete on MMA's largest stage. *Revolution's* production value is high, with the sets, lighting, staging, music, and editing producing a dramatic effect to build anticipation for the fight. The UFC premiered the video on the *Ellen DeGeneres Show*, whereas *Jessica Andrade Emerges* was likely filmed over the course of a single day and co-produced by the UFC and Combate, a sports television network in Brazil. It is evident from the production values of both that *Revolution* dwarfs *Jessica Andrade Emerges*. Yet, the latter video establishes the ways that the UFC employs social media to weave narratives of difference intended for social media that they might not for pay-per-view or broadcast television. The Andrade video is just under three minutes long, making it perfect to share and circulate on a variety of social media platforms. The UFC posted Andrade's vignette to YouTube in addition to hosting it on the UFC's main website and UFC Fight Pass, the company's subscription-based platform for streaming content. A digital trace on Facebook and Twitter reveals that numerous individuals and handles dedicated to MMA reposted the YouTube video shortly after the UFC first uploaded it. The UFC leverages the free labor that fans and prosumers, such as bloggers, perform to promote Andrade's difference.[17] Effectively, the UFC deals in niche media to generate buzz around fighters who embody difference in ways that the brand's mainstream efforts may still hedge. Hierarchies of visibility determine the scale to which various differences become visible. *Jessica Andrade Emerges* has only received 24,000 hits on YouTube since 2013, while the *Revolution* promotional trailer was replicated on numerous YouTube sites to reach millions of viewers. In sports media old inequalities exist within enduring hierarchies; however, it is important to recognize that difference is also becoming visible in networked sports media.

Book Organization

Fighting Visibility draws on feminist epistemologies, the interdisciplinarity of cultural studies, and interview and textual methods to analyze women in UFC media. I examine the UFC through the circuit of culture, a cultural studies model that examines the interrelationships between production, consumption, regulation, identity, and representation, to consider how the visibility of female fighters circulates and at what costs. Each of these aspects in the circuit are connected yet also contextual to particular moments in time, geographical locations, or type of media endeavor. Du Gay et al. (2013) note that understanding the ways in which each component of the circuit of culture joins the other in a specific context is essential because none of them exists in isolation and each is interdependent. I understand sports media as consisting of the intersections of industries, audiences, and texts that produce a symbiotic relationship among these various media forms, practices, and engagement (Arsenault and Perren 2016; Holt and Perren 2009). I weave textual analysis of an array of UFC media with interviews with UFC staff and fighters to define the contours of branded difference, and then to consider what is at stake when it becomes modus operandi in a sports brand's promotion of women. To ascertain how the UFC figures its role in promoting female athletes, I spoke with seven current or former UFC employees or contractors working in production, marketing, and public relations. My questions covered the organization's decision to include female fighters, their own perspectives on the rapid growth of the women's divisions, their primary tactics for generating buzz for women's fights, and why female fighters had become popular at this particular moment in history. I also interviewed nine current or former female UFC fighters in order to interrogate the consequences of branded difference. I asked female fighters questions about how they perceived the UFC's promotion of the women's divisions, any challenges they faced as women in the promotion, and if and how they brand themselves on social media. I also interviewed one male fighter and an attorney involved with the efforts to unionize fighters. All unattributed quotations in the book are from the interviews I conducted; a list of those interviews appears in the bibliography. I augment all of my personal conversations with UFC staff and fighters with hundreds of other interviews on podcasts, MMA blogs, and sports and brand analysis websites. Finally, I examine the representation of female athletes on a variety of UFC-produced media, such as a UFC reality show, documentaries, social media, and live fights as well as MMA blogs and news sites. I read all of the interviews and media texts through an intersectional feminist lens (Crenshaw 1991; V. Smith 1998); thus, I focus on the ways sexism, racism, classism, and homophobia intersect to construct the meaning of the female fighter within the circuit of culture.

As a feminist media scholar, I also understand my readings of each text and interview as informed by my own identities and experiences. At the time of this writing I have been training martial arts for fourteen years, and my community includes MMA fighters and other competitive athletes. My position within the community means that I deploy a feminist praxis that recognizes that research on power relations often stems from embodied knowledges and perspectives of those marginalized. I have the intimate knowledge of a White queer woman in the male-dominated practice of Brazilian jiu jitsu. Not all women's experiences in martial arts are identical to mine; rather, their identities and personal contexts engage with the sport in nuanced ways. Even though my experiences as a hobbyist are very different from a professional athlete's, Brazilian jiu jitsu is a small community that includes both amateurs and professionals. As a result, a couple of the female fighters I interviewed are in my personal networks. I am both an insider and outsider examining the sport with the critical eye of a scholar, the embodied knowledge of a queer cisgender martial arts practitioner, and the curiosity of an MMA fan. I make no claims of critical or impartial distance; rather, I position myself as embedded in the intimacies of scholar-practitioner-fan, which means this book is personal as well as political. I approach the project ambivalently—at once concerned at what the problematic UFC labor model might mean for the future of women's sports and compelled by the fact that women's combat sports are now a profitable endeavor for the first time in history.

The chapters move from the organizational context, to the symbolic and ideological, to the material as I analyze why, how, and to what ends women have become visible in the UFC brand. The aim is to both describe and critique how branded difference operates within a specific sports media context. As Amanda Lotz (2015) argues, "though academic inquiry tends to prioritize analysis, there is much work to be done in first developing more basic descriptive knowledge of actual operations from which to build empirically based analyses" (20). In this first academic book on UFC media, I map the terrain of the sports media brand to follow Lotz's call for describing how branding logics operate within the broader context of the UFC's development as a promotion. My deep dive into the UFC branding logics allows me to explain the nuances unique to that specific context while extrapolating how media culture informs and is impacted by these meanings. I use the descriptive work to spring-board into analysis on how these luminous representations of difference cast shadows on labor inequalities.

Chapter 1, "Developing a Millennial Sports Media Brand," sets the stage by considering the characteristics of the promotion that have created the context in which female fighters now experience greater visibility. I trace the infamous origins of the UFC from its early days of "no-holds-barred human cockfighting" to the global sports media powerhouse that it is today. I demonstrate how the brand developed using cultural and technological rationales of the millennial generation by becoming early adopters of social media, by orienting the brand globally, and by targeting diverse fighters and fans. This chapter argues that the UFC's evolution into what I have coined a "millennial sports media brand" created a perfect storm for integrating diverse female fighters from around the world. The brand maxim "we are all fighters" purports that having diverse fighters on the UFC rosters draws a greater range of audience demographics. Thus, this first chapter establishes *why* the UFC included women in the brand in the first place, while the next two chapters examine *how* branded difference makes female athletes visible and claims unparalleled opportunities for women within the promotion.

Chapter 2, "Affect and the Rousey Effect," contextualizes the UFC's branding of sportswomen within a cultural moment when representation matters and girls and women's empowerment is *en vogue*. To do so, the chapter asks "what 'representation matters' *feels* like in the UFC" to reveal how the promotion circulates the visibility of female athletes in affective economies. By "affective economies," I mean marketing practices that seek "to understand the emotional underpinnings of consumer decision-making as a driving force behind viewing and purchasing decisions" (Jenkins 2008, 62). In other words, brands turn their promotional tactics into capital through a process of facilitating emotional or sensationalized attachments to the brand. The UFC trades gendered difference within affective economies to appeal to new demographics and grow its viewership through identification with diverse fighters. Yet, more pertinent overall, the circulation of affect in the brand has an additional benefit for the promotion: the affective economy of the UFC also attracts female fighters. This convergence of affect, branding, and difference has facilitated the splintering of a representational glass ceiling for women within combat sports by drawing both fans and fighters. These trends suggest progress for female fighters in combat sports; nevertheless, the chapter shows that the discourse of "If she can see it, she can be it" recruits female fighters through its luminous sentimentality.

Chapters 2 and 3 scrutinize how branded difference creates luminous discourses that are attractive to fighters and fans while diverting attention away from the way these discourses only benefit a handful of fighters in the UFC. Chapter 3, "Gendering the American Dream," considers the ways the UFC has integrated women into the American sports hero trope that celebrates the underdog rising out of adversity. The American dream myth is a popular storytelling device in real and fictional sports stories, but the discourse has historically appeared less frequently in women's sports. The sentiment "it doesn't matter where you come from, it matters what you're made of," marries success with individual determination, a discourse that now includes women. The sporting American dream myth asserts that women can achieve greatness in the millennial sports media brand if they just work hard enough; yet, the reality is that only a relatively small number of sportswomen achieve fame and fortune. The mythology of the American dream is a key ideological mechanism in the UFC's use of branded difference to attract a diverse and expendable labor force of fighters. Many fighters are willing to endure poverty and jeopardize their long-term health because they assume the risk for their success while absolving the UFC of responsibility for their livelihood. Chapter 3 provides an explanation as to why fighters willingly endure the UFC's precarious labor model while the next two chapters examine the material consequences of these labor conditions.

Chapter 4 centers the voices of female fighters to examine how they navigate the economic conditions they face as contracted employees of the UFC. "The Labor of Visibility on Social Media" analyzes interviews with female fighters describing how and why they use social media to promote themselves as fighters. Self-promotion becomes an unwritten aspect of the job of professional UFC fighters—work that lacks guaranteed social capital or financial rewards. The UFC deploys this model to shift the risk and responsibility for visibility to its athletes while ensuring that the promotion benefits from that visibility to a greater degree than the athletes themselves. On the one hand, many of the female fighters I interviewed feel the responsibility to promote themselves and their sponsors online, since the UFC fails to pay most of them a realistic living wage. On the other hand, all of this unpaid or undercompensated work is also gendered in particular ways. Social media is a difficult space to be a woman in a "man's sport" since overt sexism and trolling are epidemic and exhausting. Female athletes must navigate labor exploitation, the labor of self-branding, and the emotional labor of self-protection online.

"The Fight for Labor Equity," chapter 5, continues to problematize the UFC's labor model by examining the unionization efforts spearheaded by Leslie Smith, a fighter who was cut from the UFC while making labor inequalities visible and attempting to organize athletes into a collective voice. Smith's experience shows how the wrong kind of visibility in the UFC, such as exposing and speaking against fighter exploitation, produces precarity. Drawing on interviews with Smith, her attorney, and other fighters as well as analysis of the legality of the UFC's labor model, I consider how the UFC secures contracts with fighters that leverage a large degree of control over the athletes without affording them the rights of employees and how the promotion quells unionization efforts through fears of retaliation. While visible unionizing is met with precarity for UFC fighters as independent contractors, political visibility and collective action are central methods for combating branded difference's ability to obscure labor inequality. The unionization of fighters is a key avenue for remedying the current labor conditions for athletes in the UFC, particularly for women and/or people of color. I cannot foresee a viable future for women in combat sports without better working conditions and greater fighter agency in their careers.

The UFC's branding of difference is an ambivalent cultural discourse that elevates minoritized genders, races, ethnicities, sexualities, and nationalities in order to grow the visibility of the brand with diverse and global audiences. The initial success of the UFC's women's divisions might seem to suggest that the UFC's efforts to incorporate female fighters into their brand is a promising tactic for increasing the visibility of women in sports. Representation matters, and promoting fan identification with diverse fighters appears to achieve what feminist sports scholars and activists have been advocating for decades—meaningful engagement with diverse female athletes. In this book we see how a lesbian marine, an Iraqi refugee, a Navajo champion, and the empowered White heroine all have degrees of luminosity in hierarchies of visibility. However, this surface-level celebration of difference bolsters an untenable labor model. This spectacle of difference masks the disparities that minoritized fighters face within the organization around issues of labor and exploitation, in particular. Diverse women in the UFC are exploited for the difference they represent. They receive low and unequal pay, minimal benefits, and endure contracts that benefit the UFC to a greater degree than the fighters. The UFC's branding strategies reveal that "positive," "accurate," or "meaningful" representation is a fraught endeavor without fair working conditions. This state of affairs instead means that analysts and fans of women's sports must now grapple with what happens to sportswomen when they become celebrated *and* exploited in sports media. *Fighting Visibility* throws the first punch.

CHAPTER 1

Developing a Millennial Sports Media Brand

The UFC's origin story provides a curious backdrop to the brand's eventual inclusion of female fighters almost twenty years later. The no-holds-barred contest among martial arts disciplines at UFC 1 (November 11, 1993) displayed some infamous results that continue to impact the reputation of MMA to this day. The first fighters to enter the large metal cage called the Octagon to square off against each other were a sumo wrestler, Teila Tuli (née Taylor Wiley), and a much smaller kickboxer, Gerard Gordeau. Despite being the smaller opponent, Gordeau won the fight with a kick to the head of his grounded opponent, a move now illegal in the UFC because of the risk of serious head injury. UFC lore recalls one of Tuli's teeth flying across the cage to the front row of the crowd and another tooth lodging itself in Gordeau's foot (Gentry 2011). UFC 1 and subsequent tournaments were contests without rules—eye gouging, biting, and fishhooking were finable offences, but not prohibited outright—and referees had no authority to stop fights to prevent serious injury ("Brutal Beginnings" 2013). Promoters established the premise of the UFC as a means to pit one martial style against another in a tournament to determine the world's most dominant martial artist. The origin story of the UFC brand drips with brutality, rhetoric of violence, and a fascination with testing the limits of men's bodies—a brand ethos that drew niche crowds with alacrity early in the promotion's history but proved distasteful for mainstream sporting audiences.

Gordeau (left) and Tuli (right) at UFC 1. UFC Fight Pass.

Fast-forward to the present and the sport and the UFC brand have changed dramatically. MMA rules have evolved to promote greater fighter safety and make the UFC more palatable to mainstream audiences around the globe. Even though the fighter roster was ethnically and nationally diverse at the UFC's inception, the brand's orientation toward promoting difference has increased substantially since the early 2010s. As of 2018, 55 percent of UFC fighters were from outside the United States and represented 60 different nations (Epstein 2018). Perhaps most surprisingly, a woman—Ronda Rousey—became the sport's most recognizable star in 2015 after the promotion spent years vehemently excluding female athletes. Diverse rosters that include women have been proving themselves successful for the promotion. The UFC is currently more popular with men and women ages eighteen to thirty-four than U.S. leagues such as the NBA, NFL, or MLB (Stainer and Master 2018; Epstein 2018). The brand's seismic shifts beg the question: how did the UFC go from a barbaric gladiator's contest barely capable of staying on air in the 1990s to a sports media powerhouse promoting female athletes from around the world in the 2010s?

This chapter examines how the modern sports media context has transitioned from the early years of the UFC to its present-day configuration, which provides the context for the integration of diverse women into the UFC brand that becomes the greater focus of this book. Numerous factors enabled this growth over the UFC's short history as an MMA promotion. New ownership, innovative business practices, new media technologies, niche marketing and shifting audience demographics, and an attention toward the global have each co-facilitated organizational shifts that give rise to what I call a "millennial sports media brand." The UFC developed acumen with social media and digital platforms because the promotion's teeth-extracting reputation limited avenues for distributing content to mainstream sports audiences compared to major professional sports leagues. The UFC implemented a few different millennial brand strategies to grow the promotion into the global entity it is today, including innovation with digital and social media platforms and an explicit orientation toward a diverse global market. When combined, these intersecting strategies form the impetus for the promotion's development of branded difference: a brand strategy that grants unparalleled visibility for female athletes in combat sports. Incorporating difference becomes a key strategy for the millennial sports media brand, as it allows the UFC to entice diverse fighters and fans through the representation of athletes who look and speak like them. This strategy has proven lucrative for the promotion. The UFC's efforts to become digital, global, and diverse shifted the scope of the UFC brand and eventually contributed to the sale of the promotion in 2016 for $4 billion—the largest sale of a sporting entity in history (Douban 2016). The year after the sale, the UFC was the seventh most valuable sports business brand in the world, with an estimated worth of $2 billion (behind the likes of Nike at $29.6 billion and ESPN at $15.8 billion) (Gough 2018). UFC president Dana White has since claimed that the UFC is now worth $7 billion (Reinsmith 2018a).

I use the term "millennial sports media brand" to signal a brand identity that both takes on qualities of the millennial generation within its business practices and attempts to appeal to target audiences within that same generation. Millennial brands value a synergistic relationship with digitally savvy users and attempt to benefit the brand through the collaborative engagement of the consumer. The UFC isn't out to simply sell pay-per-view events but to draw audiences into the fold through connections with the brand. Alison Hearn (2012) writes that a brand "literally and figuratively becomes culture" because "branding practices produce sets of images and immaterial symbolic values in and through which individuals negotiate the world" (27–28). This creates a slippage between what constitutes creative culture and what constitutes promotional culture, giving rise to brand culture wherein the line between making media and selling media is blurry. The UFC's in-house media team creates and distributes a plethora of content revolving around the promotion's fighters, events, sponsors, and other brand features. For example, the UFC films a thirty-minute segment showing athletes weighing in the day before an event and distributes it live via its subscription streaming platform UFC Fight Pass. The digital media team simultaneously distributes Instagram posts showing fighters squaring off against one another at the weigh-in spectacle and Tweets information about how to watch the upcoming fights. Through its partnerships with ESPN, the UFC airs a talk show with commentators before and after its pay-per-view and broadcasts events. Each bit of media content has entertainment value in its own right; yet, each social media post or television special also works to promote the organization's live events on ESPN or streaming pay-per-view. The millennial sports media brand, as I show, uses these various channels of promotional communication to create meaningful connections with its diverse millennial audiences and fighters around the globe.

Becoming a Digitally Savvy Millennial Sports Media Brand

The first feature of the millennial sports media brand is dexterity with digital media platforms and a fluid cultural understanding of how audiences use those platforms to engage with the brands they follow. In order for the UFC to grow into the powerhouse it is today, the promotion needed to adopt innovative digital branding and marketing strategies in order to survive. Interestingly, the early years of the UFC showed no real indication that the promotion would eventually become the global sports media empire it is today and instead drew a very narrow audience. War of the Worlds (WOW) Productions and Semaphore Entertainment Group (SEG) developed the first UFC live event and pay-per-view broadcasts respectively (Gentry 2011) and continued to produce UFC tournaments throughout the 1990s. The major premise of testing unbridled masculinity in a contest of martial disciplines initially marketed itself. UFC 1 brought in 86,000 pay-per-view buys despite not promoting the event on television or other legacy advertising venues. As MMA journalist Jonathan Snowden (2010) writes of UFC 1, "It's an unwritten rule that you can't sell on pay-per-view without television, but somehow the show sold" (37). News of the first event spread by word of mouth through fans fascinated with the premise of testing one martial artist against another of a different style. These early tournaments indeed brought in a very particular type of fight fan: one fascinated by the spectacle of a man testing himself against physical adversity in a large metal cage where "two men enter, one man leaves" in a contest with "no rules" ("Brutal Beginnings" 2013; Gentry 2011). The promotion wore its brutality on its sleeve to draw extreme combat sport aficionados—a marketing tactic that drew a significant but narrow fan base at first. The UFC embraced the small crowd that gathered around it in the beginning but had difficulty bringing in new audiences, which in turn made the enterprise challenging to maintain. The promotion almost went under numerous times in its first decade because it faced scrutiny from political critics and failed to gain support through mainstream sports media distribution channels.

THE UFC'S DARK AGES

After some initial success marketing the sport to a niche group of fans, the UFC entered a period when many mainstream media organizations refused to support them, creating a need for alternative communication channels in order for the promotion to stay afloat. Early fandom around the UFC had tapered a bit in the late '90s at the same time politicians began taking notice of MMA. U.S. senator John McCain led congressional efforts to prohibit the sport, and numerous other lawmakers voiced similar opposition to the level of violence displayed in the matches. The first UFC events aired on pay-per-view, but cable companies no longer wanted to air events with such controversy; as a result, the UFC lost a way to broadcast the fights nationally. MMA moved almost completely to the Internet underground in the late 1990s, surviving only through a small cohort of media savvy fans who were writing about the sport online (Gentry 2011; Cooper 2014). The niche community of fans circulated information via news sites, fan forums, and even a daily email list of information. MMA writer Steve Dawson (2016) argues that there was a natural affinity between MMA and Internet-based communities of that time: "Back in the beginning of the new millennium, the internet was a different place from the crowded commercial market it is today. There was a wild-west feel of lawlessness to many of the dark corners of the early web, and disturbing underground content would often appear in such places." These fan efforts proved to be enough to keep the sport on life support until the Zuffa years began in 2001 (Gentry 2011). In other words, new media-savvy MMA bloggers and Internet-based fans kept the UFC and rival promotions afloat during this difficult period for MMA.

MMA's dark ages illustrate a moment of transition between a media culture almost exclusively dominated by legacy media and the emergence of digital media technologies that became second nature for millennial fans and marketing professionals alike. In the 1990s, the sport had a dedicated niche audience, but cable companies refused to broadcast the events. Large segments of audiences drew the focus of cable channels, while streaming platforms were more than a decade away from ubiquity. Instead, being a UFC fan in the MMA underground required knowledge of burgeoning technologies to circulate information about the sport, including building websites to host forums and blog sites to circulate commentary and recaps of events. Casual fans were almost nonexistent because of the skills and labor required to locate and distribute information. As a result, UFC fan demographics in the 1990s were predominantly young, educated, and male with a tendency toward being early adopters of new communication platforms.

ZUFFA'S TRANSMEDIA MARKETING

MMA might have faded into obscurity if a couple of Las Vegas entrepreneurs hadn't purchased the UFC and developed the brand using innovative marketing strategies. Casino owners Lorenzo and Frank Fertitta and their childhood friend Dana White formed the company Zuffa (Italian for "fight") to buy the UFC in 2001 (Vahey, Bolyard, and Vahey 2012). The men bought the organization with the goal of making the sport more palatable to a wider (read: more profitable) audience. The trio went to work attempting to sanction the UFC with the New Jersey and Nevada state athletic commissions and brokering a three-year deal with In Demand television network to air the UFC on pay-per-view. They were able to accomplish both feats by initially investing a substantial amount into the organization and making the sport's rules more appealing to mainstream audiences (Snowden 2010). In its first four years, Zuffa spent millions of dollars in targeted ad campaigns in *Playboy*, *Maxim*, and *Stuff* and acquired actress Carmen Electra as their spokesperson, all in an effort to appeal to their target eighteen-to-thirty-four male demographic (Snowden 2010). Yet, the UFC's reputation for unrestrained brutality had damaged its ability to enter the mainstream and gain a new fan base apart from dedicated followers.

Zuffa lost $44 million in the first four years of owning the UFC and almost sold the company (Snowden 2010). White and the Fertitta brothers began testing other strategies for increasing their audience size because of their inability to appeal to mainstream audiences through traditional channels (e.g., airing fights on TV). For starters, Zuffa welcomed any type of "press" it could find for the UFC, including credentialing bloggers with press passes for the events. Several bloggers and MMA journalists I spoke with as I researched this book observed that just creating an MMA or UFC blog on a self-publishing site was enough to obtain UFC press credentials. The UFC embraced bloggers and Internet-based fandom in the beginning because social media was an avenue for free promotion when the UFC was failing to get traction in mainstream media.

Despite the efforts to promote UFC cards through blogs, it wasn't enough to keep the UFC afloat without more traditional media outlets like major magazines or network coverage. Zuffa began to brainstorm other innovative strategies to entice more fans to the sport out of dire necessity. In 2005, they hit on an idea that worked: *The Ultimate Fighter*—a reality competition show that bridged live sports television with reality TV in order to promote the sport with new audiences. UFC president Dana White convinced the Fertittas to try *The Ultimate Fighter* as a last-ditch effort to revive the floundering promotion and propel MMA into the mainstream (Snowden 2013; Gentry 2011). The newly rebranded Spike TV network, with the accompanying tagline "television for men," was seeking inexpensive sports programming to add to its lineup. The UFC agreed to pay 100 percent of the production costs for *The Ultimate Fighter* in order for Spike to agree to the deal. White's basic premise for the show included a roster of unsigned fighters competing on a weekly basis for a chance to debut in a live UFC event and win a contract with the promotion. Producers distributed athletes between two teams that were coached by UFC veterans. White believed *The Ultimate Fighter* could leverage the strengths of the proliferating reality television genre to appeal to Spike's target demographics, educate audiences on the sport, and draw in new fans—a mutually beneficial endeavor for both Spike and the UFC. In his interview with me, Chris Kartzmark, senior vice president for production and programming at the UFC, called *The Ultimate Fighter* a "Trojan horse." Kartzmark explained that *The Ultimate Fighter* allowed the promotion to "ride the wave of popularity of reality programing and introduce people to mixed-martial-arts at the same time."

The UFC's marketing strategy, namely, using *The Ultimate Fighter* to promote fighters and events, proved effective. After thirteen weeks and $10 million in production costs, the final contenders on the reality show fought for the title of Ultimate Fighter, while two veteran fighters headlined the first live UFC event to air on a television network (all other events had been on pay-per-view or nothing at all). The gamble paid off for Zuffa as fans followed from *The Ultimate Fighter*, to the live finale, to pay-per-view, which remains the UFC's primary source of revenue ("Brutal Beginnings" 2013). Before the first season of *The Ultimate Fighter*, the largest number of pay-per-view buys was UFC 40 at 150,000 buys. The first pay-per-view contest after *The Ultimate Fighter* aired had 280,000 buys (Gentry 2011). Dana White and other executives have cited *The Ultimate Fighter* as the reason the company survived the mid-2000s (Torres 2016). The finale and the entire first season of *The Ultimate Fighter* proved the reality show was a profitable transmedia marketing strategy for the millennial sports media brand.

The Ultimate Fighter formula became an effective promotional venture for the UFC because of the creative links between reality television and fight promotion. Reality television is a paradoxical genre, but one that lends itself to creating drama around a combat sport. Producers and creatives establish "reality" as representations of the "real" and the "authentic;" yet, much of the work of creating an entertaining episode, story arc, or season relies on manufacturing drama or intrigue, editing countless hours of footage to create a concise twenty- to forty-five-minute story, and putting "real" people in contrived situations. LeiLani Nishime (2014) describes reality television as "rigidly framed representations of reality," which are purposefully unrealistic and extreme that viewers understand as inherently unreal (123). Mark Andrejevic (2009) further argues "Contemporary image culture teaches both the inevitability of contrivance and, paradoxically, the need to penetrate it not just out of casual curiosity but in order to avoid the risk of being seen to be a dupe who is taken in by the lure of the image" (233). Thus, reality TV provides a pleasurable gaze behind the scenes coupled with the satisfaction of knowing one cannot be duped into believing the stories are fully organic. From a creative standpoint, producers and editors function as they would on "a scripted show, with the difference that the raw material creating the fiction of the [reality television] series is footage of real people doing real things: the magic happens in the editing room, through the decisions of producers and TV workers" (Dubrofsky and Hardy 2008, 375). The paradox unfolds on the production end as a negotiation between the scenarios created by the producers and the subsequent manufacturing of a narrative through the raw footage collected.

Fight promotion shares an affinity with reality television and seems a logical partner for MMA fights. Fight promotion is steeped in underdog narratives, life obstacles overcome, conflict, and charisma, much like reality television. Doug Hartling, former vice president of sales and marketing at the UFC, described the marketing of athletes and their fights as similar to that of daytime dramas. He says that audiences enjoy following the drama:

> These people are together, these two are fighting, or these two are plotting against one another. Nothing in the UFC is scripted, but sometimes you get a certain level of tension because it's human nature. You put enough people in a room together and sooner or later they will clash.

Conflict can be understated, such as "a clash of nations" to show the national pride associated with fighters of different nationalities or explicit, such as two fighters who have previously engaged in verbal sparring matches in front of the cameras. Dave Sholler, former senior vice president of marketing and public relations at the UFC, says, "one of the secrets to the fight business is, if there's legitimate bad blood between two fighters, the fight usually sells pretty well." Consequently, fighters who can perform "bad blood" increase their chances of being selected for high-profile matches. As in reality TV, promoters place "real" people into contrived but unscripted settings and reward them with airtime for exaggeration, conflict, and drama.[1]

The successful creative links between fight promotion and reality television show that transmedia marketing is a product of digital and interactive media culture that creates avenues for information and entertainment media to flow across genres and platforms. The millennial generation is accustomed to liking, sharing, revising, and making digital media across multiple devices and mixing genres of entertainment in the process. Millennial marketers have adapted to fan expectations by developing strategies that cross one media genre or platform to another in order to engage consumers and audiences in multiple media ventures (Jenkins, Ford, and Green 2013). Hutchins and Rowe (2012) observe that there has been a "parallel readjustment of the sport media industries and cultures" as the broader media environment has been altered with the increased use of personal computers and mobile devices along with the growing popularity of social media platforms such as Facebook, Twitter, Snapchat, and YouTube (5). With *The Ultimate Fighter*, the UFC adapted its promotional efforts to leverage the strengths of an entirely different genre of television that could do the promotional work while producing revenue in its own right. Innovation, such as developing a reality TV show to promote the sport, became part of the UFC's organizational identity and they developed a fascination with the power of social media to extend their fan base beginning late in the first decade of the new millennium.

THE UFC AND DIGITAL NATIVES

A driving factor in the UFC's newfound love of social media was the UFC's ability to bypass legacy sports media channels in order to speak directly with millennial audiences on various platforms. Other entities could be classified as a millennial sports media brand today; however, the UFC enthusiastically pursued connections with their fans online because they experienced greater challenges gaining visibility on legacy media. Dana White described the organization's early adoption of social media, "We're different from all other [sports] leagues. We embraced social media. Our fighters would tweet in between rounds if they could. We would let them do whatever they want with social media. And it's been very successful for us" (quoted in Cooper 2014). White is signaling the trepidation—circa the mid- to late 2000s—that many brands felt toward social media (Jenkins, Ford, and Green 2013). The capacity for anyone in an organization to tweet or post on digital platforms and have that message circle the globe meant that it became much more difficult for companies to control brand messaging.

To curb these effects, the NFL and NBA initially developed policies to prevent athletes from tweeting ninety minutes before sporting events and until after the postgame press conferences in an effort to manage how information was disseminated (Hutchins 2011). The UFC, on the other hand, gave bonuses to their fighters for social media engagement before, during, and after UFC events. Dave Sholler remembers hiring a former public relations director for the MLB to join Zuffa who was shocked that the UFC encouraged fighters to use social media. Sholler recalls in our interview that "he was dumbfounded because it was such a dangerous . . . risk" the MLB wasn't willing to take. "For us, we've very much grown because of our digital presence and prowess." Even though the UFC had a smaller viewership overall, the brand became one of the top-ten trending sports topics on Twitter in 2009 overtaking World Series Champs the New York Yankees and just behind the NFL. The same year, Dana White reached a million Twitter followers by "humanizing the UFC brand" through "genuine, two-way communication and interaction" with fans (UFC 2010).

Popular and academic discourses often describe millennials as digital natives because the generation came of age with digital media technologies and have integrated social media, streaming platforms, and mobile technologies into their interpersonal relationships, work life, and leisure time. Much of the commentary advising businesses on how to "reach" millennial audiences or consumers describes a process of engaging on digital platforms. Sports media organizations are no exception, and analysts debate how to best engage millennial sports fans. They even attribute the NFL's and MLB's shrinking audiences to these sports' inability to reach millennial fans via the digital content they crave (Singer 2017). In fact, "Heavy-Twitter-using millennials speak a new language and value a new currency: social media speak and social media savvy. Many established brands with high brand equity are trading in the old currency of print, broadcast, and outdoor media, and displaying a disappointing failure to adapt" (Sashittal, Hodis, and Sriramachandramurthy 2015, 326). The UFC demonstrates that even new brands with low brand equity can increase exposure through digital and social media. The UFC's legacy branding and marketing strategies had failed to produce the mainstream visibility the promotion desired; instead, they went after a more accessible millennial audience via social media.

Dana White was one of the promotion's key drivers of online engagement with fans after joining Twitter. He responded to fans, retweeted them, and featured contests to attract more followers and engagement—Twitter strategies that encourage brand attachment. Heavy Twitter users, many of whom are millennials, form emotional and cognitive attachment toward brands they like—a marketing strategy that works best when they promote the product in seemingly authentic ways (Sashittal, Hodis, and Sriramachandramurthy 2015, 326). White's charismatic and boisterous persona draws the social media crowds. He says, "I'm brutal on Twitter. . . . If you say stupid [expletive] to me, you'll get stupid [expletive] coming right back at you. But I think that part of the appeal is that it's not some corporate stiff Twitter account" (quoted in Ortiz 2013). Yet, White also understands how effective the medium is for promoting the sport: "There's no greater marketing tool in the world than social media. . . . It doesn't cost you anything. The only thing you're limited by is your imagination and how fun you want to make it and what you want to do" (quoted in Ortiz 2013). Maria Burns Ortiz (2013), a journalist with ESPN, observed White work with his social media team prior to a UFC event in 2013. She said, "White's no-holds-barred persona is certainly a fit for a social space where being engaging and unfiltered are assets."

Dana White and the UFC engage with fans on social media, but they also promote fan word-of-mouth communication via social media platforms. In 2011 the UFC experimented with airing fights streaming on Facebook, which was "the first time a major sporting event has offered exclusive content through the social networking king" (Ferenstein 2011). Fans could simply like the UFC's Facebook page to receive access to a fight streamed exclusively on the social media site. Dana White explained that during live events, not all fights on the card were broadcast so that airing some on Facebook would give the fans the means to watch every contest scheduled during the event: "Facebook gives fans the opportunity to watch fights that you'd normally have to be in the arena to see" ("2 UFC 127 Bouts" 2011). Yet, the UFC wasn't interested only in airing fights that had no distribution strategies; it wanted to generate buzz around UFC events through word of mouth. Katherine Taken Smith explains that "millennials often look to peers to determine the merit of a product or service. This generation considers the opinions of their peers or fellow consumers to be more credible than traditional media or company sources of information" (2012, 87). The promotion was eager to hype events through word of mouth on Facebook. Dana White told *Fast Company* that "one of the great things about Facebook is that it reaches 600 million people . . . even better than that, all these people can talk to each other and let their friends know the fight is on" (quoted in Ferenstein 2011). White and his team had tapped into the millennial generation's preference for word-of-mouth recommendations over traditional advertising and marketing.

The UFC's engagement on social media isn't unique when surveying the multimedia engagement of major sports brands today. Numerous sports leagues, sponsors, and networks have integrated millennial brand tactics into their promotional practices and no longer cling to traditional public relations and marketing strategies. For example, the NBA became the most tweeted-about sports league in 2018, causing one sports journalist to describe the NBA's Twitter-sphere as "a sports bar that doesn't close, a barbershop with unlimited seating, a family cookout where the NBA stars show up to hang" (Maese 2018). Like the UFC, the NBA has embraced the interaction among its fans and athletes on Twitter and understands that its fanbase is younger, tech-savvy, and more likely to watch a game online than the NFL or MLB's core group of fans. The league and its sponsors don't fear an athlete's voice in the same way that legacy public relations professionals might have and instead see an NBA player's authenticity online as a key avenue for connecting with his fans (Maese 2018). Additionally, various soccer leagues and sponsors around the globe have adopted similar tactics and view athlete engagement online as one of the key avenues for increasing brand awareness. Leagues, teams, and sponsors analyze and measure soccer star Cristiano Ronaldo's 177 million Instagram followers to justify his $44 million in sponsorships annually (Badenhausen 2019). Engagement with fans on social media is now a hallmark of sports brands like the NBA, Ronaldo's team Juventus Turin, and the UFC. The reason the UFC becomes so fascinating when describing the millennial sports media brand is that it was those branding and marketing tactics that allowed the promotion to pull itself out of obscurity and into the mainstream. Thus, the UFC's love affair with social media gave it access to a generation of "digital natives" ready and eager to consume sports content in ways that mirrored other types of content they consumed online.

The UFC's dependence on social media becomes more important to the greater arguments of this book when considering how millennial sports media brands now can monetize athletes like Cristiano Ronaldo or USWNT forward Alex Morgan through social media engagement. The UFC, in particular, uses social media as a means to determine what sort of exposure it will give any given fighter. Marketing professionals view social media engagement as a predictor of pay-per-view buys, which had long been the promotion's bread and butter because it generates greater revenue from pay-per-view than from its gate audiences.[2] This is a contrast to the history of team sports, which usually relied more on gate revenue, although professional teams now derive at least half of their revenue from televised broadcasting (Tainsky, Salaga, and Santos 2013; Noll 2007). Sports management analysts agree that the biggest ways to increase pay-per-view revenue is to include marketable stars and at least one championship fight on the card (Tainsky, Salaga, and Santos 2013; Reams and Shapiro 2017). Booking stars with the most followers and the greatest interaction online can also predict who might buy a pay-per-view fight (Reams and

Shapiro 2017). As a result, the UFC now often books two or three championship bouts per large event as a means to ensure strong pay-per-view buys. The UFC monitors analytics on athletes online engagement and decides if that fighter will be on a marquee Las Vegas pay-per-view card that generates greater exposure and payouts for the athletes or if it will include the athlete on a Norfolk, Virginia, card that airs on ESPN+, a streaming platform that is less lucrative than pay-per-view. This system of identifying stars and the UFC's reliance on social media to do so have particular impacts on female fighters that I discuss at length in chapter 4.

Courting Globally Diverse Audiences

The shift toward using digital and social media to create engagement also produced another effect that has a profound impact on the millennial sports media brand. Millennial users now have a greater ability to locate and consume content that reflects diverse identities and interests and the growth of customizable media for diverse audiences aligns with neoliberal market logics (Gray 2013b). A Brazilian fan may watch a UFC and Combate (a Brazilian cable channel for combat sports owned by Globosat) coproduced mini-documentary following Brazilian champion Cris "Cyborg" Justino the week before her fight, watch replays of her previous matches on the UFC's YouTube channel, read Facebook posts about the fighter in Portuguese and Spanish, and buy UFC brand apparel featuring the featherweight champion—all from handheld devices or a computer. Digital technologies facilitate this choice because media organizations no longer have to rely on mass broadcast television as their sole form of storytelling, which was a hallmark of twentieth-century brand culture (Banet-Weiser 2012). Media brands provide multiple choices that diverse individuals may select from and difference becomes an individualized trait that each person possesses in some form or fashion. For example, Laurie Ouellette (2016) shows that lifestyle TV builds itself on a logic of customization in order to reach particular taste groups: "the term lifestyle also refers to the fragmentation of the mass market (and the TV audience) into increasingly specialized consumer niches defined on the basis of demographics (age, income, gender, race, ethnicity, religion, education) as well as 'psychographics' (values, attitudes, interests, beliefs, behavior)" (4). Sports media has adopted a similar proclivity for customization. Victoria E. Johnson (2009) observes that mobile applications affiliated with sports television "directly appeal to the individual viewer with strategies that emphasize 'a la carte' information addressed to individual fan passions on a 'micro'-scale, in everyday use" (128). Branded

Brazilian UFC fighter Cris "Cyborg" Justino. Photo by Amy Kaplan.

difference is one such strategy the UFC can use to customize its marketing and programming according to the variety of audiences that constitute its viewership. UFC cameras can follow athletes the week before their fights to give the public a glimpse into a Muslim man's daily prayer ritual or a mother's relationship with her young daughter. These stories are inexpensive to produce and easily distributed on YouTube and circulated via Instagram or Twitter. Racial, sexual, gendered, and national difference all become customized iterations of a brand that desires to provide greater choice to a growing number of market segments (Banet-Weiser 2012; Aronczyk 2013).

The task of brands, then, is to either spin their content to reach additional demographics or to introduce content for niche groups. Either way, the imagined sporting audience no longer consists of a singular desirable demographic and allows media brands to produce a much wider array of content featuring more diverse identities. The millennial sports media brand becomes imbued with difference as a key strategy for reaching more consumers and that strategy seems to be working. As of 2018, 18 percent of the UFC fan base in the United States is Hispanic, which is larger than the NFL, NHL, NBA, or MLB's share of that same racial demographic. African American fans make up 15 percent of the UFC's audience, which is larger than every other major league except the NBA's at 17 percent (Epstein 2018). Additionally, the UFC boasts 284 million fans worldwide in 164 countries, resulting in 43 percent awareness of women's MMA in eight global markets ("awareness" in market research is used as an indicator for potential brand growth) (ibid.). Let's turn now to how racial, ethnic, gendered, and national difference each became desirable markets for the brand to promote because the representation of difference became a tenable method of growing the brand in the United States and abroad.

The UFC's orientation toward millennial values and consumption preferences motivated them to embrace their diverse roster of fighters and cadre of fans and expand internationally.[3] A 2018 Pew Research Center report found that U.S. millennials are more racially diverse than previous generations, with 40 percent of the age group identifying as Latinx, Black, Asian, Native, or other minoritized racial group. Millennials are also more liberal than previous generations, with more than 70 percent of the age group maintaining favorable stances on issues of immigration, marriage equality, and "openness to the world" (Pew Research Center 2018). Christie Smith and Stephanie Turner (2015) also show that there has been a fundamental shift in the way millennials view diversity and inclusion compared to previous generations. While their predecessors, Generation X and Baby Boomers, are more likely to frame diversity as an issue of morality or equality, millennials expand the very definition of diversity to include "previous work experience, where you were born and raised, and any unique factors that contribute to your personality and behavior" (Smith and Turner 2015, 7). Millennials see diversity—both domestic and international—as adding valuable perspectives that strengthen the organization as a means to gain stronger business outcomes. Put simply, diversity improves the bottom line and increases opportunity for businesses. For a millennial sports media brand, international expansion and the inclusion of diverse athletes can grow the audience for that sport outside the boundaries of the domestic audience while also appealing to U.S. millennials' global orientation toward the world.

The UFC has evolved as a brand that values diversity and internationalization as a good business practice. As Andrew Billings, Michael Butterworth, and Paul Turman (2014) remind us about sports and global consumption: "because sport is a valuable commodity, leagues and players alike seek new opportunities across increasingly fluid geographical, economic, and political borders" (179). Early in their ownership of the UFC, Zuffa assumed that with some legwork, they could expand to linguistically diverse audiences both in the United States and abroad. Their preliminary attempts at internationalization included broadcasting events abroad, which mirrored major professional sports leagues like the NFL and NBA who sought to expand their global reach by broadcasting games outside the U.S. beginning in the late 1990s (Andrews 1999). Likewise, Zuffa brokered deals as early as 2002 to broadcast UFC events and other MMA media content in Brazil and Japan where MMA already had a significant fan base (Hedges 2002). Currently the UFC is the "largest pay-per-view event provider in the world," reaching "nearly 800 million TV households worldwide" (UFC n.d.). In 2013, an estimated 40 percent of the UFC's revenue came from countries other than the United States (Chandran 2014).

Former UFC executive Dave Sholler maintains that Dana White and the Fertitta brothers always envisioned the UFC as a global sport. White has said on numerous occasions that fighting is just something that people "get" around the world.

> The reality is nothing in this country is bigger than the NFL. . . . I don't care if you just watch one football game all season, everybody watches the Super Bowl. It's huge. The NFL is spending billions of dollars to break into other countries, but it's never going to happen. Nobody cares about the NFL in other countries. They don't understand the rules, and they don't get it. But I can get two guys, I put them in the Octagon, and they can use any martial art they want, it transcends all cultural barriers, all language barriers because it's fighting. At the end of the day, I don't care what color you are or what language you speak, we're all human beings and fighting is in our DNA. (Quoted in Willis 2008)

The UFC president claims that fighting is universally understood and, consequently, the reason the organization has sought international audiences. In White's mind, fighting becomes a homogenizing force to bring global and linguistically diverse audiences together. Dave Sholler and Doug Hartling both echoed these sentiments about the global nature of fighting in my conversations with each of them.

The UFC began adapting its content for specific linguistic and national audiences beginning in the early 2010s (Snel 2013). In 2011, the UFC launched UFCLatino.com, a Web presence dedicated to Latinx UFC fans in the United States, which was distinct from the Latin American version of the site and boasted content in English and Spanish. Dana White said of the launch,

> The UFC has become a really popular sport with Hispanic fans based in the U.S. . . . We've seen the fan base grow and grow, so we're excited to launch UFCLatino. com as a way to continue to serve Hispanic fans. We're fortunate to have great Hispanic champions such as Cain Velasquez and Dominick Cruz and we want our fans to have access and feel connected to our athletes. (UFC 2011a)

White describes the organization's desire to build connections with U.S.-based Spanish-speaking fans through identification with "Hispanic champions." He wants them to "feel connected to our athletes." Although the UFC later folded the Latin American and Latino sites into UFCespanol.com, the organization still maintains Twitter and Facebook handles dedicated to content targeting their various Spanish-speaking demographics. The UFC's efforts to sustain connections between Spanish-speaking athletes and fans remains strong and has since expanded to include other nationalities, languages, and differences. The UFC began circulating the new brand maxim "we are all fighters" in 2016 as a means to represent these commitments to domestic and international diversity.

We Are All Fighters

> Fighters are at the heart of everything the UFC does; they're a symbol of how we fight every day to overcome challenges large and small and are designed to make a meaningful impact in communities where UFC events are held. It takes courage to step into the Octagon, and it takes courage to stand for your convictions. Our pride gives us strength, and our determination makes us lionhearted. 100 percent of UFC proceeds from the We Are All Fighters Shirt will go to LGBTQ organizations and initiatives.
>
> —Online description of the "We Are All Fighters" T-shirt

In July 2016, one month after a man killed forty-nine people in a LGBTQ nightclub in Orlando, the UFC began selling a T-shirt to show support for Pulse nightclub victims and their families.[4] The black T-shirt repeated the phrase "we are all fighters" in primary colors, which together made a rainbow symbolic of LGBTQ identities. The promotion unveiled the new product during its "International Fight Week" in Las Vegas where one could see fighters and fight fans from around the world wearing the T-shirt. The UFC designed the T-shirt to express solidarity with the queer community and the promotion donated 100 percent of the proceeds from the shirts to LGBTQ organizations in Las Vegas, where the UFC is headquartered. The online description of the T-shirt declares that fighters are "a symbol of how we fight every day to overcome challenges large and small." UFC merchandizing asserts that fighters are symbolic of other individuals—be they queer or straight—who face hardship and persevere to overcome. The description continues by proclaiming that "it takes courage to stand for your convictions" but, "our pride gives us strength, and our determination makes us lionhearted." The word "pride" has a two-fold meaning: pride for the hard work required to succeed against adversity and pride as a word associated with the LGBTQ community. The use of "we" and "our" extends beyond queer identities to further interpolate the UFC's audiences into the brand: "we" are

Left to right: Cain Velasquez, Dana White, and Travis Browne and "We are All Fighters" T-shirt. YouTube: Submission Radio.

fight fans because their fight is "our" fight. As a millennial sports media brand, the UFC can draw on discourses that "everyone is different" in some way as a means of appealing to millennial audiences.

The UFC has since expanded the meaning of "we are all fighters" beyond LG-BTQ identities so that now the phrase represents one of its eight brand maxims (Epstein 2018). The UFC's articulation of the meanings of the phrase outlines how and why the promotion brands difference. In essence, "we are all fighters" aims to "celebrate the fighter in everyone and lend support to organizations that help individuals overcome adversity" (UFC 2019). The promotion deploys the brand maxim to include marginalized identities as well as those who are more privileged within society, noting that everyone "fight[s] every day to overcome challenges large and small." The UFC used the maxim on the Pride T-shirt, to promote fighters donating their time to the Special Olympics, and also to describe the induction of former UFC fighter Rich Franklin into the UFC Hall of Fame. The "fight" in each of these contexts becomes similar if "we are all fighters." According to the press release discussing Franklin's induction, the former middleweight champion helped the UFC overcome the "meathead" stereotype of its early days. He was "not only a world-class fighter, Franklin was everyman, a former high school math teacher who chased a dream, espousing all the virtues we ideally want in our sporting heroes" (Gerbasi 2019a). The press release affirms that Franklin embodies the "we are all fighters" maxim because he had to overcome his personal brand of adversity. Branded difference explains that as a middle-class teacher from somewhere in Middle America, one might not expect Franklin to be a fighter. His personal brand of adversity—failing to fit the stereotypical mold of UFC fighter—was the obstacle he needed to overcome. In this logic, Franklin has a fight that White middle-class UFC fans can relate to,

UFC fighters meet and train with British Columbia Special Olympics athletes ahead of UFC Fight Night Vancouver. YouTube: UFC.

just as LGBTQ fans might identify with a lesbian fighter, or disabled fans might see themselves represented in the UFC through the promotion's work with the Special Olympics.

Dave Sholler, the former public relations front man at the UFC, summarizes the promotion's attempts at including diverse audiences through the "we are all fighters" maxim this way:

> I firmly believe we like to be fans of people who've come from where we come from, who've walked in our shoes, and who've seen our experiences. I grew up in South Jersey, which is a huge Philadelphia sports market. . . . There's a player named Mike Trout who grew up one city away from me in South Jersey and now plays for the Los Angeles Angels. I'm a Phillies fan, but I root for the Angels because of Mike Trout, the South Jersey guy. He went to the same schools as me, got his hair cut at the same place as me, and ate at the same restaurants as me. He's my guy. I have to think that when an Asian fighter from Japan is competing in UFC 198, there are many fans in Japan rooting for that fighter. In Brazil, when Cris Cyborg makes her walk into the Octagon this weekend in her hometown of Curitiba for her first fight in the UFC, there's going to be 45,000 fans from that region watching her as she carries the flag. We root for people who come from where we come from, that have overcome the obstacles that maybe we've overcome. . . . In order to become a truly global sport, we have to have ambassadors that are different races and colors and who speak different languages, who come from different backgrounds, and who are gay or straight. Whatever you may be, the UFC is a representation of who we are as a society.

Sholler's articulation of difference in the UFC draws on the premise that "we are all fighters" regardless of nationality, race, religion, sexuality, or gender. Sholler illustrates this by centering his own experiences as a White man growing up in South Jersey and his connection to an athlete of a similar background. He acknowledges an individualistic vantage point that differs from other perspectives. Sholler then applies this awareness to the multitude of UFC fans and believes that audiences want to see fighters who look like them represented in the UFC mediasphere. The "we are all different" or "we are all fighters" maxim centers audiences as both a niche group with specific cultural affinities or differences as well as a part of a more homogenized global community of fight fans. "We" all have faced hurdles even as those hurdles are customized to appear as diverse experiences. "We" all seek fighters who look like us and come from the places "we" have come from. The UFC understands difference as facilitating feelings of belonging and identification, which means that each fan wants to feel as if they belong because there is a fighter that represents them. Difference becomes a homogenous aspect of human nature—we all seek people who are like us to root for in sports.

Research on millennials affirms that the UFC's perception that difference "encapsulates the unique attributes and experiences that each individual brings" is common to a generation that values diversity (C. Smith and Turner 2015). Over the past decade of teaching millennial (and more recently Generation Z) undergraduates, I have observed this popular usage of difference when teaching about issues of diversity and inclusion to students new to the concept of identity privilege. I don't want to disparage the optimistic way some of my students embrace diversity; however, I would like to highlight how their definition of difference does have its limits and can be co-opted by brands to appeal to those of us who value inclusivity. Many of my students believe that everyone has a unique combination of identities or repeat the refrain that "we are all different in some way." In this logic, an individual might face adversity for being Black, dyslexic, transgender, a veteran, gay, a single mother, a first-generation college student, unemployed, or any other manner of difference. In their articulations of "we are all different," these students decontextualize identity from the structural forces that produce some of those differences and understand all identities as being ultimately "the same" because they all face some form of hardship in life. Likewise, in the UFC's millennial brand identity, the White Irishman from an impoverished background is the *same* as the Black American female fighter because they are different from one another and both may have faced obstacles to reaching their goal of becoming UFC fighters. The UFC, and broader media culture, appropriates the millennial definition of difference as something everyone possesses without full recognition for the struggles marginalized genders, races, and sexualities face. If "we" can all be different, then this logic of production functions to make difference read as sameness. Difference in a millennial sports media brand carries a sameness that is devoid of the cultural, political, economic, geographic specificities that make the White man from the Bronx and the lesbian fighter from the favela actually different. The "we are all fighters" brand maxim reveals that branded difference in the UFC is an ambivalent cultural discourse that fluctuates between depicting difference as individualized and presenting it as a homogenous feature of our collective humanity.

As I show in the remainder of the book, branded difference in the UFC serves as a key mechanism to make diverse female fighters visible while glossing over inequalities that disproportionately impact those fighters on the roster who are most different, such as women of color, lesbians, and gender-non-conforming women. Branded difference evacuates politicized meanings and instead deploys a watered-down "we are all different" mentality that is more palatable for mass consumption. Kristen Warner (2016) describes the dance between difference and sameness in media culture as "universalizing." She says, "Universal discourse underscores the historical precariousness of minorities in the creative industries whose labor always existed under this double bind structure that equates success with being both similar to and different from the normative order" (182). In this way, female fighters are both similar and different from male fighters. The UFC includes female fighters in the maxim "we are all fighters" and there is a degree of acknowledgement that they have endured social scrutiny for participating in a "man's sport"; yet, because "we all face adversity," all challenges become equal. Any gender hurdle in the sport is the unique obstacle women must work to overcome to be successful in the UFC.

Many of the narratives the UFC weaves appear meaningfully diverse (Beltrán 2010) at face value because they focus on the trials and tribulations located in essentialized understandings of difference and even cursory understandings of social and economic barricades for particular identities. However, inserting any individual difference into a brand maxim can also make those differences formulaic, flat, and mired to the idea that everyone possesses it. Gender, race, sexuality, and/or nationality become customizable features that may be plugged in and played according to the particular niche group the millennial sports media brand may be seeking to attract. Difference becomes slavish and devoid of its uniqueness or particular identity politics because difference includes *all*. The cultural, political, economic, or geographic specificities that make the White man from Jersey and the lesbian fighter from the favela distinctive are obscured. If "we" can all be different, the global socioeconomic conditions that have created the Brazilian favelas or the farming regions of Iowa remain vague. "We are all fighters," and thus difference itself, becomes evacuated of politicized meaning in favor of a branded difference that works to obscure the ways our differences produce inequalities for certain groups.

The UFC gives digital natives what they want: diverse fighters from around the world that audiences can access on multiple platforms and through various transmedia products. In many ways, the brand has made exciting inroads into making diverse female fighters visible within the sport, but at what cost? The millennial sports media brand may value diversity to a greater degree than previous generations, but structural roadblocks leveraged against women, people of color, and/or the LGBTQ community are often explained away as similar to the personal trials of straight White men. The remainder of this book unfolds how branded difference is a discourse that is appealing to fans, but it can also motivate a tremendous amount of labor on the part of a global roster of fighters. The next chapter considers how branded difference can evoke powerful affective responses that make the visibility of female fighters meaningful to audiences and fighters alike.

CHAPTER 2

Affect and the Rousey Effect

Joan Jett's iconic voice belted over the loudspeakers as the corresponding drum-beat signaled the frenzied beginning of her punk anthem: "I don't give a damn 'bout my bad reputation!" At the same time, the lights in the Rio de Janeiro Olympic arena dimmed to black as the crowd awaited Ronda Rousey's imminent approach to the Octagon. I was sitting on an upper deck of the stadium, attending my first live UFC event and waiting to see how Rousey would be received as a U.S. fighter in front of the Brazilian crowd. The ferocity of Jett's voice intermingled with a rush of exhilaration that bounded around the arena from all directions and surged through the bodies of the thousands of fans in attendance. The fervor for Rousey caught me by surprise, and the thrill of the moment subsumed me. Rousey, dressed in her signature black hoodie and surrounded by her team of coaches and security guards, appeared from a corner of the stadium just beneath me and made her determined march toward the cage. I couldn't see her face from the distance but could conjure the stern scowl that often adorned her face prior to her fights. The queen had entered her court. Partly fueled by the crowd's ardor, partly reacting to Jett's defiant punk voice, and partly awestruck by Rousey's embodied charisma, involuntary tears rushed to my eyes and my breath coalesced in my chest as I gasped. An overwhelming and unexpected force emanated from and through me. The curious scholar in me rushed to analyze the moment to identify an emotion that I was feeling or to justify my response with some logical explanation, but my attempts to intellectualize the

The Rousey mean mug. Photo by Amy Kaplan.

moment escaped me. Never in my life had I witnessed a crowd reach such a fever pitch for a female athlete. I didn't know how to process the sensations I was experiencing; rather, they radiated, beyond any rationalization I could surmise, all around me. Rousey seemed to carry the same unnamable energy into her fight and went on to overwhelm her opponent early in the first round.

Scholars have a name for the energy, the force, the bodily sensations I experienced watching Rousey enter the Brazilian arena at UFC 190 (August 1, 2015). The word "affect" describes the embodied, visceral forces that are an undercurrent to conscious thought and expressed emotion and that connect social bodies to one another (Gregg and Seigworth 2010; Rentschler 2017). In the crowd in Brazil, I sensed a collective energy that undergirded both my later analysis of the event and my attempt to identify the emotions I was experiencing. Scholars often study affect by identifying the emotional currents present in real or mediated events. As Anna Gibbs (2002) says, "Media and bodies appear as vectors, and affect itself as the primary communicational medium for the circulation of ideas, attitudes and prescription for action among them" (339). Thus, media facilitates the circulation of affect across time and space and can cause intense emotion to surge within people physically disconnected from one another even though affect isn't just a synonym for emotion. Zizi Papacharissi

(2015) argues that while affect contains feelings, attachments, and emotions, "it both precedes and sustains or possibly annuls feeling and emotion" (21). Thus, emotions can be identified, cataloged, and explored, whereas affect is broader and contains an unconscious precursor to being moved or motivating action. Affect influences both rational thought and emotions and becomes a lucrative method for marketing sportswomen in a millennial sports media brand.

This chapter considers how the UFC harnesses affective attachment to the brand through the representation of Rousey and the image of powerful female fighters. In the UFC, the visibility of sportswomen engenders an affective response that courses through people in both real, physical spaces and vicariously through a vast array of media content. Giles Deleuze (1988) theorizes clear connections between visibility and embodied sensations: "visibilities are not defined by sight but are complexes of actions and passions, actions and reactions, multisensorial complexes, which emerge into the light of day" (50). Thus, I interrogate what representation mattering *feels* like. I argue that while branded difference leverages the affective resonance of the strong female fighter to tap into the current popularity of women's empowerment in media culture, the UFC has also created a seductive mirage of possibility for female MMA fighters themselves. The UFC describes the brand as "revolutionary" or as "breaking barriers" for female athletes; however, I caution through the pages of this book that the symbol of the female fighter in the UFC is also deployed in problematic ways despite the intense sentimentality and feelings of empowerment it generates. Even though women and girls may *feel* empowered by Rousey and the UFC, branded difference remains a veneer for progress rendered hollow when considering the precarity of the fight profession for female athletes discussed in this book.

By focusing on what these images of powerful women feel like and to what effect, I follow Herman Gray's (2013a) call to move beyond the questions of representation often posed in media research by instead asking "how (and where) media gather and mobilize sentiments and affective investments" surrounding difference (253). Gray suggests that the study of affect can illuminate what is made to matter in the media and what attracts emotional intensity. This focus abandons questions of whether or not the representation of Black men, for example, is accurate or representative of the diversity of identities that make up the group of people racialized as "Black men." Instead, Gray suggests that asking "what does it feel like" and "what feelings do the structures of media produce" can provide new avenues for researching difference in the media. In the case of the UFC, the visibility of gendered difference generates affective currency that the UFC can spend to facilitate strong connections to the brand by depicting the

UFC as breaking barriers in women's sports and empowering female athletes. While I take no issue with the visibility of strong female athletes in their own right, this chapter sets the stage for my later analysis of what is missed when we culturally respond with such a positive affective response to those images without interrogating the broader consequences of their visibility. Just because the visibility of sportswomen *feels* good it doesn't mean the positive feelings produced outweigh the costs of that visibility. To begin, I consider how the UFC began to facilitate affective connections with fans through the image of Rousey before shifting to consider how the same tactics motivate female MMA fighters.

Harnessing the Power of Affect in the UFC Brand

I vividly remember anticipating the first UFC fight between women in early 2013. Similar to my experience watching Rousey's fight live in Brazil, the moment that Liz Carmouche and Ronda Rousey walked into the Octagon on my television screen felt exhilarating because it held the promise of progress for women in a decidedly male-dominated social sphere. Their success in the UFC might mean change for women everywhere in martial arts, including in my own training of Brazilian jiu jitsu. A corresponding feeling of trepidation accompanied my excitement because much was riding on that particular fight. Their failure in the UFC might confirm the dominant discourse about women not belonging in MMA. I was also unconvinced that the UFC would be the promotion that could elevate women in combat sports to the next level. As a new fan of MMA at the time, my own assessment of the sport still stereotyped the UFC as a hotbed of muscle-bound "meatheads." I remained skeptical for the few months leading up to the Rousey vs. Carmouche fight and was unsure how the UFC would promote these fighters, how commentators would assess their fighting skills, and how UFC fans would receive them. To my surprise, the UFC emphasized the historical significance of the fight and promoted the two women in ways similar to male professional fighters. The crowds in attendance and the audiences at home also generated visceral and palatable exhilaration to propel these female fighters into MMA history. Carmouche felt the same affective currents circulating through the fans in attendance as she "walked through that threshold." She said, "I felt all the energy in the entire crowd. I, to this day, have never felt anything like that. It was almost like an energy and a static in the air is the best way to describe it. You could physically feel the excitement of everybody there" ("Breaking Barriers" 2019). Women's MMA exploded at that moment, and the UFC centered a narrative of women's empowerment in the sport in a way that fans and pundits at the early UFC events would never have imagined.

The UFC tapped into a visceral pulse in popular culture that propelled Rousey's stardom in particular.

The entrance of women in the UFC at this particular moment in the sport's history begs the question: how did a brand once labeled "human cockfighting" get into the business of women's empowerment? The answer is twofold. First, branded difference is a logic deployed by the brand to expand its viewership to diverse demographics by depicting fighters that represent those target demographics. The UFC had created a strategy where it could plug-and-play a variety of identities into its storytelling formula featuring fighters succeeding against adversity, including women. Second, Ronda Rousey's stardom peaked amid a cultural moment that amplified her stardom and the UFC's branding and marketing teams recognized the potential for selling the athlete as a role model for women and girls. Branded difference latched onto the affective resonance of women's empowerment to facilitate the rise of female fighters in the UFC.

The UFC's foray into leveraging fan affective responses to branded difference began with efforts to market to Black and Latinx audiences in the United States before later translating the same principles to the branding and marketing of female fighters. "Representation matters" developed as a central logic in the millennial sports media brand's use of branded difference to promote fighters and those same approaches could be modified for gender, sexuality, and nationality. As the previous chapter articulates, difference is visible in the UFC because audiences are diverse and the millennial generation expects media representations to reflect that reality of U.S. demographics. Some of the first examples of the UFC's attempts to draw different fan demographics focused on courting Black and Latinx boxing fans. Doug Hartling, the former director of marketing at the UFC, describes the challenges the organization faced breaking into the "Mexican market" in the early 2010s, a story that poignantly illustrates how the UFC configures difference in its brand identity. Hartling says the UFC had tried to market the sport to Latinx fans in the United States for several years because of the popularity of boxing in that particular demographic. Marketing professionals commonly seek out existing brand communities, such as fans of particular sports, in order to introduce a new audience to their brand. Jenkins, Ford, and Green (2013) write that organizations "'court' existing communities whose broad interest predispose them towards the kinds of conversations the company seeks to facilitate" (164). For example, Hartling also described acquiring marketing data on the 2015 Women's World Cup finale, which featured a victorious USWNT and drew the largest U.S. audience for a soccer match ever (Chappell 2015). Hartling and his team wanted to determine who was watching that match in order to market the UFC's women's divisions to the same demographics.[1]

Hartling's tone shifts to reveal the way affect features in branded difference when he tells the story of how he realized his team was beginning to make inroads with Latinx fans. A member of his marketing staff, Fabiola Rangel, was watching Cain Velasquez's first fight in the UFC with her Mexican American family. Hartling mentioned that Rangel's family wasn't the UFC's "typical market" because they weren't boxing fans, nor did they really watch sports at all. However, Rangel recalled that the mood in the room shifted as her family watched Cain Velasquez walk into the arena before his fight. The family became animated at the sight of Velasquez sporting the Mexican flag across his shoulders and his Virgin of Guadalupe and "Brown Pride" tattoos during his walkout.[2] Hartling said "even *abuela* came running into the room" when she heard a traditional Mexican folksong accompanying Velasquez's entrance. Hartling's retelling of Rangel's story reveals that the UFC marketing team targets a more diverse fan base and that the promotion seeks avenues to reach new markets both domestically and internationally. The marketing director discussed how important it was for that family to see themselves reflected in the UFC because inclusion is a socially significant value in media culture today. He seemed to delight in the fact that the UFC was able to make the family *feel* membership in the UFC's fan community. In his marketing role, he also spoke of this moment as a synergistic opportunity because it also meant the UFC could reach new audiences. For Hartling, it was a win-win scenario: the Mexican American family felt included, and he achieved his goals of increasing the UFC's audience size.

Hartling's story brings up an interesting paradox within the MMA promotional machine that is the UFC. At the various levels of production that this book examines, it's clear that representation matters. One of the primary tactics the UFC has used to reach new racial, ethnic, national, and now gendered demographics is to connect the race, ethnicity, nationality, and/or gender of its diverse fighters with fans that share those identities. At the same time, Hartling's perspective as a marketing professional doesn't mean the broader organization treats diverse identities equally or fairly. Various media outlets have criticized Dana White and numerous fighters on the roster for racist, homophobic, transphobic, or Islamophobic comments (McClearen 2015a; Zidan 2019; Mazique 2017; Buzinski 2011). Conor McGregor has used racist rhetoric to insult opponents and generate interpersonal conflict in order to promote his fights while the UFC generally turns a blind eye to his tactics. McGregor further has two pending cases of sexual assault levied against him that the UFC fails to address (Zidan 2020). It's important to continue to view the UFC's engagement with diversity as ambivalent. These examples of condoning bigotry or rape culture fail to erase the fact that representation of diverse fighters is simultaneously a desirable pursuit for the millennial sports media brand. The UFC dances clumsily between promoting representational diversity and empowerment and condoning overt bigotry.

Despite the inconsistency the UFC shows in its treatment of minoritized identities, Hartling reveals that representation has inherent value to him personally and that branded difference is an effective tool for encouraging affective brand attachment. The marketing executive told the *abuela* story as an example of the resonance people feel when they see themselves represented. Hartling's description of the moment with *abuela* carried an affective tinge. He was proud that the UFC was able to make even *abuela* feel connected with the brand and believed that creating this affective connection made him a successful marketer. Henry Jenkins (2008) is among the scholars who show us that generating positive consumer sentiments is a key component to branding and marketing. Marketing professionals seek to understand how consumers make decisions about consumption through emotive response—a process called affective economies. As Sara Ahmed (2004) explains, affective economies work to "align individuals with communities . . . through the very intensity of their attachments" (119). In other words, marketing and branding professionals seek to understand consumers' affective motivations for participation in a brand and create a brand that facilitates that attachment. The UFC understands that its fans identify with fighters who look and speak like them and circulates ethnic identification within affective economies. Hartling used the story as one example of the UFC's efforts to expand its brand into households in the United States and abroad. Velasquez became tagged as the UFC's "first Mexican champion," while Joanna Jedrzejczyk became the "first Polish champion," and Conor McGregor became the "first Irish champion."[3] Each athlete represents a slice of the UFC's narratives of ethnicity and nationality that attempt to attract audiences who may identify with these fighters. Branding strategies such as these "encourage consumers toward highly cathected and deeply emotional relationships to brands" (Mukherjee and Banet-Weiser 2012, 19). The UFC understands branded difference as facilitating feelings of belonging and identification, which means that each fan wants to *feel* as if they belong because there is a fighter that represents them.

The sense of connection is particularly strong in sporting spaces, and sports marketing professionals like Hartling understand these fan attachments. Katie Mox, a corporate public relations manager, explains why sports brands become meaningful to fans: "What makes sports and specifically teams so special is really just the camaraderie—you feel like you are a part of something. When you see a total stranger wearing your team's clothing, you are inclined to give them a high five, compliment their shirt, or simply say, 'Go team!'" (quoted in Garrison 2016). Oftentimes these connections begin at a young age, and many sports fans recount experiences seeing their teams or favorite athletes compete when they were children. Brands like the NFL and the NBA cultivate sports nostalgia by hosting kids' club events during their seasons while the UFC sponsors children's jiu jitsu, wrestling, and karate tournaments during its International Fight Week Fan Expo. Tim McDermott, chief marketing officer of the NFL's Philadelphia Eagles, explains that his team's efforts to market to children ensures nostalgia for those experiences later in life. Rather than being a big source of revenue, the Eagles' "kids' club" encourages a sense of belonging that ensures those children continue to identify with the Eagles brand throughout their lives (quoted in Neisser 2012).

I begin this examination of affect by offering examples of the branding of racial and ethnic difference for male fighters because I want to emphasize that the UFC's promotional tactics evolved to include women rather than originating with female fighters. Facilitating affective connections between diverse fighters and fans is an ethos that the UFC has deployed to further its demographic reach in terms of ethnicity, nationality, and now gender.[4] These strategies suggest rationale for why the UFC may have taken a chance on female fighters in the first place and why the promotion has had more success at marketing female

Rousey demonstrating her judo skills at UFC 184. Photo by Amy Kaplan.

fighters than other combat sports have. Unlike the UFC, boxing promotions have failed to translate their own emphasis on fan identification into promoting female boxers. They do, however, emphasize ethnicity. Mexican American boxers often display sights and sounds of their ethnic heritage in the promotion of their fights and enter the ring accompanied by patriotic flashes of the green, white, and red flag and Mexican folk music to facilitate the affective attachments of Mexican identities (García 2013). While the UFC retains an interest in marketing pretty female fighters for a heterosexual male gaze, the promotion also began considering girls and women's empowerment as a viable marketing strategy to spur affective attachment to the UFC—largely through the tour-de-force that was Ronda Rousey.

Ronda Rousey and the Affective Resonance of Empowerment

Ronda Rousey walked onto the practice mat in Rio de Janeiro on a cool summer day in 2015 amid the hum of an adoring cadre of fans. The athlete failed to disappoint the large crowd gathered near the beach for a fan event previewing her upcoming fight. For the next thirty minutes, the former Olympic judo athlete danced across the floor, throwing her sparring partner over her shoulder, arm-barring him, and brilliantly exhibiting her skills on the mat. Her performance riveted fans in attendance and the cameras filming for streaming audiences around the world. After she finished training, Rousey wiped the sweat from her brow, only to be accosted from behind by a young fan. A small girl of seven or eight ran across the mat dressed in a blue gi (a traditional marital arts uniform) to greet the UFC star and take a photo with her. Rousey knelt down, smiling and hugging the little girl in a touching moment that later went viral on the UFC's social media channels. It was around this time that the UFC realized that Rousey was more popular with girls and women fans than with men and that discourses of women and girl's empowerment could sell UFC fights.

The star power of Ronda Rousey had a tremendous impact on the ability of the UFC to reach new audience demographics (Roberts 2015). Rousey and McGregor were the two most popular UFC names in 2015 resulting in a 65 percent increase in pay-per-view buys over the previous year (Meltzer 2015). I attribute a large part of Rousey's rise to a moment in popular and consumer culture that sought out empowered images for women and girls to emulate. Empowerment in media culture in its affective essence is a sensation, a welling up of positivity, that inspires confidence and even bravery when someone sees themselves represented. This sensation spreads through media and can be experienced collectively and even empathetically by those who hold different identities. It's the little girl in a Wonder Woman costume who stands up in her seat, raises her fist to the air and shouts "finally!" the first time she sees the superheroine she idolizes onscreen. It's the cafeteria of young Black children who joyously dance on tables when they hear they all will attend a screening of *Black Panther*. It's the little girl in Rio de Janeiro who sprints across a stage full of adults to embrace her idol. Our culture reads these moments as significant and joyous because we believe in the promises of visibility: that just seeing marginalized identities on screen means something significant that we can all feel. Brands, as conveyors and creators of culture, understand the connections between representation and empowerment. They seek opportunities to facilitate the joy that representation mattering can generate because these affective registers create loyal consumers of that brand.

Fabiola Rangel, a former member of the UFC's marketing team, recalls that after the 2015 event in Rio, the UFC realized that Ronda Rousey presented them an opportunity to increase their numbers of female fans. Rangel mused that even though Rousey displayed impressive judo skills and the Brazilian fans clearly adored her, the moment that went viral was Rousey's interaction with the young girl because, in Rangel's words, "representation matters." Rangel maintains that because of the viral enthusiasm for the video, the UFC marketing team recognized that Rousey's strength and confidence was drawing women and girls, in particular. The marketing professional says,

> You have little girls now practicing MMA. You have little girls writing to [Ronda] to tell her she's their idol and that they want to be like her when they grow up. And I think it's because of [Rousey's] confidence to act like men do and be whatever a man can.

The key takeaway is that the promotion began to understand the representation of women in the UFC as mattering to fans because women fighters inspired and empowered women and girls.

The height of Rousey's celebrity occurred during a moment in popular culture when symbols, slogans, and sentiments aimed at boosting the self-esteem and confidence of girls and women abound and feminism has achieved a "new luminosity" (Gill 2017, 611). Even when "feminist" isn't explicitly claimed as an identity category, empowerment themes materialize from all directions, such as apparel companies printing "the future is female" on T-shirts to talk show host Ellen DeGeneres declaring "girls can" in a CoverGirl makeup commercial.[5] Andi Zeisler (2016) describes these trends in consumer culture as marketplace feminism, which is a "cool, fun, accessible, identity that anyone can adopt" (xii) that also is "mediated, decoupled from politics, staunchly focused on individual experience and actualization" (xvi). Marketplace feminism, and what Sarah

Banet-Weiser theorizes in a similar vein as "popular feminism," revolves around the focus on individual solutions to inequality through consumption that rarely also consider how our social institutions, human relationships, political entities, and economic structures all work together to maintain gender inequality (2018).

Various sporting organizations have joined in the empowerment chorus reflected in popular culture more broadly. Rachel Wood and Benjamin Litherland (2018) discuss how World Wrestling Entertainment (WWE) has shifted its approach to female wrestlers over the past few years in ways similar to the UFC. For example, the documentary *WWE24: Women's Evolution* "mobilises a version of neoliberalised feminism to present a sometimes scathing critique of WWE's past management of women's wrestling, and to justify a current era of transformation" (Wood and Litherland 2018, 911). The WWE's discourse of "transformation" mirror's the UFC's focus on "revolution" (discussed below) that represents a shift from women's exclusion to celebrating sportswomen as empowered. Likewise, team sports have also taken up a degree of optimism for female athletes and the girls and women who are fans of the sport. The U.S. Soccer Federation created the #shebelieves campaign (inspired by their own players) after the women's national team won the 2015 FIFA World Cup. They describe #shebelieves as "a movement to inspire young girls and women and encourage them to accomplish their goals and dreams, athletic or otherwise" ("SheBelieves" n.d.). The campaign has included an internship program for women, a ten-city tour for the players to meet with women making a difference in their communities, and the #shebelieves Cup—a global women's soccer tournament that provides "a stage to shine the spotlight on role models (athletes and non-athletes alike) and showcase their accomplishments both on the field and in culture at large" ("SheBelieves Cup" n.d.).

Even sports that exclude female athletes have begun focusing on empowering female fans. Just ahead of the 2015 Super Bowl the NFL sponsored it's second Women's Summit. The league's vice president of marketing, Johanna Ferris, described the purpose of the summit as encouraging discussion about "pursuing your dreams" and examining "how leaders of today can share insights, and what challenges they've overcome personally and professionally" (quoted in Hampton 2017). The Women's Summit exemplifies how the NFL has worked to reposition itself as "engender[ing] civic health via individual care and empowerment" in its attempts to form connections with female fans (Johnson 2016, 14).

The UFC's interest in marketing Rousey to women continued to flourish after the video of the little girl accosting Rousey at the open workout went viral.

In October 2015, Pinterest boards flooded with a Ronda Rousey Halloween costume trend. The boards included numerous images of (mostly White) girls wearing UFC sports bras and fight shorts, hand wraps, and the signature Rousey mean-face for the camera. One board describes its young costume model this way: "Three-year-old Elsa loves boxing and quickly took a liking to UFC as well. She asks to watch 'Wonda Wousey' and is pretty disappointed when the fights are over so quickly" (Costume Works n.d.). The UFC recognized the trend and included a Halloween photo montage of girls ranging from babies to teenagers dressed up like Rousey on its Twitter, Facebook, and Instagram platforms. UFC (and Ronda Rousey) sponsor MetroPCS later created a commercial of a young Rousey look-alike trick-or-treating with the fighter. The campaign asks "would you dare to say 'no' to Ronda Rousey?" and proceeds to show Rousey and her young fan scowling at a man who opens his door and protests "but it's not Halloween" after Rousey and her mini-me chant "trick or treat." The ad ends with the girl and her idol sitting side by side eating the candy while affirming that "nobody says 'no' to Ronda." The ad continued to air during UFC events into 2018, even after Rousey has retired from the UFC.

The images of young girls emulating a UFC fighter are fascinating. If the UFC dedicated its entire brand to the "meathead" hypermasculine man, as in years past, then the representation of the small girl dressed in UFC attire would be entirely incongruent with its brand identity. However, the UFC understands that its meaning isn't singular with fans and that its constituents instead help determine what symbols become associated with the promotion. The UFC's embrace

Ronda Rousey MetroPCS commercial. IspotTV, MetroPCS Commercial, "Would You Dare Say No to Ronda Rousey?"

of Rousey as a women's empowerment figure exemplifies a key shift in twenty-first-century branding and marketing strategies on social media. That engagement—or what bubbles to the affective surface and circulates more broadly—is important information for the promotion to leverage in marketing itself. The UFC pays attention to what fans become interested in on social media and attempts to leverage that fervor in a direction that reflects positively on the brand. One of the promotion's eight brand maxims is "fans first" (Epstein 2018), which is a reflection of the millennial sports media brand's commitment to observing what garners fan interest and attachment and shift its approaches according to the fans. These examples of Rousey's viral celebrity with girl and women fans also demonstrate that marketing campaigns develop both organically from following the likes, shares, and affinities of target audiences and/or through top-down campaigns. As a millennial sports media brand, the UFC is attentive to how affective attachment becomes the impetus for fans and audiences to circulate UFC content on social media, thereby strengthening the brand and allowing the UFC to profit on Rousey's image as it circulates in more mainstream media culture.

Revolution

The UFC observed the viral success of Rousey and began considering girls and women's empowerment as also a potential top-down marketing strategy for the promotion. UFC staffers Doug Hartling, Chris Kartzmark, and Fabiola Rangel each confirmed in their interviews with me that the UFC was eager to capitalize on Rousey's growing popularity as a role model for women and girls. As a result, the UFC outsourced the promotional video for Rousey's next fight against Holly Holm to a L.A.-based production company Digital Domain, which would be able to provide a much more theatrical trailer than the UFC's in-house production team. Digital Domain producer Neil Huxley remembers a sense of excitement around creating that particular promo because the production company had the chance to tell a new story for MMA: "You don't normally see these stories about women. Look at the [UFC] promos we have seen over the years . . . it's usually heavy metal music and two guys shouting at each other face to face. . . . The fact that we got to tell a story about two fighters was great. The fact that it was women was even better because you are not used to seeing things like this." Huxley highlights that the production team sought to create a promotional spot that departed from MMA's status quo and spoke to a broader audience. Digital Domain and the UFC tapped into popular feminist discourse that acknowledges gender discrimination for women in sports and offers individual grit as a method for overcoming obstacles facing women in male-dominated spheres.

The 2015 Rousey-Holm promotional video, *Revolution*, is a narrative in under three minutes that follows the two women from their first experience with martial arts to their upcoming meeting in the Octagon for the fight (Huxley 2015). In sharp contrast to anything the UFC had done before, the promo begins with a parallel edit of Rousey and Holm as young girls growing up in martial arts and witnesses them come into their own as martial artists in their respective specialties. The short video can be divided as a three-act structure: act 1 establishes the women's first childhood encounters with martial arts, act 2 introduces the challenges to being women in the sport, and act 3 shows the women excelling in their sport and preparing for the upcoming fight between them. The UFC has produced or outsourced numerous trailers to promote major headlining pay-per-view events, but this one was unlike any other promo the UFC had ever created. UFC trailers historically featured heavy metal music, montages of fight footage, and images of fighters screaming, yelling, or pounding their chests. Another 2015 trailer, also created by Digital Domain, featured Conor McGregor and Jose Aldo walking toward each other on the empty moonlit Las Vegas strip while Jay-Z and Kanye West's "No Church in the Wind" serenaded the fighters' smooth swaggers. *Revolution*, in contrast, shows the girls grow into women who have faced adversity as they fought to stake a claim in their respective martial arts specialties. The instrumental music is much more emotive and anticipatory than "No Church in the Wind." Seeing young women face clear adversity, grow into dominant fighters, and ultimately find a space within a historically hypermasculine space produced a strangely sentimental promotional spot to advertise an MMA event—strange because sentimentality has been an atypical approach for the promotion. Since the purpose of the narrative is to market the fight between Rousey and Holm, the promo ends in a cliff-hanger that shows the two women standing across from each other in the Octagon, waiting for the referee to begin the fight. True to the promotional genre, this last part of the story is unwritten at the end of the spot and meant to encourage audiences to buy the pay-per-view and witness the resolution of the narrative.

The first time I saw *Revolution*, I cried. The emotional registry of the three-minute narrative of the two fighters reflected much of my own experience as a cisgender, White woman in martial arts. As a young White woman growing up in the southern United States in the 1980s and '90s, I was trained in emphasized femininity. For the first twenty-six years of my life, I embodied these qualities of middle-class White femininity and often feared for my own personal safety in public because of conditioned notions of weakness and inability to defend myself. When I began martial arts at age twenty-six, I started to think about my body and its experience with gendered social conditioning in new ways. I began

A young Rousey (played by an actress) in the *Revolution* promo. Vimeo, Neil Huxley, "Revolution"—UFC 193 Rousey vs. Holm promo.

walking taller, hitting harder, and renegotiated my personal understanding of feminism to include my body. Even though I still experience sexism within martial arts, the training also grants me an avenue for embodied resistance to gender discrimination on the multiple fronts that women face. The tears I shed watching *Revolution* were tears of identification even though I also identify as a critical feminist scholar who studies consumer culture and the influence of advertising on the emotions of audiences. Intellectually, I can critique what the ad aims to do and who it excludes in the process, but the affective resonance of the promo moves me despite my rationalized resistance to this form of persuasion. This is the power of the popular feminist icon in consumer culture: she inspires us even though we aren't dupes to the powers of advertising. Instead, the promo strikes a chord that connects with a cultural moment that values the empowerment of those often disenfranchised in popular media.

Digital Domain created the trailer to pull heart strings and to be inspirational. Interestingly, Huxley and Aaron Shact, the promo's writer, centered adversity and gender discrimination as the inciting incident and the key battle both women must endure to reach the climax of the story where we find out which of our heroines will succeed, that is, remain in the sport in spite of the setbacks. For example, one early scene shows Holm's trainer fitting her boxing gloves to her hands as two men stare and smirk at each other as they pass the only woman in the gym. The smirks communicate that she is not welcome in that space, where she and any other women are also likely discriminated against. Holm seems oblivious to the men's reactions to her presence in the gym. Instead, she glances up toward the ceiling and inhales an anticipatory gulp of air. The scene shifts to establish a small church, where Holm sits in a pew with her head bowed and hands clasped reverently in front of her. Her pastel clothing and reverent visage suggest the angelic purity often associated with White femininity. She lifts her head, and the camera zooms in on her pale face framed by her light-yellow hair and displays the shadows of a blackened eye. Even though Holm appears indifferent to her bruised face, a man and a woman in the congregation look disapprovingly at her while whispering to each other. Culturally, we are more likely to read White women with black eyes as being victims of domestic abuse than athletes, so women with bruises often attract concern in addition to disapproval. The scene emphasizes the contrast between the reverent young girl and the defiant fighter. Passivity and reverence in church form a sharp contrast to a White woman who fights and wears a black eye proudly because dominant constructions of gender expect White feminine passivity and assertive and even aggressive White masculinity.

The judgment that Holm faces for being in the boxing gym and for sporting a black eye in church allows a point of identification for women who may have felt marginalized in other public spheres. As I argue elsewhere, female action heroines and athletes succeeding against physical adversity often become visual metaphors for women who identify with other women succeeding in male-dominated spaces (McClearen 2015b). For that article, I interviewed university-aged women on why they enjoyed films with female action heroes. These particular viewers read action heroines as symbols of women being successful at school and in their careers rather than literal symbols of physical power. Extrapolating from this research, women identifying with Rousey and Holm might read female athletes as metaphors for women fighting for themselves in broader society rather than athletic idols that motivate them to join an MMA gym. While the UFC didn't release specific statistics on audience engagement, the promotion told Digital Domain that they were thrilled that the spot reached new fan

A young Holm (played by an actress) in the *Revolution* promo. Vimeo, Neil Huxley, "Revolution"—UFC 193 Rousey vs. Holm promo.

Holm sitting in church in the *Revolution* promo. Vimeo, Neil Huxley, "Revolution"—UFC 193 Rousey vs. Holm promo.

demographics outside their base (Martin 2015b). Rousey debuted *Revolution* on *The Ellen DeGeneres Show* and it quickly went viral, reaching nearly two million views on YouTube within a matter of weeks. Thus, the Rousey-Holm promo could breed a mass affective appeal beyond just those who regularly watched MMA or other women's sports, which is one of the reasons the ad was able to circulate broadly.

While the narrative of the promotional video displays gender discrimination specifically, Digital Domain didn't intend for the promo to appeal just to women. Huxley notes that they wanted to tell a story of outcasts overcoming discrimination, and they intended the emotional register of *Revolution* to encourage empathy with the underdog: "That was an interesting angle for me. . . . even though they were treated as outcasts, it never stopped them from doing what they wanted to do . . . what they loved doing." Huxley confirms that the intended affective register of the promo establishes both women in popular feminist narratives positioning them as heroines inspired to compete in a man's space and succeeding against adversity. It was important to the two men at Digital Domain to tell that story in a sincere way. For example, the only words in the entire promo come at the end when these words appear on the screen: "Every revolution starts with a fight." During our interview, Huxley said that he and Shact bounced around the idea of using "fight like a girl" as the tagline when first conceiving of the promo, but they felt that phrase cheapened the story. They wanted the promo to have a universal appeal and weren't aiming to make a trailer that would just appeal to women. The "every revolution" tagline, by contrast, suggests that these women symbolize change within society. Huxley and Shact conceived of Rousey and Holm as the beginning of a revolution, and both of these women had to overcome cultural obstacles to continue in their sport. They persevered against adversity in judo and kickboxing, respectively, and fought for acceptance in MMA—an underdog story with universal appeal because fight storytelling has long featured adversity and eventual victory as key narrative strategies (see chapter 3). *Revolution* celebrates Rousey and Holm's hard work and determination against gender discrimination, but it also shows that popular feminism can be a discourse molded to appeal beyond women and girls. Rather, it is also a discourse that can stand as an inspiring visual metaphor for other types of adversity an individual fan might face because "we are all fighters."

The UFC offers its brand as a solution to the crisis of empowerment (Banet-Weiser 2018) for the disenfranchised (predominantly White) feminine body, thereby facilitating the UFC's connections to the affective currents already circulating within its fan communities. This discourse extends beyond just women and girls to affirm that representation matters within branded difference and particular women, such as Rousey and Holm, can connect with certain sentiments, ideas, or priorities circulating at distinct moments within broader culture. Young girls can attach the Rousey brand to their bodies and dress like her for Halloween. Adult women can challenge the assertion that women's physicality is purely decorative by donning a Ronda Rousey T-shirt and training kickboxing at their local UFC gym.[6] The UFC positions Rousey and Holm as inspiration for overcoming obstacles to equality on the playing field. Thus, a chief aim of these branding and marketing tactics is to spur confidence that girls and women can *feel* within their own bodies. Fitness and athleticism are a means of embodied empowerment that *some* women— but not *all* women—may access through sport and fitness brands. Rousey and Holm both exhibit particular ideals of emphasized femininity, such as Whiteness, conventional attractiveness, and hyperfeminine clothing. As I discuss in the introduction, there are hierarchies of visibility within the UFC that still privilege pretty White women and beautiful light-skinned women of color over all other women.

The UFC found marketing gold with Rousey because it could appeal to a more mainstream audience and join a lucrative trend in marketing and advertising: a popular feminist ethos that encourages women's and girls' empowerment. The ability of the UFC to ride the popular feminist wave combined with their growing facility at using representations of difference to draw diverse fans both enabled the introduction of women into the UFC. Empowered female athletes had become profitable, and the UFC could now integrate them into its brand identity because they were outcasts rising out of adversity just like so many of the stories about male fighters. Furthermore, it's also important to consider how brand identity isn't exclusively an outward-facing endeavor meant to solicit consumers only; rather, brands create maxims and other identity markers of who they are as an organization in order to also develop their workers' attachments to that brand. The story the UFC spins for its fans about women's empowerment can also be useful for creating brand loyalty in its fighters. In other words, the UFC can compel female fighters to work for the brand because of the strong emotional attachment to empowerment. I now examine how Rousey's visibility motivated female fighter labor for the UFC through the affective resonance her stardom generated.

Empowering Female Fighters

The UFC's production team created a series of short films for its twenty-fifth anniversary, including *Breaking Barriers: The Story of Ronda Rousey and the Rise of Women's MMA*. The fifteen-minute film features interviews with several of the UFC's most famous fighters including Ronda Rousey, Liz Carmouche, Miesha Tate, Cris Cyborg, Rose Namajunas, Claudia Gadelha, and Michelle Waterson. Footage of two teenage fighters preparing to meet each other in an amateur MMA fight propels the film's narrative of girls' empowerment. The film opens with a montage of close shots on the young fighters' faces, on the wrapping of their hands, and on their anxious feet as they dance rapidly across the floor. Stringed instruments accompany the montage at a frenetic pace signaling anticipation as we watch the girls exude nervous energy. The film continues to follow the young fighters and intersperses interviews with female UFC athletes. A key

A young female MMA fighter featured in the UFC's *Breaking Barriers* short film. Vimeo, Dennis Fye, UFC 25 Years in Short—Breaking Barriers.

theme throughout *Breaking Barriers*, other UFC-produced media, and interviews with current and former female MMA fighters is Rousey's centrality in inspiring girls and women to train MMA and in affirming that the UFC held possibilities for women. We've considered how women's empowerment rhetoric evolved in the UFC as a response to the affective attachments of its audiences, but how do the images of Ronda Rousey circulate *affect* that has an *effect* on female fighters?

In order to understand the impact of Rousey on female fighters, we must examine how those fighters constitute another demographic of the UFC's audience. MMA practitioners are current or prospective UFC fighters and a niche fan demographic that the UFC brand actively engages. I don't want to suggest that female fighters comprise a large constituency of the UFC's fan base; instead, I propose that the promotion flourishes by maintaining a brand identity that can recruit a ready supply of prospective UFC fighters. Human interest stories highlighting the fighter's American dream is one brand message appealing to fighters that I discuss in chapter three while the women's empowerment narrative recruits female fighters. As *Revolution* also shows, the UFC tells and retells the story that women have endured gendered obstacles to break barriers in the sport. These stories have a perhaps greater consequence for fighters than for its audiences.

Stories about women breaking barriers in the UFC is a narrative that facilitates an "intimate public" of female fighters. Lauren Berlant (2008) describes an intimate public as a virtual or imagined community that

> operates when a market opens up to a bloc of consumers, claiming to circulate texts and things that express those people's particular core interests and desires. When this kind of 'culture of circulation' takes hold, participants in the intimate public feel as though it expresses what is common among them, a subjective likeness that seems to emanate from their history and their ongoing attachments and actions. (Berlant 2008, 5)

In other words, marginalized identities become unified through consumption that meets their collective needs and wants and acknowledge the perception of shared experiences. Berlant discusses media created for women as one form of address that makes American women feel connected to shared experiences and histories of other women. Berlant explains that media meant for niche, minoritized audiences "tell identifying consumers that 'you are not alone (in your struggles, desires, pleasures)': this is something we know but never tire of hearing confirmed, because aloneness is one of the affective experiences of being collectively, structurally unprivileged" (ix). Thus, the image of the powerful female fighter breaking barriers in the sport could speak to "identifying consumers" in the UFC audience who view themselves as facing collective struggles with other women.

What is more, women training in a male-dominated sport with historically fewer opportunities for female fighters become one such community that thrives on images of other women with the same goals, dreams, obstacles, and victories in their sport. Female fighters rarely experience a community of other women when they train MMA because gyms normally have much fewer women than men. Jessica-Rose Clark explains that female MMA fighters are surrounded by men and have to advocate for themselves as a result:

> I still struggle to speak up about what I believe in with certain people. [This is] especially [true] for the women involved in this sport. . . . All our coaches are men. All our management are men. All our promoters are men. So we're constantly being told what to do by strong, dominant men. It's hard to speak up for what you want.

Barbie Beeman (pseudonym) further notes that fighters tend to be an isolated group who train with a tight-knit community in their gyms but rarely spend a great deal of time with fighters outside their own gym. It stands to reason that female fighters who are mostly training with men have fewer opportunities to develop support systems within groups of other women. UFC media, then, becomes the avenue for communicating the shared experience of being a female fighter. When they see other women shining on the male-dominated stage of the UFC, the stories of other women prevailing can develop an intimate public among them.

Fighters often talk about who first inspired them to begin MMA and oftentimes it's a female fighter who had a moment in the spotlight. For those of Rousey's generation and earlier, names like Gina Carano, Cris Cyborg, and Julie Kedzie feature prominently. Rousey, for example, was first exposed to the idea of MMA through a famous women's fight: "I couldn't help but think of doing MMA one day because I saw Gina Carano and Julie Kedzie fight, and I didn't even know women fought in MMA. And it just planted that seed in my mind" (quoted in Harkness 2016). Of course, Rousey and others went on to inspire women both within the sport and outside of it. Nina Ansaroff cites the shift that has occurred in women's MMA in an interview that also featured her fiancée and fellow UFC fighter Amanda Nunes:

> There's a huge future in women's MMA where a 10-year-old girl can dream to be a successful MMA fighter. It's not something that's a crazy thing to chase anymore. Back when we [Ansaroff and Nunes] both started, it was kind of laughed

at to be like, "I'm going to live a successful life off of fighting." That didn't exist, so it was hard to keep chasing that dream. But now it's more realistic. You can look at Amanda, you can look at Ronda, you can look at all of these other girls in the UFC and think, "That's what I want to do one day!" And it doesn't seem crazy anymore. (Quoted in Kurchak 2017)

Ansaroff highlights that fighters like Rousey and Nunes prove to other female fighters that their UFC dreams are indeed possible now and they can find a great deal of inspiration in seeing women succeed in the promotion. UFC fighter Alexa Grasso agrees with Ansaroff and attributes Rousey as fueling her drive to endure the daily grind of training: "I saw [Rousey] and I want[ed] to be like her . . . I'm doing my best every day and I'm training hard" (quoted in Raimondi 2015). Thus, in addition to drawing fans to the sport, the UFC star image of Rousey motivated some female fighters to pursue the sport in the first place and embody the popular adage "if she can see it, she can be it."

"If she can see it, she can be it" is the anthem of the intimate public unifying women through empowerment discourses in media and consumer culture. It centers visibility as a key tool for providing more women avenues to thrive in whatever profession they choose. As Berlant argues, "an intimate public is a place of mediation in which the personal is refracted though the general, what's salient for its consumers is that it is a place of recognition and reflection. In an

Alexa Grasso. Photo by Amy Kaplan.

intimate public sphere emotional contact, of a sort, is made" (2008, viii). Berlant reveals how visibility, then, becomes a way for consumers to see a version of themselves refracted from the light shining on the image of the empowered girl or woman. In the case of aspiring UFC fighters, the version of themselves they see faces injury, defeat, and discrimination, but ultimately breaks through those barriers. Rousey, for example, provided many of her peers hope that her visibility in the UFC would break the glass ceiling for women. Michelle Waterson, who was already a standout fighter in Invicta FC—the first and only women's professional MMA promotion in the United States—when Rousey burst into the UFC, says this of Rousey's significance to women's MMA: "Ronda Rousey came around and became dominant in the sport . . . [and gave] . . . women visibility and a voice. We were always there, but . . . [because she was] outspoken [she] helped open the floodgates and let more of us get recognized for performing at the highest level of fight sports, which is UFC" (quoted in Frye 2019). Waterson wasn't inspired by Rousey to join the sport, but Rousey gave her increased confidence that women could now thrive in the promotion. I asked several fighters that I interviewed if they had been skeptical that women's MMA would flourish after Rousey and Carmouche fought at UFC 157. They all responded that they knew women just needed the opportunity to shine and that everything would change after that. Cortney Casey said, "As soon as they signed [Rousey], I knew we were going to have a career in the UFC as women. Just because the door needs to be opened . . . once people saw that we could do this, people were going to want to watch more girls fight." Roxanne Modafferi agreed with Casey: "I think that we [women] just needed a star to be stuck in there and convince Dana White [that women could fight]." Rousey's success in the Octagon generated feelings of optimism and even a collective pride as she proved what these fighters already knew: women could fight and draw fans. Even though fighting is an individual sport and contemporary empowerment discourses also privilege the individual, the feelings that women's visibility in the sport generate are collective and spur them to action.

Female fighters even cite making big life decisions as a result of Rousey's success in the UFC. According to UFC fighter Cynthia Calvillo, "Ronda came around and changed the game. She changed the game for all professional [MMA] athletes. This is the highest we've ever gotten paid." For Calvillo, the fact that the UFC paid Rousey so much meant that she too might find similar success in the UFC and that was when she decided that MMA could be a career. "I knew that [the UFC] was the biggest paying organization, so that was one of the biggest reasons why I pursued it professionally and quit my job." Other fighters have echoed the same sentiments as Calvillo. Mackenzie Dern says she was always against transitioning from being a professional Brazilian jiu-jitsu fighter to MMA, but Ronda changed her mind. She thought, "'Okay, I can do this . . . I saw Ronda, how much she opened the doors for girls, even outside of MMA. All the success that she had, it was like, man, we can make a living off that too" (quoted in "Dern" 2016). Rousey's own assessment of the opportunity that women like Calvillo and Dern could find in the sport supported the up-and-coming fighters' aspirations: "MMA is the only women's combat sport that offers enough money so they can make a living. And so every single other discipline where the best women are, they all have incentive to move to MMA" (quoted in Luther 2015).

I've illustrated in the fighters' own words that Rousey's success and stardom in the UFC became a huge motivating factor for other women and girls in MMA. The UFC brand generated an intimate public of female fighters moved by the narratives of Rousey "breaking barriers" as a "revolutionary." These stories spilled over into the fighters' own understanding of what Rousey's success meant and what that might mean for their careers as well. For these fighters, representation generates feelings of inspiration, motivation, and affirmation for a group of women long struggling in a male-dominated space. The allure of Rousey's stardom was powerful for them even if they didn't idolize her in the same way some fans do. Rather, her visibility meant that the floodgates opened and now things would change for women in MMA. *Breaking Barriers* even ends with these statistics to underscore the point. A slide flashes on the screen to declare: "Since 2013, when Ronda Rousey defeated Liz Carmouche in the UFC's first women's fight . . . over 300 women's bouts have taken place inside the Octagon. Women have headlined 5 of the top 10 pay-per-view events of all time. Ronda Rousey became the highest paid athlete on the UFC roster." Presumably women could now hope to support careers as professional MMA fighters because the most prestigious MMA promotion now allowed them into the limelight.

From Inside to Outside the Limelight

The discourse of women's empowerment connects with an intimate public of both audiences and fighters who view women's opportunities in the sport and in broader society with hope. The images of the powerful female fighter provoke a shared emotional register among those in the intimate public of female fighters even though the popular feminist discourse of empowerment seeks to elevate the individual rather than develop strategies for women to collectively fight discrimination. Popular feminism, then, produces an ambivalence between the individual and the collective. The intimate public of female fighters collectively celebrates the successes of women who excel in the limelight and feel positive associations with images of women's empowerment. Yet, those same women must individually face the gender discrimination the sport acknowledges still exists for them. Female fighters may collectively shine through a few success stories within the promotion, but many individuals labor for the UFC in virtual obscurity. The affective resonance of girls' and women's empowerment is one of the key tricks of the light that enables these working conditions to persist with little objection from fighters or fans.

The positive affect that circulates around these female athletes has the distinct ability to favor the purity of the pursuit of greatness over the reality that the quest is mired in the realities of the business. As Victoria E. Johnson (2019) shows, love and attachment to sports teams or athletes is culturally perceived as pure and as outside the constraints of the market. When athletes leave those teams for financial reasons, for example, fans come to the realization that sports are "a market rather than a potentially utopian community" (162). Likewise, women who fail to achieve their UFC ambitions remain invisible because that would contradict the lore of the empowered female athlete the UFC has crafted and that fighters and fans enjoy so regularly. The strong affective pull of the empowered female athlete prefers that these market realities remain invisible because that lore *feels* good. In actuality, the chances that the women who sign contracts with the UFC will succeed at the level of Ronda Rousey or even Holly Holm is exceptionally rare. Dana White even admits this when he tells female fighters that "the sacrifice that you have to put in to make it into the top five or top three in the world is hard. It's almost impossible" (ESPN 2019). White's comment points to the discrepancies between the sparkle of women's empowerment and the obscurity of the hardship and toil that marks the path of the female fighter. Even though he admits to these realities, the glittering image of the empowered sportswomen persists. Luminosity in the media is the power to make certain things sparkle while producing an effect of the light that casts shadows over others. As with all tricks of the light, we must continue to ask "what is invisible?" when the light shines so brightly on certain images and creates shadows elsewhere even if it feels better to ignore what lies in the darkness.

The next chapter begins with another sparkling discourse but then shifts to further examine how branded difference also works to exploit those seeking the spotlight. Chapter 3 investigates how the UFC perpetuates the American dream myth that encourages fighters to labor for the promotion while facing low pay and minimal benefits as independent contractors of the UFC when the rewards for these sacrifices are fleeting and few. The result is a roster of fighters who remain optimistic about their chances if they can just work hard enough, which obscures the fact that very few fighters achieve their UFC dreams. The affective force behind the women's empowerment and the American dream discourses unite to convince us that anything is possible for women within the promotion even though the UFC currently maintains a structure that severely limits its capacity to deliver on those promises.

CHAPTER 3

Gendering the American Dream

One evening during season 26 of *The Ultimate Fighter*, UFC president Dana White visits the house where a group of female fighters live while filming the reality show (Piligian et al. 2017). Shortly after his arrival, Lauren Murphy, one of the contestants, asks White "what kind of car did you roll up in?" The executive smiles widely as he tells the group of aspiring UFC fighters that he drives a BMW M760i, adding that there are only twelve of that particular model in the United States. After Murphy asks if they can see the car, White takes the group outside to show them around the luxury vehicle. Murphy later reflects: "I just thought we were going to look at it. I didn't think we were going to get to sit in it and push all the buttons. That car has more class in it than I will ever have in my whole life. I was happy to just sit in it." The reality show positions Murphy's reflection on the BMW as aspirational. Financial success is discursively possible within the UFC brand, and the presence of White and the car suggests this explicitly. Murphy was already signed to the UFC in another weight division and has been fighting for them since 2014. She has been ranked as high as eighth in that division. Despite this relative success, she has never experienced even a fraction of the financial benefits afforded to White or UFC superstars Conor McGregor and Ronda Rousey. Earlier in the year, Murphy told the Bleacher Report that UFC fans are often surprised that she drives a rusty 2004 Dodge Neon. She recalls an encounter with one fan: "There was a [Cadillac] Escalade parked outside . . . and [the fan] goes, 'Is that your Escalade out there?' And I just laughed and laughed" (quoted in Harris 2017). Scenes like the ones with White and Murphy amplify a perception of wealth in the UFC. Yet, the reality for many fighters is much starker. Murphy says, "You wake up every day, and you're hurting, and you wake up and you're f—king exhausted. . . . Where's all the money? Where's the rock star stuff? You've got to love what you do. It makes me cry a lot. This life is actually pretty hard. You have to love the grind" (quoted in Harris 2017). Murphy grapples with remaining optimistic while acknowledging the adversity she faces daily to continue on the path of a UFC fighter. Her reflections accentuate the fact that financial gain and "rock star stuff" are isolated to a relative few within the UFC.

Dana White claims in the same episode of *The Ultimate Fighter* that "There's no other organization in the world where if you truly believe you are the best in the world or can be, where you make millions of [bleep] dollars . . . women are making millions of dollars. That's the place where we are now. You look at all these other sports and women don't make what men make. Women made more in this [bleep] sport than the men. That's what you're capable of doing." When White says "women" can make more money than men, he may just be referencing Ronda Rousey, who was the highest paid UFC fighter in 2015. White emphasizes that women have an equal chance to rise to the top of their game and make millions in the promotion. The UFC can ride the popularity of women's fighting and proclaim that women can be successful in the promotion because Rousey was. Yet, as I've already noted, the athletes who "make millions" comprise a small percentage of fighters and the remainder of the roster, like Lauren Murphy, must resign themselves to "just sit" in the UFC president's BMW. Despite White's assertions that women make more than men, most MMA analysts agree that the pay gap between male and female fighters is stark after removing Ronda Rousey from the equation (Brennan 2016; Scott 2017). The UFC instead exploits the myth of the American dream to motivate fighters to continue on a quest to achieve the same success as Rousey or the UFC president himself.

The American dream is a popular discourse that views all social inequalities as conquerable by "pulling oneself up by the bootstraps" and striving to achieve one's goals despite setbacks. Yet, one of the grand failures of the myth is a disregard for the ways structural forces inhibit social mobility and maintain inequality. The dream myth instead deflects blame for immobility onto the individual. As Diane Negra and Yvonne Tasker (2014) further explain, neoliberalism shifts the responsibility for poverty onto individuals by continually peddling "capital-friendly narratives that call on the working class to deal privately rather than publicly with economic exigencies" (25). This results in much greater emphasis on hiding one's economic woes until those troubles have been surmounted.

Dana White offers a cautionary tale for the aspiring UFC fighters like Murphy that illustrates how the myth functions in the promotion (in Piligian et al. 2017). He acknowledges that the road is rocky and that the women vying for success in the UFC will have to "make sacrifices" and experience "bumps" and "scratches" along the way (quoted in ibid.). But, he continues, "If you're that [bleep] good and you believe in yourself, you can make a lot of [bleep] money. This is the toughest thing you will ever do, throughout your entire fight career." White's acknowledgment that the road is long affirms the struggles of fighters like Lauren Murphy, who admits that she cries about her financial situation as a UFC fighter. The American dream would claim that this is a necessary pain on the road to success and that, if she quietly endures, she will prevail. The UFC celebrates female fighters for their difference and folds them into a narrative of hard work and reward while the structure of the organization only allocates that reward for a few superstars.

This chapter examines how the branding of diverse female fighters in the UFC facilitates the myth of the American dream in fighter promotion, in sponsor relationships, and in fighters' own rhetoric. In the UFC's branded image of itself, female fighters have unbridled potential to achieve their dreams of becoming UFC champions. Branded difference is a promotional tactic that supports the notion that hard work overcomes any obstacles no matter the position one begins from. While these narratives are appealing for fight fans, I argue that the millennial sports media brand customizes the American dream to entice a continual stream of diverse and expendable labor willing to sacrifice their livelihood and health to chase their UFC dreams. The American dream myth allows the promotion to elevate the visibility of gender, ethnic, and sexual difference; yet, it simultaneously absolves the UFC from any real responsibility for the well-being or financial stability of its athletes. Instead, the promotion insists that if fighters just work hard enough, money and success will follow. Sports films, documentaries, and shorter vignettes have long used the myth to tell captivating sports stories, but the UFC brands the American dream sports narrative in ways that have been rare for female fighters.

The chapter begins with considering how the UFC deploys the myth in its promotional and storytelling tactics in order to fully examine how discourses of the American dream operate in this context. I start with the representational before moving toward an analysis of how UFC athletes incorporate these discourses into their understandings of the working conditions in professional MMA. The interplay between the representational and the material allows us to better examine what is shiny and new within the UFC's treatment of difference and what labor conditions remain hidden from view because of that luminosity.

The American Dream as Storytelling

The unity between branded difference as a promotional strategy and the American dream as a storytelling tradition in sports has been effective for the UFC because these discourses are appealing to both fighters and fans. Fighting as a metaphor for the American dream came to prominence long before the UFC began promoting MMA fights. The American dream is the muse of the underdog—a Rocky Balboa who defies his life circumstances to shock the world with his gritty rise to greatness. Underdog stories are some of the most thrilling memories of live sporting events, such as the United States' triumphant win over the much favored Soviet hockey team at the 1980 Lake Placid Olympics or Matt Serra's thrilling knockout of champion Georges St-Pierre at UFC 69 (April 6, 2007) despite the Las Vegas betting odds heavily favoring St-Pierre. While a come-from-behind underdog narrative can be found in most sports, a physical fight between two athletes symbolizes the very ethos of a down-and-out hero overcoming the trials he—and it usually is a *he*—faces along the way. Pugilists must endure intense physical pain and mental exhaustion to keep punching in the ring, and fans then celebrate the fighters who endure the most suffering to overcome their own bodies' limitations.[1]

It's important to consider the ways the drama of fighting also becomes fictionalized in UFC American dream storytelling even though UFC fights are "real." As I argue in chapter 1, fight promotion as a genre of media shares an affinity with reality television because it is steeped in interpersonal conflict and personal charisma per *Keeping Up with the Kardashians* or the *Real Housewives* franchises as well as underdog stories told on competition shows like *The Voice* or *American Idol*. Reality competition shows often provide backgrounds on the show's contestants that emphasize personal tragedy and setbacks they've undergone to reach the competition stage. As Jo Littler (2017) points out, "Wildly successful transnational franchises such as *Idol, The Apprentice*, [*The*] *Voice, Got Talent* and *Top Model* repeatedly address ordinary subjects who can 'make it to the top' of their particular profession, particularly in the performing arts and business, through hard work and self-fashioning" (59). In many ways, the UFC presents fighters as relatable and ordinary in their quest for the top.

UFC media also shares an affinity with a long history of sports film championing meritocracy. As Samantha N. Sheppard (2018) writes, "sports film is a genre that uses sports figures, history, events, and iconography to narrativize inspirational and cautionary tales about athletic success and, to a lesser extent, athletic failure" (162). The constant tension between success and failure in the Octagon reflects in the ways the UFC tells stories about individual athletes in a similar fashion to Sheppard's description of the sports film genre. She adds, "Perseverance and victory over adversity are common themes in sports films, and these tenets produce predictable story lines: hero faces obstacles, overcomes obstacles, and wins the game and gets the girl, too!" (163). Similarly, narratives of fighter adversity and persistence against obstacles permeate the UFC's prefight promotional vlogs following fighters, are displayed across the large screen monitors in the UFC event arenas, and become infused within the sponsor relationships the promotion builds. The UFC weaves tales about individual fighters that frame their personal lives as extensions of the fight that takes place in the ring. A UFC 194 (December 12, 2015) promotional video declared that José Aldo fought his way out of a Favela to become a Brazilian national hero. Season 20 of *The Ultimate Fighter* (2014) introduced contestant Randa Markos as an Iraqi refugee who now must overcome her father's distaste for her profession. Various types of UFC promotional media highlighted that Ronda Rousey slept in her car for a time between winning an Olympic medal and becoming a UFC champion. Yet, as Aaron Baker (2003) notes about sports films in particular, "what is less connected to social reality in many sports films is the overly simplistic explanations they offer for how star athletes achieve these successes" (12). The UFC promotes perseverance and tenacity in the ring and in life as the singular characteristics that lead to athletic success, but there is little acknowledgment for any other conditions beyond the fighter's control that might require more than grit to overcome.

The Fighting Spirit

A series of commercials and short YouTube videos titled "Fighting Spirit" exemplifies the American dream storytelling tactic in the UFC, which also extends to the promotion's sponsor relationships. The thirty-second commercials for Modelo, the UFC's official beer sponsor, focus on fighters who have overcome some sort of challenge in their lives or careers by cultivating a "fighting spirit." These ads prominently feature athletes who persist against setbacks. The slightly longer YouTube videos follow Chris Weidman, Michael Chiesa, Felice Herrig, Tatiana Suarez, Amanda Nunes, Nicco Montaño, and other fighters before big events. Each of the videos are between three and four minutes long; feature interviews with the fighters, their coaches, and their friends and families; and depict the fighters drinking Modelo. Similar to the *Revolution* promotional video, the Modelo ads and YouTube videos emphasize what each athlete has overcome to enter the Octagon with their "fighting spirit." Chiesa survived the death of his father while competing on *The Ultimate Fighter*. Weidman persevered when he lost his house to hurricane flooding. An adolescent Suarez overcame discrimination from boys who wouldn't wrestle against her because she was a girl. Montaño dug herself out of poverty. Like other American dream storytelling in the UFC, the Modelo ads weave narratives of adversity that climax when that fighter proves themselves in the Octagon. The customization of adversity is a promotional strategy designed to appeal to a variety of demographic markets thereby making difference hypervisible and commodifiable. In this vein, it doesn't matter if you are a Polish woman or, as the next section articulates, a lesbian fighter from Brazil—you too can achieve your UFC dreams.

In late 2017, the UFC announced it was trading its official beer sponsorship from Bud Light to Modelo Especial, a Mexican beer brand owned by Groupo Modelo. The change in business partnerships was an interesting one considering the Budweiser brand is an American sports staple found in ballparks all over the United States. The UFC had secured Bud Light sponsorship in 2008, when the promotion was still trying to gain legitimacy in mainstream sports media. Ike Lawrence Epstein, the UFC chief operating officer, said of the Bud Light sponsorship that "It gave us a tremendous amount of credibility with other sponsors. And not just sponsors. Television networks and venues and, frankly, anybody involved in the business of sports entertainment around the world" (quoted in Associated Press 2017). Yet, after the vast growth of the UFC worldwide, the promotion changed its beer sponsorship for a few key reasons. First, the Bud Light deal formed an exclusive relationship between the UFC and Anheuser-Busch that prevented the UFC from establishing partnerships with local beer companies outside the United States. The new partnership gave Modelo exclusive domestic rights yet allowed the UFC to seek other beer company sponsorships outside the United States, thereby allowing the promotion to form relationships in local markets around the world. Second, as Jim Sabia, chief marketing officer of Modelo, affirms, the UFC "wanted to get into more multicultural consumers" (quoted in Associated Press 2017). Modelo promotes its Mexican roots and prominently features American Latinx identities in its U.S. advertising, such as a commercial highlighting Hispanic American football players and another celebrating the first Latina fighter pilot in the U.S. Air Force. The UFC's move away from Bud Light to the Mexican beer brand signals the promotion's commitment to "multicultural" expansion of its brand both within and outside of the United States.

Modelo's tagline "brewed with a fighting spirit since 1925" further seemed like a logical partnership with a global fight brand. Modelo released a series of commercials claiming "it doesn't matter where you come from, it matters what you're made of" and featuring prominent Hispanic Americans and later

UFC fighters. Modelo described the rationale for its rebranding in the United States as an effort to expand the brand while maintaining allegiance to its core consumers:

> Modelo has been successful by growing with core Hispanic consumers. However, in 2016, we were approaching the end of that runway. To further grow, we needed to drive penetration with a new audience and not alienate our core Hispanic brand lovers. To do that, we identified a compelling, unifying and culturally relevant insight that grew the brand with new audiences while maintaining loyalty with Hispanic brand lovers. How? By proving that even in today's divided America, it doesn't matter where you come from, it matters what you're made of. ("Modelo Fighting Spirit Stories" n.d.)

The message of unity among differences for Modelo is clear. The brand speaks directly to current immigration debates in the United States by emphasizing both a celebration of Hispanic heritage and a focus on what it believes can unite ethnically diverse people in the States—being made of the fighting spirit. The latter narrative allows Modelo to extend its brand to other identities, namely UFC fighters who also display the same fighting spirit in the Octagon and without.

A major tactic of Modelo, both in the ads that promote UFC fighters and the others featuring stories of Latinx Americans, is to focus on the identity of immigrant as a fundamentally American experience. Modelo narrates Stipe Miocic's ad by emphasizing his American dream story: "UFC Heavyweight Stipe Miocic fights for more than just a gold belt. The proud son of immigrants, Stipe fought for his dreams while working two jobs and fighting fires for his community. Stipe still fights fires and still proudly fights for his heritage" ("Modelo TV Commercial, n.d."). The commercial describes Stipe Miocic as a "proud son of immigrants," signaling his identity as first-generation Croatian American. This plays into a central feature of the American dream myth—no matter what your national origin, the same formula for success yields the same results. Miocic worked two jobs and fought fires to achieve his UFC dreams. He symbolically fights outside the ring and literally fights within the ring with the same resolve. In this way, a traditionally Hispanic brand can connect with other ethnic identities through the discourses of immigrants coming to America, working hard, and achieving success.

In many ways, Miocic fits the stereotype of the desirable immigrant and admirable prizefighter. He is a White working-class American who, as a firefighter, is the epitome of masculine heroism in the ring and in life. Michael Butterworth (2007) reminds us that rugged individualism embedded in the

Nicco Montaño wins the flyweight championship. YouTube, UFC, UFC 228: Nicco Montano—Fighting Spirit, presented by Modelo.

American sports hero narrative often centers around White athletes while Kath Woodward (2006) observes that these stories are almost exclusively about men. She chronicles the long history of fictional and nonfictional storytelling about boxers using masculine ideals of physical power to find "a route out of poverty and into acceptance, wealth, and celebrity" (164). This pursuit of the American dream through literal fighting has long been the purview of White men and to a lesser extent men of color, while female fighters have been almost invisible as American dream heroes. Woodward illustrates this by examining the critically acclaimed film *Million Dollar Baby*, which features a female boxer. Woodward reasons that although the subject of the film is a female boxer who fights her way out of poverty, the narrative pays more attention to the men in her life, who became the real heroes in the film's narrative.

Read as a singular text, one might deduce that the Miocic ad relies on generations of heroic narratives about White male boxers from working-class communities. Yet, reading Modelo's promotional content intertextually, we can begin to see how the UFC Fighting Spirit campaign welcomes a variety of identities into the fold, including women. The promotional spot for Nicco Montaño customizes the campaign for her Navajo identity:

> Winning the flyweight belt has changed my life. I was living in a basement with no water pressure, no AC, just my boyfriend and I and our two cats. You could definitely say we were poor in cash, but I was never poor in spirit. The fighting spirit comes from my Navajo blood and adversity. (UFC 228 2018)

Montaño rhetorically echoes Miocic and the other fighters as they define and give examples of their own fighting spirit. They describe hard work, determination, and adversity along the way and identify failure, disappointment, and challenging life circumstances as tests of their resolve as fighters. The promo also emphasizes Montaño's identity as a Native woman. The spot begins with her speaking Navajo after winning the flyweight championship in 2017. Later in the video she says that she considers herself a representative of her family, tribe, and land and that "coming from a land of resilience and a tribe of strength gives me the strength to pull through." Thus, "no matter where you come from," be you a working-class White hero or the first Navajo champion, "it just matters what you're made of." The former part of the slogan shows that fighters are diverse, while the latter requires that they exemplify the same fighting spirit in order to succeed in MMA. Branded difference ultimately serves to uphold unified myths of meritocracy and the American dream; yet, the brand strategy executes these narratives differently depending on the specific identities featured. I now consider how the UFC incorporates lesbian identities into the "we are all fighters" brand maxim in order to illustrate how the UFC nuances the stories it tells about difference and the American dream according to the various identities represented.

Crafting UFC Dreams for Lesbian Athletes

A promotional spot for UFC on Fox: Johnson vs. Moraga (July 27, 2013) called *Jessica Andrade Emerges* "spend[s] a few minutes with Jessica Andrade in her native Brazil as she takes you through a typical day and tells you the *unique* story of how she broke into MMA" ("UFC on Fox 8" 2013, emphasis mine). Presumably, the goal of the three-minute video is to introduce an unknown fighter to the UFC audience prior to her first fight in the promotion. In Portuguese (with English subtitles), Andrade explains how she works by day and rides the bus across town to train jiu jitsu at night. As she speaks, images of her neighborhood in Rio de Janeiro flash across the screen: people on motorbikes navigating Rio, a roughly patched roof decorated with a colorful array of laundry drying on a clothesline, and Andrade taking down the laundry while sporting a backward-facing baseball hat and Combate T-shirt. The images suggest Andrade comes from a lower-class neighborhood, though not a favela. Just thirty seconds into the video Andrade says, "Ever since I was a kid, I knew I was different. I liked to play ball, play with action heroes and toy cars. I even had a little girlfriend when I was ten. My mom didn't know about this, but now she will!" The video presents Andrade's disclosure of her lesbian identity as one of the key elements of how audiences can understand her.

Jessica Andrade Emerges exemplifies how branded difference crafts specialized narratives for lesbian fighters that can still be folded into universal

Jessica Andrade. Photo by Amy Kaplan.

characterizations of the nature of adversity and success on the path to their American dreams in the UFC. Because branded difference as a promotional strategy and an ideology dances ambivalently between difference and sameness, we can understand Andrade both for her national and sexual diversity as well as the things that make her similar to everyone else: the quest to realize her dreams. The promotion does so by emphasizing the national roots of its lesbian fighters, thereby extending the dream discourse from poor White men, Latinx men, and Black men to now include lesbians from around the globe. Nationality, gender, class, and sexuality all feature prominently in the first thirty or forty seconds of *Jessica Andrade Emerges.* In fact, the description of the video on YouTube declares that the video will be about her "unique" story. The fact that she began training Brazilian jiu jitsu before transitioning to MMA is unremarkable because many fighters specialize in one art before taking up MMA. The fact that she is preparing for an upcoming fight by watching video of her opponent is a common strategy for fighters. Andrade's uniqueness stems from her female masculinity, her Brazilian national and ethnic identity that is tied to a class identity, and her sexuality.[2] Each of these subjectivities contribute to the individual story of difference that the UFC seeks to tell and to sell. Andrade's Brazilian ethnicity, race, and class are visually front and center to the story, but her lesbian identity becomes central as well. As a result, *Jessica Andrade Emerges* shows how UFC's homogenizing discourse of "we are all fighters" incorporates lesbian identities into a millennial sports media brand that touts global and domestic diversity as business values.

Another perspective on how nationalism and queer identity intersect in the UFC's American dream discourses is offered by examining Liz Carmouche. The UFC explicitly promoted Carmouche as a lesbian and a former marine while sounding much less fanfare for her than Rousey in the lead-up to the first women's fight in the promotion. In *UFC 157 Countdown: Rousey vs. Carmouche* (2013), a forty-five-minute documentary preview of the upcoming fight card headlined by the two women, the narrator begins the story of the first women's fight in the UFC with this declaration: "Ronda Rousey launches the women's bantamweight division against marine Liz Carmouche." The emphasis placed on Rousey as "launching" the women's division coincides with the narrative the UFC prefers to spin about the beginnings of women in the organization. Dana White has said on numerous occasions that Rousey was the reason he changed his mind on including women, and all of my interviews with UFC staff and fighters have supported this narrative. Rousey's ability to perform emphasized femininity and belligerence simultaneously was marketing gold for the UFC. This acknowledged, the selection of Carmouche to fight Rousey and the UFC's efforts to market the "out lesbian" and "the former marine" bare some scrutiny.

These two identity markers, marine and lesbian, signal one of the ways the UFC has included queer identities in the brand. In *UFC 157 Countdown*, the narrator begins Carmouche's story by describing how she grew up on a military base in Okinawa, became a marine, and served three tours in Iraq. Establishing Carmouche's military background first speaks to the relationship among support for the U.S. military, U.S. nationalism, and sports. Butterworth and Moskal (2009) argue that "Americans are implicated in a structural relationship between government, the military, and entertainment industries to the extent that it has become functionally impossible to live outside the rhetorical production of war" (413). Sports are one such entertainment industry wherein military celebrations and nationalism become features of the spectacle, as Mia Fischer (2014) analyzes at length in her article on the NFL's commemoration of 9/11. Carmouche's military service becomes a core narrative about her in the introduction to the UFC's first female fighters. *UFC 157 Countdown* establishes Carmouche's national identity and patriotism first and foremost before telling her American dream story.

UFC 157 Countdown also reveals how the UFC marketed the first women's fight as significant not only because it was the first time the organization featured women but also because it was the first time the promotion booked an out

member of the LGBTQ community. Talk show host Larry King (2013) interviewed Carmouche and Dana White just prior to UFC 157 and asked the fighter
about her military service, the military's "don't ask, don't tell" policy that dis-
couraged out servicemen and women, and Carmouche's lesbian identity ("UFC
President Dana White" 2018). Carmouche frames her identities as a lesbian
and as a marine as facing adversity. In the interview, Carmouche embraces the
significance of her ability to openly disclose her sexuality in sports—a cultural
institution that has long festered homophobia and encouraged closeted athletes.
Larry King then asks Dana White about the UFC's response to Carmouche as
the organization's first out fighter. White responds:

> We could care less. People have been asking me this question for a long time.
> What are you going to do if one of your athletes comes out and says they're gay?
> I could care less. Look at the way we responded when she came out. We've em-
> braced it. We've reached out to the gay community about this fight. (Quoted in
> "UFC President Dana White" 2013)

On one hand, White's "I could care less" remark suggests he is open to including
queer athletes. However, arguing that a fighter's sexual identity doesn't matter at
all can work to minimize the fact that gay athletes face challenges in the UFC or
in other sports because they are gay. On the other hand, he explicitly discusses
reaching "out to the gay community about the fight," alluding to UFC efforts
to market Carmouche with gay and lesbian fans. These efforts align with the
promotion's orientation toward branded difference as a strategy for reaching
new fan demographics.

Liz Carmouche's marketability as a fighter in both "UFC 157 Countdown"
and the interview with Larry King strays from the dominant paradigm for promoting women in sports: sexual desirability, compulsory heterosexuality, and
emphasized femininity. It is also different from the popular feminist discourse of
empowerment surrounding Ronda Rousey or Holly Holm discussed in chapter
two. Carmouche is queer, of multiethnic descent, and performs female masculinity to a greater degree than Rousey, so she represents an entirely different
discourse than the more famous fighter. Instead, the brand can emphasize a
narrative that draws on American patriotism to incorporate normative gay and
lesbian identities and position the UFC as modern, progressive, and cosmopolitan. Carmouche is a patriot and proud out lesbian who has been battle tested
from the marines, to the social sphere, to the Octagon. The UFC presents her
ability to overcome adversity in Iraq as a soldier and at home as a lesbian athlete
as significant and even groundbreaking for its viewership. Much of Zuffa's work
since purchasing the UFC in 2001 had been rebranding MMA's reputation as

more sophisticated and less of a brute sport in order to draw fans from outside of its niche base. Featuring an out lesbian on the UFC roster further allows it to extend the American dream discourse beyond just heterosexy straight women to include female athletes who sport media rarely considers "marketable."

The entanglement between queer identities and nationalism is a contemporary discourse implemented by millennial brands that value global engagement. Jaspir Puar's (2007) work on "homonationalism" is useful for making sense of this discourse. Puar describes homonationalism as a "collusion between homosexuality and American nationalism that is generated both by national rhetorics of patriotic inclusion and by gay and queer subjects themselves" (39). In other words, homonationalism is discourse that incorporates gays and lesbians as rightful citizens of the nation-state rather than sexually deviant outliers. This LGBTQ assimilation into nationalist rhetoric becomes a method for representing the nation as progressive and tolerant compared to regressive states that disenfranchise or persecute queer identities. The comparison—between the progressive state and the regressive one—becomes a method for elevating Western nationalisms through the traditional binary of Us versus Them. Homonationalist narratives work to normalize certain sexual identities, namely monogamous gay and lesbian relationships, while suppressing Othered sexual identities and racialized subjects. International sporting events have been one such location where homonationalist rhetoric has increased since the 2010s (Sykes 2016; Travers and Shearman 2017). For example, the 2012 London Olympics "represented a moment when particular ideas of sexual cosmopolitanism were deployed to regulate, order and normalize the variegated sexual landscapes of a world city" (Hubbard and Wilkinson 2015, 598). The inclusion of gay and lesbian identities at the Olympics allowed London—and Brits by extension—to position themselves as tolerant and cosmopolitan. The UFC brand similarly normalizes lesbian fighters as part of the tapestry that is the UFC nation. Borders dissolve so the millennial sports media brand can offer opportunity for athletes worldwide while also drawing in new global audiences who identify with those diverse athletes. By crafting each of these fighters' stories as overcoming an obstacle, the fighter belongs to a gay-friendly UFC brand built on individualism and the American Dream—something that UFC fighters presumably have access to regardless of their nationality, gender, or sexuality.

The examples of Carmouche and other out-lesbian fighters signal a degree of visibility for queer women in the UFC just as there is an important degree of visibility for Native female fighter Nicco Montaño. At the same time, if we declare an American, straight, White, middle-class female UFC fighter as part of the "we are all fighters" brand just as the Brazilian, lesbian, native, lower-class fighter, then both women's challenges to achieving her UFC dreams are the same even as branded difference emphasizes the ways these two identities are simultaneously dissimilar. Furthermore, the ambivalence between the unifying "we are all fighters" and ways the UFC tells stories unique to specific identities has an important ideological function that equates hard work with success and failure with lack of effort. In the UFC imaginary, fighters can overcome obstacles only through individual hard work—a logic that places the responsibility for success on the fighter themselves while absolving the promotion from having a role in the outcomes of a fighter's career. I now consider the material consequences for UFC fighters as they chase their MMA dreams.

The Cruel Optimism of the Fighter's Dream

Because branded difference works so diligently to prove that a Native woman from a poor reservation or a lesbian war hero can achieve UFC glory, the dream appears open for all. Many athletes maintain an allegiance to the pursuit of becoming a UFC fighter or achieving glory in the Octagon even though the structure of the sport ensures that a relative few will actually do so. Hundreds of fighters in the promotion toil away at their UFC dreams without guaranteed income or insurance in a sport that is notoriously punishing on the athlete's physical health. Indeed, many fighters forego income via other avenues in order to sacrifice their bodies to the possibility that they will be one of the few who rises above the rest or at the very least that they can continue in the sport. Scholar Lauren Berlant (2011) calls this mentality of self-sacrifice "cruel optimism," which is "a relation of attachment to compromised conditions of possibility whose realization is discovered either to be impossible, sheer fantasy, or too possible, and toxic" (94). In other words, cruel optimism occurs when an individual faces precarity and choses optimism as a means to deal with that uncertainty even with the odds stacked against them. Berlant describes this particular affective phenomenon as a condition of neoliberalism, an economic discourse that creates a greater degree of uncertainty for career advancement and financial security. A combat athlete's drive to fight professionally is cruelly optimistic when fighting takes an enormous toll on the body and rarely leads to fame and fortune. The structure of the UFC as well as the "fighter's mindset" coalesce to sustain cruel optimism as fuel for the American dream myth. The UFC has a ready supply of fighters willing to work for low pay and few guarantees because they love the sport.

The "fighter's mindset," an athlete's continual mantra that no amount of adversity in the ring or without will prevent them from success, further supports the athletes' willingness to endure poor working conditions. UFC fighter Roxanne Modafferi explains the fighter's mindset as such:

> I think that every fighter knows that they need to believe in themselves in order to win the fight. If you say you're going to lose, you're 99 percent sure you're going to lose. So fighters have to believe in themselves and believe in their training. Even if they had a bad camp, they have to convince themselves they're going to pull through this. That's just part of mentally preparing for the fight. So every fighter who says, "I'm going to win," has to convince themselves that they're going to win.

Pre-fight interviews with UFC athletes regularly consist of the fighter envisioning their own success through specific strategies and a projected sense of invincibility. Self-belief and perseverance become central to the mentality that the fighters attempt to maintain throughout their preparation and for the fight itself. In the ring, these discourses translate to fighting even when injured, persisting when exhausted, and relentlessly pursuing a knockout or submission finish when the scorecards say that's the only way to win. Out of the ring, resilience against adversity might mean overcoming injury or personal heartache to compete at the sport's highest level, such as Daniel Cormier's loss of an infant child or Jessica Eye's broken back. After recounting a horrific car accident that killed her childhood friend as well as another crash a year later that broke her back, Eye describes this adversity as becoming part of the fighter's mindset that she carries with her into the Octagon. She now says that hard experiences in life become part of the process: "I love those barriers because I love to break them down and I love to show people how to break them down" (quoted in Gerbasi 2013). Adversity discourse weaves previous failures, defeats, and setbacks into the athlete's story as battle scars that authenticate their resilience.

Fighters' persistent rhetoric about prevailing against affliction through the fighter's mindset and the UFC's penchant for highlighting fighters' hard-knock life histories intertwine discursively to support the idea that the UFC dream is accessible to everyone who works hard enough. In a *Rolling Stone* article describing Henry Cejudo as an "immigrant son" fighting for his "American Dream," the UFC flyweight describes his resilient mindset that led him to success in Olympic wrestling and the UFC: "You can accomplish anything that you dedicate yourself to. Think how many people struggle across the world, across the country . . . I know anything is possible if you set your mind, your body, your soul and your faith to it" (quoted in Bohn 2015). Cynthia Calvillo echoes Cejudo's sentiment when discussing her relentless pursuit of her dreams despite injury: "If you have a dream, there's always going to be adversity and obstacles, and it looked like I was seriously swimming against the current, but if you really believe in

Cynthia Calvillo on Instagram. Used with permission.

something, you can make it happen" (quoted in Gerbasi 2017). Success in the form of glory, wealth, or championship belts become evidence that the American dream is alive and well for fighters. The belief that diverse identities can achieve their UFC dreams is certainly an appealing narrative for audiences drawn to the affect that branded difference circulates.

Many fighters endure financial strain, personal sacrifice, and health risks because discourses of fighting and the American dream map so neatly onto one another. In addition, the fighter's mindset might further mean enduring economic hardship, injury without adequate insurance coverage, or lack of guaranteed income. As independent contractors, fighters bear the risk and responsibility if fights fall through or if they become injured and are unable to fight because the UFC diverts the costs of fight preparation, canceled bouts, and health insurance to fighters (see chapter 5). Communication scholar Gina Neff explains the corporate trends of mitigating a company's risk:

> The increase in contract and temporary work increases companies' options and flexibility by distributing part of the burden of risk to external subcontractors and self-employed freelancers. When times are good there is work, and in downturns contracts are not renewed. This is an explicit *externalization* of costs by a firm onto workers. (Neff 2012, 8, original emphasis)

Thus, the UFC's practice of hiring fighters as independent contractors ensures the promotion can mitigate its own financial risks by drafting contracts that require fighters to absorb much of the responsibility for the precarious business of fight promotion. Investing in fighters *is* risky because injuries are so commonplace that it's impossible to guarantee an individual fighter will be able to compete when scheduled.

Cortney Casey explained in our interview how much fighters risk when they invest themselves in preparing for a fight. She is dating a fellow UFC fighter, Drakkar Klose, and the two help each other prepare for bouts by investing time, energy, and financial resources into a fight camp, which is a preparatory period of typically eight to ten weeks for fighters to train for a bout and prepare to make weight. Casey says that camp preparation also includes medical screenings, specific nutrition and weight cutting, and sports therapies, all of which involve financial investments by the couple. Casey and Klose arrived in California, where the Klose fight was to take place, a few days before the bout only to find out that his opponent had to withdraw due to an injury. The UFC then attempted to find a replacement. According to the contract between fighters and the UFC, the promotion has no obligation to pay for the time and resources spent and in most cases will not pay a fighter for a canceled bout. If the promotion was unable to find a replacement, then Klose wouldn't receive any compensation for the fight and the couple would have invested time and capital, only to wait weeks or months for another fight. Klose described the several days while the couple waited for word from the UFC about a replacement for Klose's opponent as an "emotional rollercoaster" (quoted in Gerbasi 2019b). The UFC called at one point to say they had found a new opponent for him, only to call two hours later to say that the state commission couldn't clear the fighter in time for the fight. At this point, Casey and her boyfriend had already invested so much money in preparing for the fight that their stress was high. Casey explains the emotional labor involved in attempting to maintain the fighter's mindset in these conditions:

> Now his mind is already gone, in regard to fighting. Now we're just stressed out about money. If he doesn't fight, that's $10,000 dollars [we have invested] down the drain. . . . Now he has to psych himself up to go fight again without having an opponent and knowing we have all those bills from last camp, from this camp, and my upcoming camp. And he has to try to make it work and still go into the cage to perform and do his job and try not to think about it all.

The fighter's mindset, then, can support neoliberal logics that incorporates financial risk and failures into the many struggles that athletes in the UFC face. As a consequence, individual fighters become expendable since the UFC doesn't have a long-term investment in its independent contractors. As Casey says,

> I think that's a reason why we get cycled through so quickly as fighters. We put a lot of wear and tear on our bodies without the proper recovery, with all the weight cutting. . . . Then add the stress put on us of having to fight short notice

sometimes because that's our only option. Then we're cutting drastic amounts of weight. Then we get more hurt outside of practice. I feel like it's this snowball effect, but everyone is in it, you know. Everyone is in the same boat.

Casey describes the physical toll training and competing takes on fighters and how much additional risk fighters must absorb in order to potentially reap the rewards for their investments. She describes a vicious cycle of cutting weight and fighting with injuries in order to be paid for that labor. Yet, UFC contracts don't guarantee a return on the fighters' investments in their training and preparation prior to an event.

Nicco Montaño provides further evidence of the ways discourses of the American dream filter into fighter rhetoric about working for the UFC and further reveals the limits of branded difference. We might interpret Montaño's championship win as achieving the pinnacle of success in her sport except that her experience also shows how expendable UFC champions can be. Her historic win as the UFC's first "Native champion" was a short-lived modicum of success that exposes the American dream for the mythology that it is. Illness and injury prevented Montaño from training or competing, so she was unable to defend her championship title for almost a year. She finally booked a title defense against Valentina Shevchenko for September 2018. The night before the fight, Montaño was forced to withdraw due to hospitalization from a difficult weight cut (Lee 2018). She elaborated in an Instagram post:

> I had stopped sweating early, my kidneys shut down, and I had an imbalance of electrolytes, my sodium levels were way too high. When I got to the hospital the doctors told me that it was the best idea, that if I had waited even 30 minutes longer it could've led to cardiac issues. (Quoted in Reinsmith 2018b)

Like wrestlers and boxers, MMA fighters restrict calories and hydration in order to weigh in lighter the day before a fight. After the official weigh-ins, fighters then replenish the nutrients and water loss to return to a heavier weight before the bout. This process can lead to a variety of medical conditions related to severe dehydration and calorie restriction.

The toll that weight cutting takes on the body is a common occurrence in combat sports; yet, Montaño's participation on *The Ultimate Fighter* compounded her health issues. The reality show's tournament-style competition requires that fighters make weight multiple times during a season. Generally, fighters "walk around" heavier than their fight weight and then cut calories and water leading up to weigh-ins in order to be on weight and then gain a significant amount back once they rehydrate. The process is quite challenging on the body for the typical MMA fighter who fights a couple times a year, but the frequent weight cuts in a short period of time for *The Ultimate Fighter* tournament are even more difficult. Additionally, Montaño broke her foot while filming the reality show but chose not to wear the medical boot to stabilize it until after she fought for the championship. After winning the flyweight title, she was inactive while healing her foot, gained weight, experienced frequent upper-respiratory infections, and had a tonsillectomy. She attributes the deterioration of her health to the drastic weight cuts from participating in *The Ultimate Fighter*. As a result, she delayed defending her belt for nine months due to these health concerns.

In an interview with Luke Thomas of *The MMA Hour*, Montaño said she had originally wanted an October or November 2018 contest date, but the UFC strongly encouraged her to schedule the fight against Shevchenko for UFC 228 (September 8, 2018)—a full month earlier than she wanted ("Nicco Montaño" 2018). Montaño recalls feeling that she had limited options. She needed more time to prepare for the weight cut now that her health had improved, but she feared the UFC would strip her of the belt if she didn't fight on the September UFC card. Thomas asks her directly if the UFC explicitly stated that they would strip the belt if she didn't fight. She admitted that the UFC didn't use those words directly, but she was under the distinct impression that failing to fight in September would lead to that consequence. In the end, Montaño agreed to fight earlier than she had hoped. She was heavier than normal when she started her preparations to make 125 pounds. In the end, the weight cut proved to be disastrous for Montaño, who had always made weight for her previous professional bouts. As already noted above, the day before the scheduled September fight, Montaño was admitted to the hospital for kidney issues because of the severe dehydration. Since Montaño was unable to fight, the UFC stripped her of the title and moved the division forward without her.

Of the title stripping, Montaño stated, "if you ask me it's completely uncalled for—there have been plenty other fighters who have not been punished for a lot more" ("Nicco Montaño" 2018). Montaño's assertions have merit when considering that the UFC doesn't simply rely on a fighters' stats and skill to determine who will compete for championships. Instead, the UFC decides who it will feature in marquee events and championship bouts. The subjective nature of the sport places emphasis on the fighter's popularity and charisma to determine who the promotion will support and how tolerant it will be of delays because of health concerns or other setbacks. Max Holloway, for example, had to withdraw from three championship fights in 2018 due to health issues ranging from a broken leg, to concussion-like symptoms, to symptoms from drastic weight cutting. The UFC never stripped him of his title, and he was finally able to defend his belt in December 2018. Both Montaño and Tom Vaughn, Montaño's coach, insist that she wasn't given the same chance as a fighter like Holloway because "unfortunately I'm not one to be running my mouth so I don't bring in the big bucks." She suggests that her status as a champion failed to give her any sort of job security because she isn't contentious in how she promotes herself and she doesn't "bring in the big bucks." Vaughn continues that he understands that the UFC made a "business decision" when they took Montaño's championship status. He further concedes that Shevchenko is more "marketable" because she's "technically sound" and has a huge social media following already. He continues:

> The UFC makes the biggest fights they can make all the time. I get that. They're a money machine. I understand that. . . . All businesses are like that. I'm not one of those guys who wants to bash the UFC for making as much money as they can make. That's what big business is . . . I get it. But there does need to be some set of rules. (Quoted in Erickson et al. 2018)

Montaño echoes a sentiment similar to Vaughn's. She says she can "kind of understand" the UFC's choice to strip her of the title from a "business perspective," but she also thinks the promotion should institute rules governing title defenses in order to prevent inconsistencies. She further points out that she doesn't have any "personal vendettas" against any individual decision maker, but she generally felt disappointed in her treatment. She reminds herself: "F this. You just almost died for a company that doesn't even call you to make sure you're alive" ("Nicco Montaño" 2018).

Montaño's story reveals the ways that fighters deploy discourses that an entity's drive for profit, or pursuit of their own American dream, can justify the expendability of fighters. Montaño and Vaughn find it unfair that the UFC stripped her of her title despite having never previously missed weight and having risked her health to compete for the promotion. Neither the fighter nor coach seem to be able to identify a singular culprit in the promotion for this state of affairs; yet, they both identify consistent UFC policies as the means to prevent these sorts of inequalities in the future. Montaño's story shows that logics supporting profit-driven organizations are used to justify decisions that negatively impact individual fighters while freeing the promotion itself of any responsibility for this situation. Both Montaño and her coach believe the UFC treated her unfairly; however, they also verbally support the promotion's "right" to make decisions that allows the UFC to "make as much money as they can."

Montaño and her coach illustrate that neoliberal societies generally support an entity's right to pursue its own American dream and "make as much money as they can" regardless of the impact on individuals also trying to "make it." In fact, there is another Fighting Spirit promotional spot for Modelo that describes the risks and rewards that Dana White and the Fertittas undertook to grow the UFC into the millennial sports media brand that it is today ("Fighting Spirit" 2018). The video opens with White declaring that "there's one guarantee everyday when you wake up: life is standing there ready to kick you right in the teeth, and you have to fight." White goes on to describe how he and his partners bought the brand that was little more than the three letters and "broke the rules" fighting to make the UFC into what it is today:

> A lot of people will tell you that you can't change this and you can't change that, but that's bullshit. It's not true. All the rules can be broken. Everything can be changed if you believe in what you're doing and you work hard at it every day.

The Fighting Spirit spot highlights White's diligence at building the brand despite his early challenges at Zuffa. Although the UFC is much bigger than just White, his fighting spirit represents the corporate face of the promotion for many. White is a central decision maker and the figurehead. When Montaño and Vaughn say they understand the UFC's right to make money despite consequences for the fighter herself, they understand the promotion as having its own fighting spirit and right to achieve its dreams, just as Modelo frames White's right to his success. Interestingly, the ideological support of White's American dream and the UFC's by extension means that he and the broader promotion are justified in making decisions that exploit individual fighters like Montaño.

To be clear, I'm not faulting fighters for rationalizing the UFC's treatment of them; rather, I want to point out that neoliberal culture so broadly supports the myth of the American dream that it normalizes exploitative work relationships. The UFC diverts much of the financial risk to the fighters in a manner that seems normal and even expected in contemporary society. Montaño, for example, remains optimistic for her future in the UFC despite her inability to make a living at fighting for more than a year and a half, despite her apparent expendability, and despite the risks to her health. She says, "When you're stuck in between a rock and a hard place you stick up your dukes and get down to it and that's precisely what I did and will continue to do" (quoted in Reinsmith 2018b). Again, Montaño returns to the fighter's mindset to optimistically fuel her dreams. The pressure she felt to take a fight before she was ready, the dangerous weight cut, and the subsequent loss of her title all became folded into those discourses of adversity that all fighters must overcome to succeed rather than any fault of a promotion that's pursuing its own dream.

Branded difference and the American dream are powerful bedfellows for the UFC brand because these discourses allow the promotion to attract fans and fighters from "all walks of life" and divert the risk and responsibility for achieving the dream to the fighters themselves. Thus, the dream discourse embedded in UFC promotional content motivates hundreds of diverse independent contractors to remain cruelly optimistic in their quest for UFC glory. The UFC relies on the dream ethos to make clear that a fighter's life is challenging, and that hard work is the only method for success. This conveniently allows the promotion to shirk much of the financial responsibility for making the path easier for fighters. In order to do so, the promotion folds gendered difference into the dream discourses in novel ways for combat sports. Stories of the American dream are luminous within the UFC, while the toll that dream exacts remains overshadowed.

Thus far this book has examined how branded difference operates symbolically to make diverse female fighters visible while hinting at the material consequences of working for the UFC. Representation matters to millions of people who have long been invisible in sports, such as White women, women of color, lesbians, women from all corners of the globe, and women whose identities intersect with these categories in multiple ways. Branded difference further uses discourses of the American dream to claim that all female fighters have access to the same opportunities granted superstars like Ronda Rousey. Yet, the UFC has failed to deliver on this promise. On the contrary, discourses of the American dream fuel the cruel optimism of fighters, while the UFC continues to profit on its athletes' aspirations and labor. The next chapter digs further below the exterior of branded difference to interrogate the material labor of visibility on women in the UFC. I examine how female fighters navigate precarious working conditions in the UFC through labor on social media to increase their own visibility and gain sponsorships.

CHAPTER 4

The Labor of Visibility on Social Media

A small crowd gathered around a stage in July 2015 during the UFC's International Fight Week Fan Exposition in Las Vegas, Nevada. Several female UFC fighters, including Rose Namajunas, Paige VanZant, Johana Jedrzejczyk, and Liz Carmouche, sat in the spotlight to take questions from a group of men, women, and children all attending the "Female Fighters Panel." One man asked the panelists why women's MMA had recently exploded given that female athletes in other sports struggle for visibility. Liz Carmouche, the first woman to enter the Octagon against Rousey just two years before, jumped at the chance to answer the question: "In MMA, [fans] actually have a chance to connect with the athletes. You don't see that as much in the other sports. Particularly in the UFC, Dana White has made us so accessible" ("Female Fighter's Panel" 2015). Carmouche identifies the ways that the promotion has encouraged fighters to embrace social media in order to grant UFC fans greater access to its athletes. The UFC's alacrity for social media has been a key factor in the promotion's growth into a millennial sports media brand that facilitates new levels of visibility for female fighters (see chapter 1). Yet, sitting in the audience as Carmouche celebrated the opportunities social media affords, I wondered about the labor and costs involved for the fighters. Self-promotion online takes work. That work requires intellectual and social skills but also demands a degree of emotional resilience. Were the benefits of self-promotion online worth the labor or the emotional costs of exposing oneself to the dredges of the internet? How much did individual female fighters benefit from this labor compared to the UFC itself?

This chapter examines the labor of visibility that female UFC fighters perform on social media platforms. While I integrate a variety of sources into the analysis, I center the voices of nine female UFC fighters I interviewed to understand the promises and pitfalls of using social media to promote their personal brands as athletes. I argue that the labor of visibility online is a hidden and undercompensated aspect of a UFC fighter's job that primarily benefits the promotion and excises specific gendered labor for female fighters. Making oneself visible online is work that often rests squarely on the fighters themselves because the UFC encourages them to be active on social media until they have theoretically "made it," at which time the UFC presumably increases the promotional labor to augment a fighter's star power. Several fighters have created successful personal brands that prove that self-promotion can work. Famous love-to-hate-him villain Colby Covington made a name for himself as an agitator only after the UFC told him it wouldn't re-sign him even though he had a professional record of twelve wins and just one loss. On hearing that he was about to be cut from the promotion, Covington immediately began posting controversial content and insulting other fighters. The tactics worked, and he has since remained in the UFC as one of the promotion's most visible heels. The negative press Covington produced was enough to save his UFC career because he generated a form of visibility that the UFC could market (Rothstein 2019). Former UFC fighter Barbie Beeman (pseudonym) explained to me that "Being in the UFC does not constitute making it. It doesn't. Being a Conor McGregor is making it." Beeman marks a clear distinction between being an average or lower-tier fighter and being a UFC celebrity, even if that means being the bad guy like Covington. Beeman's comment punctuates the fact that visibility online often yields underwhelming outcomes since the number of fighters who "make it" as UFC celebrity athletes is a very small proportion.

Fighters must work at their own visibility online. They perform that labor while hoping to generate enough interest to convince the UFC that they are a viable investment and/or to gain the attention of potential sponsors. Media scholar Brooke Erin Duffy can offer insight on the cultural logics that motivate many UFC fighters to labor online with little to no reward. Duffy (2017) coined the term "aspirational labor" to describe "a mode of (mostly) uncompensated, independent work [on social media] that is propelled by the much-venerated idea of *getting paid to do what you love*" (4, original emphasis). Duffy examines fashion and beauty content creators who toil for hours at creating videos or posts for social media because "they love it." The work is aspirational because content creators expect to eventually reap the benefits of that labor in terms of the fame and fortune that promises to accompany visibility. For UFC fighters, the act of promoting oneself on social media isn't necessarily *the thing* that they love. Rather, social media is a means to an end for many of them. It is the thing they believe will get them into the Octagon frequently enough to do what they love. For some of them, social media is a "necessary evil" while others take a more positive outlook and view the creative process or the fan interaction as enjoyable. Much of the content fighters generate online is unpaid or underpaid, but the promises of visibility in the UFC suggest that it will pay off eventually through "material rewards" or "social capital" (Duffy 2017, 4, 5). Yet, as with the content creators that Duffy studies, someone is benefiting *now* from the labor of fighters. The social media platforms themselves make money from the content posted through advertising revenue and the UFC can identify potential stars based on a fighter's popularity on social media.

The UFC's practice of diverting the labor of visibility onto fighters is another feature of the millennial sports media brand (see chapter 1). The UFC embraced social media before other sports brands because it allowed the promotion to circulate inexpensive content to grow its fan base. The UFC's practice of encouraging fighters to be accessible to fans on social media has now been embedded in the promotion as a key business tactic that mirrors marketing strategies used by a variety of other brands courting millennials. Furthermore, social media engagement is a method of predicting which fighters will appeal to broadcast or pay-per-view audiences. If fighters generate significant followers, clicks, likes, and comments, then the UFC often takes notice, schedules them to fight, and may potentially spend additional resources in that fighter's promotion via more mainstream, that is, more visible and lucrative, media channels. All the while, the more the fighters hashtag the UFC and generate content with the promotion's name attached, the more the UFC can justify the brand's worth to sponsors and partners. In the end, the labor of visibility in the UFC is a pyramid scheme bolstered by the success of a few fighters who have gained celebrity status online and become millionaires in the sport.

Social Media: "It's Part of My Job"

The unwritten bullet point on the job description of UFC fighter is "grow your fan base online by gaining followers and interacting with them on a regular basis." From the perspective of the millennial sports media brand, that implicit job requirement aligns with a broader culture that assumes that everyone should be self-promoting. Since social media and other innovative media practices became so important to the growth of the UFC worldwide, the athletes' use of social media becomes expected and taken for granted. In brand culture, some of the responsibility of marketing and promoting products, services, or personalities, now shifts to individuals instead of falling on professionals in communication roles. As London-based boxer and the Africa Zone Featherweight Champion Ramla Ali explains,

> being a millennial athlete means you have to manage your own image correctly, appeal to fans, respond to requests and stay current through fashion, music, or sports, all while still training at an elite level and competing around the world. (Quoted in Pitcher 2019)

Any and every "self" in contemporary culture can be incorporated into brand logics, including sportswomen such as Ali. As Alison Hearn (2008) writes, "the function of the branded self is purely rhetorical; its goal is to produce cultural value and, potentially, material profit" (198). I would posit that this transferring of responsibility from the marketing professional to the individual person becomes even more pronounced in a work climate that hires independent contractors instead of employees. We rarely see universities promote the scholarship of an adjunct faculty member, but we frequently see them highlighting the latest work of a tenure-track professor.

I asked several fighters what other things they considered central components of the MMA fight profession beyond training for bouts and the fights themselves. They all included social media as "part of their job." While the ones I spoke with felt that social media was important and something they "should" do to gain visibility, sponsors, and the attention of the UFC, their level of engagement on platforms varied from enthusiastic participation to ambivalence to reluctance. Additionally, only one of them vocally questioned whether social media should be a part of a fighter's job. It is possible that some fighters don't perceive their work on social media as performing free or underpaid labor for the UFC and that others feel uncomfortable criticizing the UFC's business practices publicly due to fears of repercussions (chapter 5 outlines some reasons why these fears of repercussions have merit). Regardless, brand culture necessitates promoting oneself online as a form of participation in a variety of cultural and economic spaces, so the fact that UFC fighters would also participate in this labor goes largely unquestioned.

Some fighters actively embrace social media as central to their profession even though the UFC rarely gives them specific feedback on what types of content they should post. Jessica-Rose Clark is a UFC fighter who believes that social media is a key element in her career and she generally enjoys the work of self-promotion:

> I definitely believe that marketing and advertising yourself and your fights and training is a huge part of [the job]. There's a reason that people like Conor McGregor and Ronda Rousey made so much money. It's because they turned themselves into a name. And you can't do that without self-promotion or self-marketing. You don't get paid unless people want to see you fight. And whether people want to see you fight because they love you or hate you, it doesn't matter. Either way, the way to get big fights and to get more money is to have more eyes on you when you fight.

Clark emphasizes the labor that MMA stars like Rousey and McGregor undertook in order to become brand names. Clark also coaches up-and-coming MMA fighters and one of the things she emphasizes to the athletes she trains is how social media enables them to "do what they love." She says, "We're entertainers. If we don't entertain and people don't want to see the entertainment we provide, then we don't have a job, it's as simple as that. So, I feel like that is as equal, and in some respects more important than the actual fight itself." Roxanne Modafferi also views herself as an "entertainer" who understands creating content on social media as a way to expand her role as entertainer beyond the Octagon:

> I think what most people don't understand is that mixed-martial arts is half sport, half entertainment. The fighters are told that their job is [training and fighting], but [the UFC isn't explicitly] telling you that the other half is being entertaining. What that entails is half the job, whether it be trash talking . . . or [posting] butt pictures [online], or whatever. . . . I believe that social media should be part of the job because it's part of the entertainment.

Modafferi agrees that the job of fighter doesn't come with an explicit description of self-promotion on social media, but that savvy fighters understand how the fight business works. UFC fighter Laura Brown (pseudonym) agrees that the UFC doesn't give specific strategies for social media, but she adds that sometimes managers train fighters in the business of self-promotion.

> My manager did help me a little bit. He was like "look, you need to get on Twitter, in the morning when you're pooping, go ahead and answer your fans, or Tweet something out." After my last fight he texted me because I was Tweeting at people, and he told me I need to keep up the chatter on Twitter because I've gained like 2,000 followers in the last four days. So a good manager will follow [your social media engagement], and monitor it, and tell you how to do that.

Clark, Modafferi, and Brown demonstrate that gaining fan attention through social media is an unquestioned requisite of the fight profession. They generally accept that a UFC fighter's job is to self-promote because so much of modern culture rests on the idea that branding oneself is key to cultural and economic capital. A fighter performs unpaid or underpaid labor in the hope that if they are appealing enough to fans, then they can reap the promises of visibility. The UFC adopts the meritocratic approach that if a fighter works hard enough at MMA and at self-promotion online, then they will prove themselves worthy of financial rewards. If visibility fails to materialize, neoliberal logics fault the individual fighter rather than the promotion, which in turn allows the UFC to refuse to promote its fighters without demonstrated fan engagement. Invisibility becomes a fighter's challenge to overcome rather than a series of cultural and economic conditions that dictate where the light of visibility shines. The aspirational labor that fighters perform is "risky" because they remain uncertain the labor will yield the benefits promised. Instead, the fight business assumes those risks are the fighters to bear.

The growing work culture of independent contracting creates a labor force that is more expendable and perceived as unworthy of investing in until they go above and beyond to prove their worth. For independent contractors like UFC fighters, companies and institutions avoid viewing themselves as responsible for paying benefits or supporting the contractor beyond the job they've agreed to do, so they also invest fewer other resources to help them excel at their jobs. Gina Neff (2012) describes this "risk economy" as a contemporary

Jessica-Rose Clark on Instagram. Used with permission.

Jessica-Rose Clark representing a sponsor on Instagram. Used with permission.

labor discourse where the risks of employment shift from company to the individual. This discourse frames taking risks as "inevitable, necessary, and beneficial for one's career and companies, reinforcing cultural messages about the attractiveness of risk" (3). Yet, this shift also has consequences in sociologist Vicki Smith's assessment: "when corporations no longer buffer their workers from the uncertainty of production and employment workers must take risks and expend great personal and group resources to control that uncertainty themselves" (quoted in Neff 2012, 8). In other words, the UFC has shifted much of the risk of being a UFC fighter, such as promotional labor, healthcare, or income, to the fighter themselves. Largely the promotion and the fighters see these conditions of labor as acceptable because it's so commonplace in neoliberal business practices.

The female fighters I spoke with espoused a range of perspectives about social media as part of the job. Some of them adopted a cynical stance that "this is just the way it is" while others voiced a more optimistic perspective even though much of their work on social media is aspirational. Cortney Casey summarizes how she weighs the costs and benefits of self-promotion on social media:

> [The UFC] can build you if they want to build you, and you can build yourself if you wanna get built too. But again . . . do I want to put that much energy into social media when I'm not fighting, or do I want to fight? [Do I] want to spend that time in the gym or spend that time with my family? I don't know when I'm

going to fight again. So everyone is different in where they're at in their career, where they want to go in their career, and what they're willing to do.

Casey describes a delicate balance between the labor of social media and using the time elsewhere in her life. Even though she constantly weighs how much engagement she will undertake online, Casey says that she feels that promoting sponsored content is something she feels "forced to do" because that's how a lot of UFC fighters make extra income or get free products that can help offset the low pay from the UFC. However, she never articulated *who* was "forcing" her, and she didn't explicitly name the UFC as the pressuring entity, nor did I push her to name any particular source of that pressure. Casey explained her working conditions as being "how it is" even though she felt uneasy with that reality. To gain sponsorships, fighters have to agree to post a certain amount of content online to promote the product, which Casey feels is "just selling myself . . . I feel like I have to pimp myself out all the time, if that makes sense. I don't like that." She was clear that she didn't want social media engagement to be a part of her fight career, but she understood only too well how the UFC and brand culture more broadly valued and measured her online visibility. She reluctantly adopted a "this is just how it is" perspective to acknowledge her inability to change her working conditions.

Retired UFC fighter Barbie Beeman explained that one of the biggest misconceptions that people outside the MMA business had about fighting in the UFC was that the best fighters—that is, those who had the most fighting talent—booked the most fights and received the most promotion from the UFC.

Cortney Casey and family on Instagram. Used with permission.

For women in particular, if you're attractive, you're a huge draw already. If you have a large number of followers on your social network, then you're going to be a draw. If you're somebody who runs your mouth a lot, you're going to be a draw. If you're somebody that picks fights with other people and somehow makes a grudge match, you're going to be a draw. It's the things that make people want to watch you. That [could be] anything, but it's usually appearance or controversy—either you create controversy or you have [an attractive] appearance. There's a very, very small number of fighters that are a draw simply because they are amazing fighters.

Beeman pinpoints a range of factors that can make an athlete popular with fans: from attractiveness to performing the role of the heel to having a strong presence on social media, and sometimes all three. She also alleges that the UFC compels fighters to make themselves visible and heard on social media and other popular media outlets because the promotion might see those fighters as "a draw [for audiences]." Fighters can often accomplish degrees of visibility by making a ruckus online and offline so that more UFC fans pay attention. Some fighters get attention by being unlikeable, like Colby Covington, while others are just beloved by followers who want to see daily content posted online about the fighter's life. Beeman is very clear these attention-grabbing performances are central components of those fighters who have "made it." For the fighters who haven't, some of them expend considerable time and energy clamoring for visibility without making any great gains in the number of fights or sponsors they secure, nor do they see increased payouts from the UFC.

Most fighters I spoke with didn't identify the UFC as responsible for the pressure to make oneself visible online; rather, the fighters who spoke critically of their social media obligations described some unnamed force that compelled them to perform that labor, even though they acknowledged the UFC encourages the practice. It becomes difficult to identify where the pressure to self-brand originates when the whole of U.S. society supports brand culture as a way of life. The pressure feels amorphous to fighters because it goes beyond just the UFC itself. These athletes navigate a billion-dollar sport yoked to sponsors that rely on television and pay-per-view ratings and online engagement numbers to determine their worth. Even though self-promotion feels as if they are "pimping" themselves, for some of them, what alternative do they have? They can participate in that system, or they can refuse to and risk their chance to compete in the sport. These working conditions can produce an ambivalent attitude of "this is just the way it is."

Interestingly, I've seen numerous instances on MMA social media sites where fans and MMA pundits assert that if an individual disagrees with the UFC's treatment of its contracted workers, then fighters shouldn't sign contracts or agree to the promotion's terms. The attitude is "if you don't like it, then don't do it." That is, if the fighter doesn't like having to self-promote in order to receive better pay, then they should seek other work. This retort appears across a variety of sectors in American life. Teachers, for example, are notoriously underpaid in the United States. Yet millions of them choose to continue to educate young people even as they also participate in unions and strike for better pay. The "if you don't like being underpaid, then choose another profession" mentality constantly crops up in American discourse when teachers go on strike, as if educators should resign themselves to being underpaid in perpetuity. This discourse capitulates to power structures and presumes that participation in any given structure necessitates agreement and harmony with "the way things are." The logic further presumes that school districts, corporations, and millennial sports media brands are immutable and that by signing a contract the signer forfeits free thought, agency, and the desire for change. In the UFC, "if you don't like it, then don't do it," supports the status quo and resigns fighters to cope with these working conditions as best they can while Dana White, Endeavor, and their stakeholders continue to increase their profits.

Julie Kedzie, a retired UFC fighter who had a long MMA career prior to joining the promotion, was one of the only fighters to criticize the labor of visibility that fighters undertake. Her willingness to do so publicly might stem from her status as a retired fighter rather than an active one concerned with their status in the UFC; thus, it's possible that other fighters may share her opinion. Kedzie articulates a clear delineation between the role of fighter and the role of promoter. She says that the UFC tells fighters "you gotta hype yourself up, and you have to promote." However, she argues that "a promoter's job is to promote a fight, not the fighter's. A fighter's job is to fight." Kedzie details the labor required for training and preparing for an MMA bout in terms of physical, mental, and emotional energy. She believes the pressure of developing one's personal brand, promoting one's fights, and clamoring for other types of visibility shouldn't rest on the fighters, because "fighting is hard enough" on its own. Having the assumed bullet point of "self-promotion" on the UFC fighter job description adds to an already difficult profession.

A UFC fighter's worth, according to the metrics of popularity the UFC uses, becomes tied to labor that the athletes perform on social media that ultimately benefits the promotion. The UFC has a cheap method for identifying fighters with an established fan base on social media that can draw audiences to broadcast or pay-per-view events. Laura Brown explains how the fighters' use of social media benefits the UFC. She says the UFC doesn't offer specific feedback to individual fighters on how to make themselves more popular; instead,

> it saves them money not to [train us how to promote ourselves] . . . they want people that can naturally do that themselves. How terrible would it be if somebody promoted themselves, got way up there, had this media buzz, and then just suddenly fell off, couldn't do it anymore and rise to the occasion? I think they want people that can just do it on their own.

Placing the burden of self-promotion on the fighter becomes a relatively inexpensive way for the UFC to identify potential stars. The UFC doesn't accrue major overhead costs because fighters do this labor for free, and the promotion merely has to pay its social media team to monitor who is gaining attention online. From the fighters' perspective, the aspirational labor they perform integrates with the American dream discourse (see chapter 3). In order to "make it," fighters must sacrifice in the gym, in fights, and in the social media labor they perform to get there. If they work hard enough in each of these aspects of their job, then they expect to see results. Yet, as I show in the next section, not all fighters benefit equally from the labor of visibility they perform online.

Hierarchies of Visibility Online

All the fighters I spoke with also elaborated on Barbie Beeman's observation that female fighters' attractiveness is a factor in their marketability in the UFC and their visibility on social media. I now examine how these fighters develop personal brands that feel "authentic" to them while negotiating the pressures embedded in the hierarchies of visibility online. In an age of media saturation where "anyone" can become a micro-celebrity on Instagram, these female UFC fighters understand that curating a hyperfeminine, heterosexy image on social media can lead to opportunities for visibility in the UFC as well as additional income and other advantages, such as "free stuff," through sponsorships. Fighters who can perform this particular brand of femininity stand near the top of the hierarchies of visibility. However, many of the fighters I spoke with feel inauthentic if they attempt to curate an online presence that caters to a conventionally straight male gaze. Instead, they attempt to "be themselves" and post content that will attract a more niche audience of online followers. The structure of social media sites like Instagram allow these women to develop a certain level of visibility within representational culture even if the rewards are unequal to those that accrue for women who perform emphasized femininity online.

Some fighters are able to walk the delicate balance between athleticism and femininity on social media, while many cannot or decide against doing so. Several of the fighters I spoke with cited UFC fighter Paige VanZant as an example of how the "right" combination of factors can be very lucrative for fighters with heavy engagement on social media. VanZant is a young, blonde, bubbly, fitness model who is also a scrappy fighter in the cage. She has an established presence on social media and tells MMA journalist Ariel Helwani that "with endorsements, I make way more money sitting at home posting pictures on Instagram than I do fighting. . . . If I were to stop everything I do outside of fighting and just fight, I would be at a loss. By a long shot" (quoted in Andrew 2019). As of this writing, VanZant has 2.3 million followers on Instagram and posts a whole range of content including selfies with her husband before "date night," pictures with her dog, bikini shots, videos of her latest workout, and numerous product endorsements of her sponsors. VanZant stands closer to the top of the hierarchies of visibility than most female UFC fighters because she possesses the femininity, Whiteness, charisma, heterosexiness, and athleticism that make her an Instagram darling. If she had the fighting record that matched Ronda Rousey at her prime, VanZant's charisma and appearance might place her at the top of the hierarchies of visibility because attractiveness can propel one far in sports media culture. However, female fighters must also excel in their craft to achieve the same level of superstardom as someone like Rousey in her UFC heyday.

VanZant represents an athlete who successfully performs what scholars Kim Toffoletti and Holly Thorpe (2018) describe as the "athletic labor of femininity." Toffoletti and Thorpe examine sportswomen who have large followings on Instagram, such as Ronda Rousey and Serena Williams. They find that the most visible sportswomen online excel in a form of labor that accentuates emphasized femininity, or a "non-sporting labour that female athletes undertake to demonstrate successful sporting subjectivity online relative to postfeminist aesthetic and affective codes of femininity, as they are presented through the body" (312). In other words, the sportswomen Toffoletti and Thorpe examine and perform a delicate dance between femininity and athleticism while positioning themselves as women with agency and choice, which are characteristics of the "postfeminist aesthetic." The athletic labor of femininity translates into a viable income for female athletes that can adopt a pretty, powerful, and empowering image. These women stereotypically appeal to straight men through their heterosexiness and straight women for their power and strength. It is important to highlight that even though being conventionally attractive and feminine can benefit fighters like VanZant, branding and self-promotion is still work, which is why Toffoletti and Thorpe highlight the labor involved in these sportswomen's online portfolios. VanZant runs her own social media accounts and acknowledges that the labor she performs on social media is a necessity: "To be a successful person you need to have multiple sources of income. In a unique sport like MMA it's hard to rely only on your fight purse" (VanZant 2019). VanZant strategizes her online content and seeks new sponsorships and followers as she posts about her life and work on a daily basis.

THE RACIALIZATION OF THE ATHLETIC LABOR OF FEMININITY

While Toffoletti and Thorpe consider Serena Williams in their study, I would also like to point out that idealized forms of femininity privilege Whiteness on social media and in legacy sports media (Dubrofsky and Wood 2014; Mason 2016). As I illustrate elsewhere, popular feminist media has championed Rousey for being unabashed and unashamed of embracing her muscular, athletic body while U.S. and international media has long criticized Serena for being too muscular (McClearen 2018). Sexist and racist discourses about her body characterize Williams as masculine and superhuman and frequently contrast her with the emphasized femininity of athletes such as Maria Sharapova or Anna Kournikova (Wilks 2020; Anyangwe 2015; Schultz 2005). Kournikova reportedly once declared "I hate my muscles. I'm not Venus Williams. I'm not Serena Williams. I'm feminine. I don't want to look like they do. I'm not masculine like they are" (quoted in Nittle 2018). Kournikova's hatred of her own muscles becomes a point of contrast with the Williams sisters. They become the Othered reflection of what Kournikova considers ideal. Otis Gibson of the Australian *Sunday Telegraph* illustrates similar sentiments about Williams's decision to wear a form-fitting catsuit at the 2002 U.S. Open:

> On some women [the catsuit] might look good. Unfortunately, some women aren't wearing it. On Serena, it only serves to accentuate a superstructure that is already bordering on the digitally enhanced and a rear end that I will attempt to sum up as discreetly as possible by simply referring to it as "formidable." (Quoted in Desmond-Harris 2018)

Williams continues to face body shaming many years after Gibson's indictment of her choice of athletic attire. The French Open banned the form-fitting catsuit in 2018 after Williams again wore one as both a fashion statement and out of medical necessity to prevent blood clots (Nittle 2018). In contrast to these remarks and regulations steeped in misogynoir, when Rousey described her body as "femininely badass as fuck," she became an icon of the body positivity discourse that circulates within popular feminist media.[1] Actress and producer Tina Fey penned an introduction to Rousey in *Time* magazine for their top 100

Angela Hill. YouTube, MMA Junkie, UFC 238: Angela Hill full pre-fight interview.

people of 2016 issue and asked, "Could Ronda be the one to finally help us understand that as females, we define the word *feminine* and that it doesn't define us?" (Fey 2016, original emphasis) even though Williams had been in the spotlight for redefining femininity for two decades. Instead, "Rousey becomes 'revolutionary' for women's body confidence and Williams continues to earn less in sponsorships than tennis stars far less skilled than she" (McClearen 2018).

The contrast between Rousey and Williams demonstrates that Black women perform different athletic labor of femininity as they face racist discourses that perpetually position them against idealized forms of White femininity. Black UFC fighter Angela Hill describes her own experience in the media spotlight in similar terms to Williams. She says that the UFC and potential sponsors are looking for the "all American look." When I asked her to describe what she means by "all American" she elaborates: "Just that girl-next-door look. Light skin, long hair, blonde a lot of times. Something '90210.' Something that's not too scary to look at. Something that's familiar to the majority of media that you're fed by TV shows and movies." Hill identifies the ways that "all American" and "girl next door" are coded as White in mainstream media culture. She contends further that as a "Black woman" who has "natural short hair" and is "muscular," it's often difficult for White audiences to galvanize around her as fans. She then compares her own experience with Williams's:

> It's crazy to think that someone [like Williams] who has broken so many bound-
> aries is still having the same issues as someone like me, who hasn't really done
> that much yet. I feel like that's always been a struggle in sports. And I feel like
> the Black woman in general. . . . We're such an odd thing to look at for a lot of
> people when it comes to athletics because a lot of female athletes are promoted
> based on their sex appeal.

Hill identifies the ways that Black women face an uphill battle when it comes to sponsorships within the hierarchies of visibility. Hill's comments reveal how White-dominated popular culture typically codes "sex appeal" as White. Additionally, while media culture lauds Rousey for her work ethic in crafting a muscular athletic body, it often accuses Black sportswomen of having "natural" muscularity and physical skill. Hill explains:

> I feel like there's always this subconscious feeling that Black athletes have the advantage, so when they win it's not as big of a deal. I would see that a lot with women like Serena Williams, you would see her beat these women in tennis and they're like "well look at her." There's a lot more to tennis than strength and size.

The labor of being an exceptional athlete, then, often goes unrecognized in Black female athletes and instead racist scripts explain the labor away as a natural phenomenon devoid of discipline and hard work.

The athletic labor of femininity requires additional racialized work from Black sportswomen like Hill in the UFC. Since Black women have long been compared to the emphasized femininity idealized for White women, they must work to make themselves less threatening and more palatable for White audiences in order to receive endorsements. Yet, as Hill points out, White female athletes can more readily flaunt their muscularity and can be read as figures of women's empowerment compared to Black female athletes, particularly those with natural hair, dark skin, or other visual signifiers of their difference. Athletes like Hill are astute in their assessments of these realities of their professions and must learn to carefully craft their social media accounts with these realities in mind. They could actively push back by labeling the racism and sexism they experience, they can attempt to present themselves in ways that cater to a White gaze, or they can soften their antiracist efforts in their online presence through what Ralina Joseph (2018) defines as "strategic ambiguity." Strategic ambiguity is a set of tactics deployed by Black women celebrities that uses the language of postrace to subtly and calculatedly resist the microaggressions and overt racism waged against them in media culture. Regardless of the method that Black female athletes use to resist racism on and offline, the necessity to craft one's identity within these conditions increases the athletic labor of femininity required of them.

UFC athlete Michelle Waterson also provides insight into the ways that race and gender interact to impact a fighter's negotiation of the athletic labor of femininity. Waterson is a mixed-race Asian American UFC fighter who has gone by the nickname "Karate Hottie" throughout her MMA career. She is a compelling figure in MMA media because she is sometimes distinctly coded as Asian and other times read as emblematic of the postrace discourses that circulate around mixed bodies. As Jessica Chin and David Andrews (2016) note about Waterson's self-presentation online and through various MMA media sites' descriptions of the fighter, she often walks an ambivalent raced and gendered line between the "dragon lady"—dangerous and sensual—and the "lotus flower"—passive and receptive of male attention—prominent stereotypes in Western representations of ethnically Asian women. They show how her nickname emphasizes her Asianness in "karate," and her sexual availability and desirability in "hottie," to perpetuate "a historical narrative of Asian American women as mysterious, beautiful objects of desire" (166). Waterson also regularly emphasizes her roles as wife and mother on her social media accounts and even began circulating the hashtag #momchamp after declaring that she wanted to be the first mom in the UFC to be champion. Chin and Andrews contend that "the presentation of these athletes as mothers and wives reinforces their femininity, displaying a caring and nurturing side as a balance to the violence enacted during fights that bring into question their feminine traits" (168). While White female athletes who perform emphasized femininity must work to maintain a balance between pretty and powerful, Waterson must also navigate particular Orientalist tropes of her Asian femininity.

Waterson views her participation in the "Karate Hottie" image as "playing the game." She says, "if that's going to get me in the door so people can actually see how skilled I am as an athlete, that's fine. I'll play the game" (quoted in Segura 2013). Waterson is a savvy self-promoter on social media and understands that branded difference in the UFC creates value for her as a mother and Asian woman:

> The UFC loves me. They know what I can bring to the UFC as far as bringing different types of people into the arena. I am a mother. I have Asian descent. So I have all these different things that people outside of the general MMA (audience) would want to come watch. I think the UFC sees that and they're going to be putting more effort into working me up. (Quoted in Connolly 2017)

Waterson shows that as a mother and Asian woman she can reach different audience demographics than the UFC might otherwise be able to access. Thus, her propensity to emphasize these traits stems from an understanding that these identity categories are appealing to the UFC decision makers because they believe it will connect with new audiences.

Waterson's mixed-raced identity also becomes a marketable trait for the promotion that requires her to navigate discourses of femininity and postrace in particular ways. As ESPN's Katie Barnes (2017) notes, Waterson is

Michelle Waterson "Mom Champ." YouTube, UFC, Making of the Mom Champ—Michelle Waterson.

"approachable, playful and, as an added bonus, she's biracial, breaking the model of the blonde female UFC star." Barnes views her biracial identity as an asset for the promotion in similar ways that Waterson has discussed her race as marketable. Waterson's mother is Thai and her father is White American, she is married to a Latinx man, and her daughter is multiracial. While Waterson may be read more dominantly by fans and MMA media as Asian, her biracial identity and mixed-raced family are useful in examining Waterson as an Instagram darling and UFC star. As LeiLani Nishime (2014) writes in her book on mixed-race Asian identities in American media, "the liberal democratic racial project" promotes "a disembodied and decontextualized version of race. It neatly neutralizes the possible disruptive power of presenting a racially ambiguous figure" (47). Nishime makes these points while discussing Nike's advertising campaigns featuring mixed-race golfer Tiger Woods to illustrate how the advertisements amplify postrace discourses. Although Waterson is sometimes coded as monoracially Asian, she can also represent colorblind discourses that permit a malleability in her image in UFC promotional media: she can stand in as palatable evidence of the UFC's inclusivity of diverse female fighters while supporting the postracial surmounting of race that mixed-race bodies are presumed to achieve.

For example, a UFC promotional spot on YouTube featuring Waterson and her family called *Making of the Mom Champ* emphasizes how she navigates her relatable roles as mother and wife while being a professional fighter (UFC—Ultimate Fighting Championship 2019). Her racial identity is never discussed explicitly, but her mixed-race family features prominently as visual evidence of branded difference. Ralina Joseph (2009) describes postracial discourses of racialized women as an ambivalent dance between the "'post-identity' everywoman who embodies a universal appeal because of her positioning as a liberal, democratic, colorblind subject," and a more racially specific subject that represents "niche desirability" (238). Waterson can be marketed as the everywoman or as the Asian woman depending on the goals of any particular promotional effort, which speaks to branded difference's tendency to waltz between difference and sameness when promoting fighters. Regardless of whether Waterson is coded as Asian or as being beyond race at any given moment, the point is that her athletic labor of femininity is always simultaneously performing racialized labor.

NEGOTIATING AUTHENTICITY AND THE ATHLETIC LABOR OF FEMININITY

Many female fighters feel pressure to invest their labor in curating a presence online that deploys particular brands of femininity, like Waterson, but many of them feel inauthentic to their own personal brands when they do. Angela Hill explains that a lot of female athletes are compelled to post content that appeals to a straight male gaze:

> I know a lot of the girls feel pressure to post sexy pictures just to keep their names in people's mouths. That's kind of the line that a lot of female athletes have to walk. They have to be able to do both. They have to be able to be monsters in the cage but also look cute and pretty outside the cage. And I'm not against that, I feel like I do a pretty good job at doing both. But it is annoying that the guys don't have to do that. The guys can just be themselves, just be athletes. They don't have to take pictures in their underwear to promote themselves.

Hill illuminates the ways women in the promotion negotiate how to authentically brand themselves when many of them can't or won't perform the same athletic labor of femininity online as VanZant. By "can't," I am signifying those women of color and/or masculine presenting women who society measures as failing at emphasized femininity, and by "won't," I mean those who reject society's expectation that they adjust their self-presentations to fit cultural norms. The women I interviewed all understood that VanZant's place in the hierarchies of visibility correlates with her ability and willingness to perform that labor. Cortney Casey, who reluctantly engages social media, says "I could post the same picture as Paige VanZant and get 200 likes. And she's going to get 7,000 likes and 6 sponsorships out of it. But I just did the same picture and it's not worth it." Casey points to the fact that she is less visible online than VanZant and that she doesn't think posting the same types of content as the Instagram model would reap the same benefits. Instead, many of the women I spoke with discussed how it was important to them to be "authentic" and find the niche audiences that were interested in the content they posted. Jessica Rose-Clark explains authenticity and the niche audience this way:

> I've seen so many different personality types and styles marketed really well. I think the biggest thing is to fill your own niche. Find what suits you and find what's good for you instead of copying what someone else is doing. That's where I see a lot of athletes fail. They try to be like Conor. Conor found his thing. He found his shtick. He found the thing that drew people to him. Just because it works for him doesn't mean it's going to work for you.

Clark acknowledges that not every fighter can copy a specific formula for increasing social media engagement. She instead suggests fighters "find what suits" them.

Social media allows for customization and for connecting with consumers that might be interested in an athlete's personal brand even if that athlete falls somewhere in the middle or lower tiers of the hierarchies of visibility. Angela Hill and Roxanne Modafferi share some similarities in how they brand themselves on social media yet differ on their willingness to post "sexy" content. Both athletes have roughly eighty thousand followers on Instagram, a fraction of VanZant's following, and describe themselves as "nerdy." Hill explains her personal brand:

> I think the Angela Hill brand is kind of quirky. It's smart and it's seeded in a bit of pop culture. I do a lot of stuff with video games and with art. Before I got back into the UFC, one of my big things was doing cosplay, but aside from that I've always tried to take the witty side of things. I've always tried to live Tweet fight nights and stuff like that. The funnier the comments that I made during the fight, the more successful I felt I was being toward what I was trying to represent. So I've always tried to be funny in a smart way. So when I do do something sexy, it isn't just sexy, I try to keep it fun and something you would laugh at when you see it. Like saying something silly in the caption or make fun of the fact that I'm doing it. So I think what I want to show when I do stuff is that I'm very aware of what I'm doing, but I'm not afraid to be who I am, and show that nerdy artsy side of myself.

Hill emphasizes a playfulness and lightness in her self-presentation and shows she is comfortable with "sexy" in a way that doesn't take herself too seriously. Roxanne Modafferi shares some similarities in her "nerdy" self-presentation, but she differs in her willingness to portray the "sexy" female fighter. Modafferi says,

> I tend to post pictures of what I enjoy doing, like jiu jitsu or Japanese anime. [I also post] sponsor stuff. I don't tend to post glamour shots of me scantily clothed. I think that's one thing that differentiates me from other female fighters. And I gotta tell ya, the few times I've done that, like one of my costumes or something . . . I've gotten so many likes. So many likes. I'll be like hey, I just posted this awesome, fun thing I was doing, and it got 200 likes. Then I posted one picture of my butt in spats, and it got like 2,000 likes. Sex sells and that sucks for me. I'm shy, so I don't do that. But I do stay true to myself and notice that my fans are hardcore. They'll never turn on me. . . . I know I have good quality fans who might like my butt, but it's not the most important feature. You can quote me on that.

Modafferi points to an athlete's ability to find a supportive and niche following within the hierarchies of visibility. She doesn't have as many followers as VanZant, probably makes a fraction of sponsorship dollars, and hasn't had the same level of mainstream media appearances as VanZant. Modafferi even went so far as to acknowledge this reality on her Instagram page. She posted "I just realized I have 50,000 followers! Thank you so much, everyone! I don't even post bikini pictures. So nice to know 50K ppl like my heart and soul. lol Nothing against those who do, of course!" (Modafferi 2019). There is a niche market for the types of content that Modafferi promotes even without the "bikini pictures." However, I would venture that building a niche audience and connecting with a particular brand of followers may now be possible through social media, but it does require additional labor. Creating an audience without using the "bikini pictures" method requires trial-and-error labor on the part of sportswomen to see what might entice a group of followers that better reflects that fighter's personal brand. Customization and the curation of a particular audience is possible but requires considerable effort.

THE BUSINESS OF MICRO-INFLUENCERS

The experience of fighters like Hill and Modafferi shows us that there is a market for online personalities that fall outside the sexy sportswoman motif even though they attract a smaller share of the total market. Social media sites like Instagram have developed a business model that allows for people to craft distinct online identities and develop sponsor relationships that share affinities with those identities (L. R. Smith and Sanderson 2015). This model merges corporate branding and marketing strategies with personal brands and micro-celebrities online (Carah and Shaul 2016). Sites like Instagram call these personalities "influencers" because companies can use an individual's popularity and reach to connect their products, services, and content with a desirable market segment.

As such, the business of influencers directly monetizes hierarchies of visibility. Marketing professionals divide influencers into categories according to the numbers of followers they reach and how much followers interact with the content posted through comments, likes, and shares. The hierarchies of visibility range from a nano-influencer (somewhere around 1,000 followers), micro-influencer (about 10,000 to 100,000 followers), a macro-influencer (about 100,000 to 1 million followers), and a mega-influencer (1 million plus followers). Celebrity endorsements online can cost up to $250,000 a post because they can reach a mass audience, so placing one's product with a mega-influencer like LeBron James or Serena Williams is expensive ("Complete Guide" 2019; Lieber 2018; Ismail 2018). Marketing professionals are becoming increasingly interested in micro-influencers because they charge less per post and "brands can bank on their followers being interested in whatever made the micro-influencer 'internet famous'" (Ismail 2018). In other words, athletes with fewer than a hundred thousand followers are still valuable to brands for their abilities to engage a niche audience. The fact that Hill and Modafferi each cater to the MMA fan who also may like anime and cosplay has a monetary value attached in the Instagram world of influencers.

The UFC is one such brand that understands the value of its athletes posting content about the promotion even though those fighters have thousands instead of millions of followers. The UFC has explicitly encouraged its athletes to be active on social media by holding contests for "most followers" on Twitter and "biggest percentage growth in followers" (Hui 2012; Dugan 2011). UFC president Dana White explains why the promotion decided to encourage athletes to be active on Twitter: "Twitter is the greatest marketing tool in the history of the world, and it is *free*. You can talk directly to your fans instantly. There's no filter or delay; it is all real time. It's incredible" (quoted in Schrager 2012). White's framing of the platform as "free" reveals why the promotion finds the generation of UFC content online so valuable. Since UFC fighters are independent contractors, the brand doesn't have to pay them to Tweet, so the labor fighters perform is free, and the only costs to the UFC are to run data analytics on its fighters' accounts and to pay out the occasional bonus for engagement. Thus, the UFC uses many of the logics of influencer marketing to promote its brand but doesn't directly pay its athletes to do this work. Modafferi and Clark both describe the UFC's practice of analyzing its athletes' social media use and giving them individualized reports on the accounts. Clark says that each time she is scheduled for a fight she sits down with the UFC's social media team to discuss her social media accounts. She says the team looks at her engagement

Roxanne Modafferi representing a sponsor on Instagram. Used with permission.

levels and prints out a report of what types of content fans are engaging with and what days and times they tend to do so. The UFC doesn't necessarily tell athletes what to post but does recommend they increase their engagement levels.

An influencer's engagement with followers is a key consideration when brands decide how much a micro-celebrity endorsement is worth. Joe Gagliese, a cofounder of an agency that facilitates relationships between influencers and brands, explains how an influencer's stats are monitored and predicted to represent certain values for the brands that hire them: "We look at views, likes, engagement rates, watch times, click-through rates, comments, you name it, to share with brands. And the cool thing is we are able to actually guarantee a certain level of interaction" (quoted in Lieber 2018). Engagement rate becomes a central factor in predicting an influencer's ability to "convert" their followers, namely, convince a consumer to purchase a product or service. The rate is calculated by adding up all interactions on a post, including comments, clicks, likes, and shares, dividing by the number of followers and then multiplying by 100 to yield a percentage that helps determine the worth of an influencer for the brand. An average engagement rate on Instagram is 2.1 percent, while a 5 percent rate is considered desirable for influencers. Jessica Rose-Clark's engagement rate is 4.1 percent according to a website that tracks the engagement rate of accounts with more than 100,000 followers, such as Clark's (Trackalytics n.d.) while Modafferi recalls that at her last meeting with the UFC's social media team, her rate was around 1 percent. Thus, Clark's level of engagement would be more desirable to brands seeking to partner with influencers than Modafferi's. Clark and Modafferi both remember the UFC's social media team explaining that the way to increase their engagement rates is by responding to fans' comments on their accounts. Clark says: "Commenting on people's posts. That's what the [social media team] told me leads to the highest level of interaction." The personalized interactions with fans leads to increased engagement overall. Clark received this information with enthusiasm because she sees social media as "part of her job," and she generally enjoys it. Modafferi was positive overall about having a supportive fan base but wasn't so enthusiastic at the work of commenting back to fans to increase her engagement rate. She says the social media team told her "oh, you should comment more and reply to your fans. If they like your stuff you have to reply. I'm like 'what a pain in the neck.' If I want to raise my percentage, I should do that. . . . I was like 'alright.'" The tone in Modafferi's voice suggested a reluctance to spend her time and energy increasing her engagement online. As Joe Gagliese describes, "being an influencer takes hard work, it's a full-time job, and you could be working at it for four years before you hit it big" (quoted in Lieber 2018). Female fighters sometimes find themselves reluctantly laboring for online visibility in the hope that the labor will be rewarded with time in the Octagon's spotlight. For all intents and purposes, this labor is aspirational in that UFC fighters hope that their work will lead to booked fights or more sponsors. Yet, the rewards for this work are unequally distributed because the business of influencers is financially tied to hierarchies of visibility.

The rising trend of influencer marketing on Instagram attaches clear monetary values to the content female fighters generate online. This results in a sliding scale of payment wherein the most visible women make the most money. Typically, the women who gain the most from the labor of visibility are those who most successfully perform the athletic labor of (White) femininity. That said, the contemporary market for niche audiences seeking content that falls outside the mainstream ensures a modicum of success for fighters like Modafferi and Hill, who amass a following outside the mainstream models of promoting female athletes. Yet, it's the brands that connect with micro-influencers that thrive in this new era of advertising. Marketing professionals now consider micro-influencers more valuable to brands because they cater to extremely defined groups of consumers, they are cheaper, and followers are more likely to believe that an Angela Hill actually uses a product she endorses than a Kim Kardashian (Main 2017). What the world of influencers and micro-celebrities teaches us is that there is money to be made for brands who attach themselves to all sorts of people laboring for visibility online. Branded difference at its core understands that different types of content attract various UFC fan demographics, so they need multiple onramps for engagement. Yet, much of the content fighters post on their social media accounts is a form of aspirational labor that circulates the UFC's name and connects the promotion with the niche audiences that follow particular fighters without necessarily paying the fighter financially or in terms of securing fight contracts. Additionally, visibility online incurs an additional form of labor for female fighters that is often invisible: the emotional labor of dealing with online harassment.

The Emotional Labor of Fan Interaction

People aren't very nice on the Internet, especially to women. Women experience twice the rate of sexual harassment online as men and that harassment increases with media visibility ("Troll Watch" 2019; Dhrodia 2017; Duggan 2017). A study conducted in Australia found that 27 percent of Facebook comments directed at Australian sportswomen were negative (including sexist and belittling comments) (Silva 2019). The potential impact of this sort of vitriol online becomes more pronounced when considering that none of the fighters I spoke with has a team to manage their social media accounts. Even Paige VanZant manages her personal brand online. Micro-celebrities whose "job" is to post sponsor content and UFC fighters who need to remain relevant in order to book fights have to manage their own fan interactions. The fact that the UFC and other sponsors encourage them to interact more with their fans to gain higher engagement rates means they will likely have to manage their own harassers as well. VanZant says she has learned to manage negative comments:

> I definitely found it hard at first. You have to have thick skin and know that you will have negative comments . . . anytime you're in the public eye you're going to have people hide behind an Instagram page. You have to know that those people saying those things are still paying attention. You still matter.

VanZant admits that it's challenging to deal with harassment online; however, she also spins it positively since the engagement still means they're "paying attention," that is, contributing to her overall visibility. On the one hand, one might suspect that VanZant receives a greater volume of harassment and trolling because of her sheer number of followers. On the other hand, as a woman who performs the athletic labor of femininity to stand near the top of the hierarchies of visibility in the UFC, she is likely harassed differently and perhaps less frequently because of the privileged identities she holds. For example, Laura Brown describes the differences between her experiences online and VanZant's:

The number one insult I hear is "you're ugly." It's so common and it's hurtful. This is pretty personal, but I guess a big part of me believes them. . . . Paige VanZant doesn't get that. She might get one or two, but her timeline is flooded with people probably asking her nasty things. That's totally disrespectful in a different way, but mostly it is people telling her how beautiful she is and "will you marry me." I'm sure she has her assortment of guys that say things like "I want to fuck you in the ass" or the nasty stuff. That's also a form of disrespect and abuse, but to me it's not the same.

Brown points to the ways that harassment may require different degrees of emotional labor depending on how well a woman in the UFC performs the athletic labor of femininity.

Female UFC fighters have reported various degrees of harassment online, a fact that reveals the cost exacted from them as they labor for visibility. The harassment ranges from negative commentary on their performances in fights, to name-calling, to derogatory comments on their appearance, to sexually explicit photos and videos, to rape and death threats. While she asserted that "99 percent of my fans are great," Barbie Beeman listed some of the comments she received online, including "you have no boobs," "how old is she," "worst ground game ever," "you scare me," and "she is on steroids." She also recalled a fan declaring on a social media account that she was the only woman who could go from "hot chica," to "a not so good-looking dude, and back again," which punctuates the scrutiny female athletes with muscular builds experience. Since emphasized femininity and athleticism are difficult for most women to perform simultaneously, harassers relish pointing out when sportswomen fail at achieving the feat. Although Beeman remains largely unphased by the negative comments, many fighters are unable to do so. Laura Brown reveals that the vast majority of negative comments online are about her appearance: "The first thing people generally attack is the way I look. . . . When I put something on Twitter and somebody doesn't agree with it, the first and most common insult I get is 'shut up you ugly bitch.' Or 'you look like you're old.'" Brown doesn't shrug off the comments as easily as Beeman and says she sometimes cries because "it really gets to me."

Other fighters have discussed the sexually explicit content they receive on a regular basis. Brazilian UFC fighter Bethe Correa describes her experience:

They harass me on Snapchat and Instagram from seven to ten videos a day. Guys send me videos of them masturbating with pictures of me. Sometimes they get to the point of masturbating themselves while watching me fight and I'm just working, I'm doing my job, practicing a sport. (Quoted in Rezende 2016)

Claudia Gadelha. Photo by Amy Kaplan.

Correa points out just by "doing her job" she receives a large degree of sexually explicit messages online as a result of that visibility. Fellow Brazilian Claudia Gadelha cites similar forms of sexual harassment. She says she has never been harassed in person after becoming a professional fighter, yet,

> on social media [harassment] happens all the time. We get messages not only from fans, but also from pervs all the time. It's annoying, I get messages like "I fantasize about you hitting me." It's very weird. Some men send pictures of their junk. Some guys really bother me. I try to ignore them. (Quoted in Rezende 2016)

Correa and Gadelha's accessibility facilitates an onslaught of unwanted attention. When considering that the UFC has largely pushed its fighters to be accessible and available to fans, it is clear that the millennial sports media brand's emphasis on athletes using the "free" platforms of social media isn't exactly without cost. It's a cost that the fighters themselves must bear.

Visibility online, then, requires more conventional forms of labor in terms of time and effort as well as emotional labor of varying degrees. Barbie Beeman says that she mostly shrugs off the negative comments she receives online, but she recalls being angry and afraid for a close friend and fellow UFC fighter who has experienced death threats and comments like "I'm going to rape you and make your son watch." Beeman says, "It makes me mad that she has to deal with those types of threats. When you're as public as she is, you have to take it seriously." Other female fighters admit to feeling "bothered," "annoyed," "weird," and sometimes "scared." Laura Brown has had a much more difficult time managing harassers and trolls. She says that after her last fight she received so many negative comments about her appearance that she met with a plastic surgeon and considered getting a face lift. She says:

> I can't even fight back [against the harassment]. The [trolls] can tell me everything they think is wrong with me, and they're really personal and super mean. It's kind of making me emotional right now. It's making me tear up. It's harder for me to deal with than I expected. Maybe other female fighters don't take it personally, but it's something I've struggled with my whole life.

Brown admits that her response to harassment about her appearance may be more extreme than other fighters; yet, she illustrates how the pressure to be online in order to be a successful MMA fighter can exact a heavier toll for some women than others depending on personalities, life experiences, and subjectivities. The intersecting oppressions of sexism and racism result in one such glaring difference among fighter experiences.

Women of color tend to face more harassment online than White women. An Amnesty International study on violence against women and Twitter found that women of color were 34 percent more likely to receive harassing comments than White women. Black women were a staggering 84 percent more likely to experience online abuse ("Troll Watch" 2019). Angela Hill, one of only a handful of Black women currently in the UFC, has experienced this harassment firsthand. She describes her experience growing up in an affluent Black neighborhood "sheltered" from the types of misogynoir common to online spaces. She says she was shocked at the level of racist and sexist comments online in the beginning of her UFC career. Prior to joining the UFC, she had never glanced at the YouTube comment section but learned quickly that it was an unhealthy space to dwell:

> It's disheartening. When I looked at YouTube comments about me because I thought people would embrace the fact that I was the first Black American woman in the UFC . . . instead, people were like "who is this girl, we wanna see more of Paige VanZant."

Hill's experience in the YouTube comment section shows the reality that Black women remain at the lower tiers of the hierarchies of visibility online even though sports are a cultural space where Black women have thrived to a greater degree. Hill has developed her own niche "quirky" brand on social media to grant her a degree of visibility within the hierarchies; yet, she is still more likely to experience harassment for her race and gender online than White female fighters.

The assumption that the visibility of sportswomen can produce equity in contemporary sports media must also consider the costs of that exposure. Thorpe, Toffoletti, and Bruce (2017) assert that social media "provides sportswomen with opportunities to bypass the gatekeepers that control traditional media products, regain some control over how they are represented, and potentially build new audiences" (361). Their analysis is illuminating, but there are also consequences when sportswomen embrace social media as aspirational labor. Social media visibility requires sportswomen to negotiate the athletic labor of femininity (by embracing, tailoring, or rejecting it) while opening themselves to public scrutiny and harassment that they, rather than a publicist or manager, must navigate. The female fighters I spoke with reveal that fielding sexist and racist comments from fans emboldened by the screen barrier between them and the fighters is emotionally laborious. The actual physical labor these sportswomen undertake is a consequence of a risk economy that facilitates aspirational labor online to hopefully gain what visibility promises to offer: more fights, increased sponsorship, and greater job security. All the while, the business practice of using influencers to curry favor for larger companies and corporations means that these workers may never actually see the fruits of that labor in tangible terms.

Precarity and Visibility

The pressure to self-promote certainly isn't isolated to UFC fighters; other sports and professions shift this labor to the individual as well.[2] That said, it is important to consider the contextual consequences generated from the labor of visibility for female fighters in the UFC. The pressure to self-promote becomes more profound when one is struggling financially or fears losing one's job, which are common conditions for UFC fighters who find themselves lower in the hierarchies of visibility. Laura Brown outlines many of the conditions of precarity that fighters face in their profession. She agrees with Barbie Beeman that getting a UFC contract isn't "making it."

> Everybody wants to go to the UFC. They're like "if I train really hard and I go to the gym everyday and work really hard, I'll be in the UFC someday, and that's my dream. I just want to be in the UFC." To them that's the pinnacle.

Here Brown highlights how many fighters labor just for the chance to fight in the UFC but are unaware of the additional costs associated with that feat. She explains that the reality is that she has to "fight with strangers online" who say "the worst things they can about me." On top of that, she has to "deal with the UFC lowballing me and me fighting to get paid what I'm worth." She continues:

> I think people wouldn't [want to be in the UFC] if they knew they'd be worrying about all these injuries that are happening on the way to their fight and having to keep those injuries hidden until after the fight [so that insurance will cover them]. People never really think in those terms. They just think they want to be in the UFC, they want to be on TV, and it's going to be so glorious. It's only that way for 1 percent of people.

Brown articulates how the labor of dealing with harassment online intertwines with other working conditions that cause her concern. She highlights pay, but also contends that many athletes fight with injuries because they need their paychecks, or they need the UFC's insurance to cover the cost to repair an injury. For example, Cortney Casey admitted to fighting with a broken hand because she couldn't afford to forgo the income from the UFC. Roxanne Modafferi's biggest fear is getting cut from the UFC. UFC contracts are one-sided so that the promotion can terminate a fighter's contract at any time, but the fighter doesn't have the same right. Modafferi explains that "the UFC basically ties the fighter into the money and how much they're going to make." In other words, if the UFC determines that the fighter isn't worth the money allocated to him or her in the contract, it can easily cut the fighter.

Visibility in the UFC encourages specific forms of labor from female athletes including the labor of self-branding, a negotiation of the athletic labor of femininity, and emotional labor for managing their lives as women in the spotlight. All of these efforts are largely aspirational because female fighters hope this work will lead to a spot on a popular UFC card, more booked fights in the promotion, or sponsorships; yet, there are no guarantees that this work will yield these results. The working conditions for UFC fighters are precarious, and the aspirational labor that fighters perform online are an attempt to alleviate some of that uncertainty. Cortney Casey explains that

> we don't have off seasons. We're not on TV for six months or three months every Saturday. So you have to kind of build yourself in between every six months. Ideally, most fighters fight twice a year. If you're lucky, three times. If you are super lucky and you're Donald Cerrone or you're finishing fights really early, then four times. But it's rare. So you have to stay relevant in other ways.

Social media becomes one of the ways to "stay relevant" and "keep your name in their mouths," as Barbie Beeman says. All the while, these same fighters vying for visibility online have limited rights in their UFC contracts, are paid a small percentage of the UFC's overall revenue and given limited health insurance to cover all the wear and tear on the body that fighting causes. The next chapter considers how athletes in the UFC are fighting back against these precarious labor conditions.

CHAPTER 5

The Fight for Labor Equity

MMA fighters from all over the world gathered for a weekend at the promotion's headquarters in Las Vegas in summer 2017 for the first UFC athlete retreat. The festivities included celebrity speakers, seminars, informational sessions with UFC sponsors, and a concert by rapper and UFC fan Snoop Dogg. The spectacle heralded a few developments in the organization, namely the opening of a new world headquarters and the UFC Performance Institute, a branch of the UFC dedicated to studying and improving the physical skills and recovery for fighters. The retreat also offered the first chance for the new owner, Endeavor, to engage a large group of the promotion's athletes and set the tone for the next chapter in UFC ownership. In one session, former NBA star Kobe Bryant spoke about his experience as a professional athlete and opened the floor for questions from the fighters gathered around the room. UFC fighter Leslie Smith walked up to the microphone, unsure how Bryant would receive the loaded question she was about to pose:

> How essential to your personal negotiations and the success of basketball in the world do you believe a players' association has been? We're on the verge of forming a union here . . . [but] . . . some of us are on the fence about how much do we pay in or [are] worried about rocking the boat. How significant to you and your career, and basketball in the world, do you feel like the unity of the players represented by the association has been? (Quoted in Bohn 2017)

As Smith formulated her words, there was a rising sea of cheers as many of the other three hundred athletes at the retreat began to realize that she was breaching a taboo topic between fighters and the UFC. For fighters, the issue of an association or union to grant them more access to UFC decision-making and revenue is one that often takes place behind closed doors rather than in the public eye. But in this moment, Smith brought the fight to the UFC elites making her politics extremely visible for those in the room and those watching later on social media. Bryant responded affirmatively to Smith's question:

> [A union is] extremely important . . . we [NBA players] understand completely that a rising tide raises all boats. When you guys have this unity and you guys are operating together on the same page. . . . it does nothing but simply fortify the sport, make the sport better. Not just for present, but for future generations that are coming. So it's extremely important. (Quoted in Bohn 2017)

Bryant asserted that players unions were essential to the ability of NBA players to have agency in their careers. He repeated the adage "a rising tide raises all boats" to support the concept of unionization within the UFC ranks. Smith walked away from the microphone beaming victoriously to a chorus of cheering voices. Less than a year later, the UFC chose not to renew Smith's contract despite her winning record, impressive stats, and dynamic fighting style. She directly correlates her unionization efforts to her dismissal from the UFC. The timing and circumstances of her abrupt departure from the promotion raises concerns about the level of impunity the UFC has in managing fighters.

Leslie Smith. YouTube, MMA Junkie, Leslie Smith still upset at last fight, ready to shine at UFC Fight Night 85.

The moment between Smith, Bryant, and the other fighters at the retreat prompts us to consider the athletes' precarious relationship with the UFC as they expose structural inequalities in the promotion for the world to see. To fighters like Smith and Cat Zingano, the UFC retreat made the stark contrast between organizational revenue and fighters' lives more apparent. Zingano also attended the retreat and remembers that the content of the seminars addressed issues that were incongruent with more pressing concerns for the group of athletes in attendance, which largely consisted of fighters who were paid in the low to mid-tier range rather than the promotion's biggest stars (Mindenhall 2017). Zingano believed that the UFC's chief aim for the retreat was to inform the athletes about all the new developments in the promotion while spending millions of dollars on an event with carpets and wall fixtures that "will only be used once." She continued: "how much money went into bringing Snoop in and Michael Strahan in, and Kobe Bryant—what did these guys get paid to come do this when we're sitting here broke, or struggling?" (quoted in Mindenhall 2017). Zingano further noted that the UFC has cultivated sponsor relationships that augments the wealth of the UFC, but not the fighters:

> That was more insulting than anything, and I don't know if they considered that when they were creating the content when they were like look, we get this many viewers, we sell this many fights to this many homes a year, blah blah blah, and all of us are still sitting there knowing exactly what we get f*cking paid. (Quoted in Mindenhall 2017)

Zingano's experience at the athlete retreat marks the tenor of the room where Smith stood to raise the issue of a fighters' union. The palpable disconnect between the content of the corporate event and the actual experience of the fighters proved Smith's question both poignant and timely.

This chapter centers Leslie Smith's fight for MMA fighters' rights through the labor organization she cofounded: Project Spearhead. We have seen that discourses of women's empowerment and the American dream promise possibility for the droves of female fighters attempting to join the most prestigious MMA promotion in the world. Branded difference paints an attractive image of successful female fighters while disregarding the fighter labor at the center of the UFC's profitability. In addition, visibility is a key avenue to gaining fans, booking flights, and garnering other types of exposure for a fighter's career (chapter 4); yet, visibility is also a double-edged sword. Branded difference operates within economies of visibility that assume that the mere presence of female fighters has achieved some form of justice; yet, the promotion also

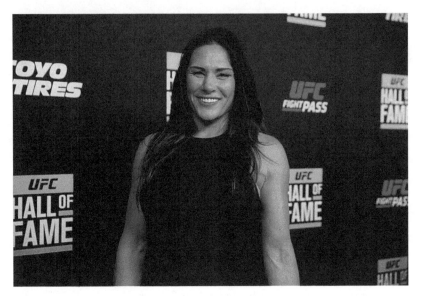

Cat Zingano. Photo by Amy Kaplan.

attempts to thwart political visibility that might draw attention to injustice. To make noise, to clamor for fairness, to stand alone in a room of UFC fighters and dare to say the word "union" is precarious for fighters. I assert that political visibility is a key avenue for illuminating labor inequalities for workers and holds promise for improving workers' rights within the UFC, and for women in the sport in particular. This chapter takes seriously the imperative within the cultural studies scholarly tradition to highlight how power operates in media culture, but also to pragmatically consider how to combat exploitative practices. As the scholar Henry Giroux (2000) reminds us, "cultural studies is more than simply an academic discourse; it offers a critical vocabulary for shaping public life as a form of practical politics" (13). The shift to "practical politics" extends the book's ideological critique by examining the legality and ethics of the UFC's use of a contract labor force. I consider the precarity facing Smith and other fighters who have brought the union fight into the light and show how unionization might benefit fighters.

This chapter's consideration of what political visibility can offer UFC athletes has perhaps no greater inspiration than the USWNT's quest for equal pay. A few months prior to the start of the 2019 Women's World Cup, twenty-eight USWNT players announced a gender discrimination lawsuit against U.S. Soccer citing stark wage disparities between the highly successful women's team and the often floundering men's team.[1] Announcement of the lawsuit was well-timed for maximum visibility: on International Women's Day, three months before the world would be glued to the pitch for several weeks to watch the sporting drama unfold during the sport's most visible event. *Washington Post* reporter Liz Clarke (2019) points out that the timing of the team's actions was also unusual: "This isn't what champion athletes normally do—launch a public fight with their boss at the most critical stage of their athletic preparation, when their focus is on shutting out distractions, rather than actively creating them." Instead, the USWNT timed their actions meticulously to coincide with when their visibility was reaching fever pitch. Much of the media coverage of the World Cup indeed focused on the team's fight for equal pay. Fans at USWNT games during the World Cup even chanted "equal pay" in response to the team's fight with U.S. Soccer. As Professor Nicole LaVoi told ESPN, "Traditionally, athlete activists have been shut down, fired, discriminated against, all of that. . . . What's happening [with the USWNT], though, is working. They're drawing attention to the issue. They're using their collective power" (Borden 2019). Likewise, leveraging political visibility through collective action is one such measure that Leslie Smith firmly believes could benefit fighters as well.

Much of my analysis of Smith's union fight and the obstacles to unionization centers on issues that impact both female and male fighters, even though the heart of *Fighting Visibility* remains fixed on female athletes. The fight for labor rights is an uphill battle that can best be won by as many fighters as possible rallying in support of one another to build strength in numbers. That said, White women, women of color, and/or women who fail to perform the pretty and powerful imperative stand to gain the most from these efforts because unions historically have raised wages and improved working conditions for everyone, but especially for women and/or people of color. Those workers who are most disenfranchised often experience the greatest gain from those organizing efforts when unions and associations collectively advocate for workers' rights to be equally applied to everyone. The latter part of the chapter considers how Project Spearhead's key platforms would benefit all fighters with added equity for female fighters.

The Peacemaker's Union Fight

Leslie "the Peacemaker" Smith began training MMA in 2008 and fought her first amateur fight a month after beginning the sport, which is a telling example of her fearlessness in the ring and outside it. One of UFC fans' most memorable moments of Smith occurred in a fight against Jessica Eye at UFC 180 (November

15, 2014) in Mexico City, when a strike from the other fighter caused a small hematoma, or "cauliflower ear," to burst and separate part of Smith's ear. The doctors examined Smith to determine if she could continue, and she yelled in Spanish to the crowd "It doesn't hurt! I can continue!" The doctors didn't share her optimism and stopped the fight. Witnessing her aggressive fighting style and durability in the ring, some might think her nickname simply refers to the Colt .45 revolver, "the peacemaker"; but Smith strongly identifies with nonviolence and sees MMA fighting as a "controlled burn" that allows fighters to express themselves in a contained environment. She says, "I grew very fond of the nickname . . . because I feel like that it is something I am trying to use, the soapbox I get for fighting, to talk about other aspects of fighting, peace and life" (quoted in Reid 2017). Smith views the MMA stage as a platform to bring visibility to the fight for social justice in the sport. Her efforts to organize fighters into a viable union and collective voice are a shining example of "The Peacemaker" in action. Politically, she exposes the ways the UFC misclassifies fighters as contracted employees and prevents its athletes from taking collective action. Smith's experience attempting to unionize MMA fighters illuminates how precarious certain forms of visibility can be for independent contractors in the UFC.

Smith has advocated for greater fighter agency in the UFC through collective organizing since 2016. She has joined other MMA athletes to form fighters' associations that demand more rights and opportunities. She was an active member in the Mixed Martial Arts Fighters Association (MMAFA), a group formed to lobby for the Muhammad Ali Boxing Reform Act to be applied to MMA and to prevent the UFC from having a monopoly on the sport.[2] The U.S. Congress passed the act in 2000 in order to curb corruption and fighter extortion in boxing. Some of the provisions of the Ali Act included limiting the length of a contract to twelve months and providing consequences for contracts that heavily favored promoters over boxers. The MMAFA argued that MMA fighters faced similar issues in their sport and that the application of the Ali Act to MMA would benefit the sport. The association also sought to curb the UFC's ability to stifle other MMA promotions, arguing that healthy competition among various MMA entities would drive promotions to elevate overall fighter salaries and benefits in order to recruit the best talent. Smith was active in the MMAFA, but the organization disagreed with her assertion that unionization was a viable path for increasing the rights of MMA fighters. Instead, it favored methods that would reduce the UFC's monopoly on the sport.

In February 2018, Smith formed a new effort to gain support around a fighters' union when she, fellow fighter Kajan Johnson, and attorney Lucas

Middlebrook created Project Spearhead. The key aims of the new association included collecting authorization cards (a signed document supporting the formation of a union) in order to form a legitimate fighter union while also operating "as an Association of fighters and secur[ing] benefits for its members such as healthcare, access to legal review of contracts and access to reputable financial planners. The ultimate goal is for all fighters, across every promotion, to speak with a unified and collective voice" ("Project Spearhead Home" n.d.). Smith and Middlebrook were clear in their promotion of Project Spearhead that authorization cards would remain confidential in perpetuity as a measure to encourage fighters to sign without fear of retaliation from the UFC.

Unfortunately for Smith and Project Spearhead, her eventual dismissal from the UFC did nothing to assuage fighters' concerns that retaliation for unionizing was a possibility. As Smith began advocating on various MMA news sites and social media for fighters to sign authorization cards via the Project Spearhead website, she simultaneously promoted her next fight scheduled against Aspen Ladd in April 2018. UFC contracts for Smith and Ladd required both women to weigh in below the 135.5-pound limit for the bantamweight division, but Ladd failed to make weight, which nullified the contract between the UFC and the two women. In many states that sanction MMA events, Smith wouldn't have been entitled to any pay for the canceled fight. UFC contracts typically exclude provisions for fighters who fulfill their obligations but whose opponent must cancel for any reason. This means a fighter could spend months preparing for a bout, attend all the prefight week fanfare, and make weight only to lose their chance for a payday at the last minute—an experience that UFC fighter Cortney Casey describes in excruciating detail (see chapter 3). Because the fight was taking place under the New Jersey Athletic Commission rules, Smith was still entitled to the fight purse she was promised if she had competed. Most states don't have a similar guaranteed payment provision in such cases, and the decision to pay a fighter remains at the discretion of the UFC.

The UFC paid Smith for the fight due to state regulations and determined that the promotion and the athlete had fulfilled the three-fight contract both entities had signed. The UFC then announced that it would not renew her contract, which was a curious move considering Smith's winning record in the UFC and her desire to remain in the promotion. For example, the UFC ranked her ninth in the world in her weight class, had recently awarded her a "Fight of the Night" bonus for an impressive performance, and celebrated her as producing several memorable fights during her four-year tenure in the promotion. Smith maintains that the UFC retaliated against her because of her visible unionization efforts. She then took legal action to prove these claims. Even if, for the sake of argument, the UFC didn't renew Smith's contract for other reasons, her case illuminates how precarious fighters are in the promotion. Smith did her job, did it well, and was still ousted from the UFC rather quickly. This is precisely the type of working conditions that she and others are trying to bring to light.

Smith and her attorney, Lucas Middlebrook, determined that the UFC's decision not to re-sign her provided a case to bring before the National Labor Relations Board (NLRB). What transpired between Smith, the NLRB, and the UFC demonstrates the ways that the UFC leverages its clout to prevent certain labor issues from seeing the light of day. The NLRB is an independent government organization established in 1935 to provide legal protections for workers and their efforts to unionize, to collectively bargain, and to protect themselves from unfair labor practices. Smith's NLRB claim argued that the UFC retaliated against her because she was actively unionizing. Middlebrook presented Smith's case to Region 4 of the NLRB, which is based in Philadelphia, in May 2018. After nearly two months of deliberation, Region 4 determined that Smith's case had merit enough to file complaints against the UFC, which is the first step after a charge has been filed. In most cases, once a claim has been determined to have merit, the parties involved would either settle out of court or go before a judge with their dispute; however, Smith's case did not advance to this stage of the process.

A few hours after Region 4 determined merit, Middlebrook received a call from NLRB headquarters in Washington, D.C., indicating that they would block Region 4's determination in order to consider the complaints before moving forward, which halted the progress given Smith's case only a few hours earlier. The attorney noted that occasionally regions would reroute difficult cases to the NLRB's headquarters in Washington, D.C., but usually with some indication in advance that the transfer would occur. Middlebrook says, "I had never experienced a situation where you were told that the region had ruled in your favor, only to hear hours later that D.C. called and said, 'no we're going to look at this first.' [It was] so suspicious. Not even enough time had elapsed for Region 4 to issue their determination in writing." Later that September the NLRB reversed its determination of merit, stating that the UFC terminated Smith's contract because of failed negotiations rather than as retaliation for unionizing. The NLRB reported that the UFC claimed that Smith demanded greater pay and that the two parties failed to reach an agreement as a result of this and other contract disputes, which resulted in their dismissal of the fighter's claim. Smith disputed this characterization of the events that took place, but to date the NLRB has not granted her an appeal of its dismissal of her claims.

Smith and Middlebrook believe that the UFC leveraged its political ties to block their efforts to voice her grievances before the board and to bar fighters from gaining more power through the NLRB to advocate for their labor rights. Middlebrook explains that the president of the United States appoints the NLRB's general counsel. Upon appointment by President Trump in 2017, Peter Robb, a lawyer with a reputation for union busting, diligently went to work to reverse some Obama-era provisions that strengthened unions (Stern 2017). This is a curious agenda for an appointee to an organization founded on the notion of protecting workers' rights. After Trump took office, the NLRB has seen an 11 percent drop in disputes filed by unions because of fears that the Republican-leaning board would be unlikely to rule in their favor (Wallender and Kanu 2019). Middlebrook also points out that the president of the UFC, Dana White, has had a long business relationship with President Trump. The UFC front man spoke at the Republican National Convention on behalf of Trump during the election and even visited the White House for dinner with the president just days after Middlebrook attended the meeting at the NLRB. Middlebrook would like to see an investigation into whether the UFC lobbied the president to ensure the NLRB ruled in their favor. Middlebrook summarizes: "It continues to be our opinion that this is just purely political string-pulling in order to cover the UFC." He believes the promotion sought to prevent a determination on the status of UFC fighters as statutory employees, which could have much larger ramifications for the financial bottom line for the UFC than Smith's singular case of retaliation.[3]

By strong-arming Region 4 into reversing its determination that Smith's claims were worthy of consideration, the NLRB prevented a serious examination of how the UFC manages its workers. The politics of visibility in this case demonstrate how power operates to keep structural inequalities hidden from view. Smith, for example, wasn't allowed to be present when her attorney was summoned to Washington to discuss her complaint before Peter Robb and the NLRB. After protesting Smith's exclusion, Middlebrook recalls Robb explaining that claimants tend to become "too emotional" at these hearings to be included. The attorney later left the meeting thinking "this woman fights in a cage for a living, and you're concerned that she's going to be emotional in this conference room in D.C.?" The sexist excuse that a woman fighting for her rights would be "too emotional" further underscores what is at stake when inequality becomes visible. Smith is a charismatic activist who challenges the status quo. She is an empowered female athlete who might stand as a role model for women and girls in the ways that the UFC marketed Rousey; yet, the promotion dismissed Smith rather than celebrate her. The UFC's trope of the empowered female athlete can be visible only if she elevates herself as an individual and toes the party line in the promotion. The UFC will not depict her as an empowered woman for speaking truth to power within the promotion or for using collective action to bring change. The power to prevent Smith from speaking for herself and for others is a political act that benefits the UFC while ensuring the agency of its fighters remains limited.

Barriers to Unionization

Smith's fight for labor equity in the UFC is precarious because standing up in the limelight to contest the UFC's business practices has damaging consequences. Organizing MMA fighters has proven to be particularly challenging because visibility is a double-edged sword: it is key to raising support around issues of inequality, and yet it can result in a fighter's dismissal from the UFC. Since even a contract with the UFC brings no job security, fighters face the promotion alone when they negotiate contracts that grant them little agency. I asked Leslie Smith, Kajan Johnson, and Lucas Middlebrook what they perceived as the barrier to fighters signing authorization cards and showing more vocal support of fighters' rights. They were unanimous in their responses: "fear of retaliation." That Johnson's contract was also not renewed after he began organizing with Project Spearhead fuels fighters' fears that voicing support for a union means they risk being cut from the roster. Or worse yet, as Smith explains, UFC athletes fear being "shelved" by the organization while under contract. Since UFC contracts prohibit UFC athletes from fighting professionally outside the organization and the fighters have no avenues for breaking contracts, the UFC could hold a contract over their head for several years without any obligation to schedule a fight. Lucas Middlebrook describes how fear of getting cut or shelved is a major deterrent to organizing fighters:

> The UFC fighters are proving to be a really difficult group to organize from a union standpoint. The reason for that is the climate of fear that's been created by the UFC. The amount of control that the UFC exerts over these fighters has done just that. It has created this perfect storm of fear of retaliation. Where the fighters don't even want to be mentioned in the same Tweet as Project Spearhead, whether they agree with it or not. In fact, the large percentage of the people who sent in cards . . . made it painfully obvious that they didn't want any mention that they had even signed a card to get out into the public realm.

Fighters fear that making the working conditions in the UFC visible may lead to dire consequences for their individual careers; so, most prefer to keep their heads down when it comes to unionizing.

Julie Kedzie adds that fighters often believe that they are all replaceable, which would make it easy for the UFC to cut them should they become visible union advocates. She says that fighters tend to believe "there will always be a replacement fighter that will come in and take [a fight] for less than the other fighter" if they attempt bargaining or asking for more. This leaves many fighters feeling that having their name associated with union efforts is a huge risk, with little promise of reward. Retired UFC fighter Barbie Beeman told me that the prospect of signing an authorization card seemed pointless to many fighters. She said, "So why would you put yourself out there to do that? It's probably not going to do anything for you. Not within your generation of fighting. So why would you put yourself on that blacklist if you don't have to deal with that shit? Because it's not going to do anything." Ulrich Beck (2000) describes this phenomenon as the "individualization" of the work force—a process that centers the individual worker while maintaining a skepticism of collective action and solidarity. Many fighters remain skeptical that there is any safety in numbers and instead view joining a collective as a potentially detrimental form of visibility that presents more risks than just working in the conditions the UFC presents.

Standing out as a unionizer seems too risky for many fighters, but that doesn't prevent them from discussing their precarious working conditions in private. Kajan Johnson clarifies that issues of labor and pay equity circulate in tightly guarded fighter circles instead of out in the open:

> In the back chats and the back channels, face to face, in backrooms and locker rooms, everybody talks about [fear of retaliation and lack of fair revenue sharing]. It's like a big joke for us, actually. Everybody laughs about how much money we don't make. And how the public perception of UFC fighters . . . is that we're on television and must be making . . . millions of dollars. That's obviously not the case.

I spoke with several other UFC fighters who wish to remain anonymous on the issue of labor organizing for many of the reasons that Kedzie, Johnson, and Smith have described. Those anonymous athletes corroborated the shared experience of fighters whispering about the precarious nature of their jobs to other fighters they trust. Many of them also warned me that it would be difficult to persuade fighters to discuss these issues openly with me. Indeed, in the course of researching this book I found their prediction to be true.

Another factor hindering the organizing success of Project Spearhead is that UFC stars have refrained from publicly adding their names to authorization cards even though they are also susceptible to labor inequalities in the UFC. As the athletes who make the highest income in the UFC, some of these fighters perceive themselves as having less to gain and more to lose from collective action than the average fighter. Leslie Smith spoke with a high-earning UFC fighter who said

> they were scared of losing their job. Someone that was at the very top of the UFC, top of their weight division, top of everything. They should have been 100 percent

secure in where they were at, but even they were saying they do not believe that fighters need to come together to get more rights. But they were worried about their job. They felt like they needed to get some more wins before they were able to stick their neck out.

These reservations acknowledged, I would venture that securing the voices of UFC stars would be a key path to growing Project Spearhead's base of fighters. Champions and other stars bring visibility to a cause. For example, there was a great deal of initial buzz around the Mixed Martial Arts Athletes Association (MMAAA), which formed in 2016 with names like Georges St-Pierre, Donald Cerrone, and Cain Velasquez at the helm. MMA analysts are unsure if the association failed to live up to its initial media buzz because of internal strife among the organizers or external pressure from the UFC (Martin 2016; Okamoto 2016). Regardless, without star athletes collectively clamoring for change, it is more difficult to draw support from non-prominent fighters, who feel even more vulnerable, experience more economic insecurity, and are more replaceable in the UFC's eyes.

An additional factor impeding Project Spearhead is that the UFC's organizational structure is so individualistic and isolating for fighters that they rarely have an opportunity to speak with one another in a larger forum. Several hundred fighters personally witnessed Smith stand to speak about a union at the 2017 athlete retreat; however, UFC athletes rarely, if ever, gather together as a large group let alone build coalitions. Middlebrook says that the geographic distance among the global roster of fighters makes unionization a challenge. Even with an event like the retreat, Middlebrook is skeptical that fighters would feel secure enough to have an open discussion: "I think they would only engage in a really [productive] discussion if they truly knew no one from the UFC is watching and no one from the UFC is going to hear about [it]." Instead, Middlebrook proposes that having Smith go from gym to gym might be the only avenue to convince geographically dispersed fighters that a union could benefit them. Even that would be logistically challenging because Project Spearhead doesn't have the financial resources to cover those travel costs.

Why Unionize?

Fighters fear making their support for a union fight public; yet, at the same time, visibility for Project Spearhead is central to galvanizing fighters as a collective front. A viable fighter's union holds promise for ameliorating labor inequalities because unions offer fighters "a seat at the table" that is difficult to impossible to obtain otherwise. A union would give all fighters greater ability to advocate for their careers, livelihoods, and even their physical health. Unions provide collective bargaining and protections from retaliation in order to make fighters' needs and priorities visible. Project Spearhead has determined several key areas of concern that they have foregrounded for the collective betterment of the fighters. Below I examine four of these issues: the misclassification of fighters, access to the financial data of the company to ensure that fighters have a fair share of the revenue, health and disability insurance, and gaining a voice in company decisions about issues impacting the fighters. More important to this project as a whole, history tells us that women of all races have the most to gain from a collective voice advocating for fair treatment because "the best trade unions strive to counter inequalities and exclusions based on gender, class, ethnicity and other dimensions of social power" (Banks and Hesmondhalgh 2016, 267). As Kobe Bryant argued at the athlete retreat, a player's union has the capacity to improve working conditions for all fighters.

THE MISCLASSIFICATION OF UFC FIGHTERS

Project Spearhead seeks to address the misclassification of UFC fighters as independent contractors. The distinction between an employee and an independent contractor largely boils down to issues of control, and numerous law review articles argue that the UFC exercises more control over UFC fighters than the legal classification of "independent contractor" allows (e.g., Salminen 2017; Gaul 2016; Birren and Schmitt 2017; Same 2012). An employer exercises control over the employee by determining when, where, and how they work, while an independent contractor typically has more freedom and determination over those working conditions (Salminen 2017). For example, a large painting company employs numerous full-time employees and determines when, where, and how those employees work, and what uniforms they wear—all indicators of the company's control over its workers. A painter who works as an independent contractor can determine which jobs they take, when they do the work, and how many projects they work on at once, which are indicators of a greater degree of agency than an employee. Fighters, on the contrary, must yield to the UFC's when, where, and how while assuming most of the financial risks, as well as additional physical risks, of devoting their careers to fighting. For example, UFC fighters must notify the USADA of their whereabouts at all times for random drug testing and must adhere to a code of conduct in order to receive their Reebok sponsorship pay for their official UFC apparel. USADA regulations and the code of conduct both suggest a level of control over athletes that extends beyond typical contracted labor relationships.[4]

UFC athletes further lack the individual agency to negotiate many labor issues within the promotion because of the ways its contracts favor UFC interests above athletes'. The UFC can void multiple-fight contracts or decide not to re-sign a fighter to a new contract, while the fighters remain legally bound to fulfill their contracts. UFC contracts also restrict an athlete's ability to participate in broadcasted fighting contests that are not UFC sponsored, which effectively prohibits them from fighting for other promotions. This contract stipulation statistically impacts female fighters more than male fighters, because the UFC books women for fewer fights on an annual basis than men.[5] A female athlete's three-fight contract and a male athlete's three-fight contract are statistically unequal because he will complete those three fights faster than she will, and she will have to wait longer between each payday in her contract. Beyond the gender inequality in the fulfilment of UFC contracts, the stipulation restricting fighters to one promotion is illogical because the very nature of freelancing is one's ability to work for multiple employers at once. For example, Uber drivers can simultaneously work for Lyft or other rideshare companies in order to ensure they have the most opportunities to work (Weed 2019).[6] Yet, once a fighter signs a contract with the UFC, that contract obligates them to fight exclusively for the promotion.

The misclassification of UFC fighters affects both male and female fighters alike; however, because there are far more federal and state labor laws for employees that are leveraged to protect women and people of color specifically, it stands to reason that the misclassification of fighters leaves these groups most vulnerable because they have less access to legal mechanisms to protect themselves as marginalized workers. As Heather Berg and Constance Penley (2016) write, "independent contractor law is organized explicitly to excuse employers from their responsibilities to workers . . . [and those workers] have little legal protection from discrimination in hiring or pay disparity" (159). Studying the adult film industry, Berg and Penley confirm that the status of independent contractor means that "rates for black women performers are a fraction of those of their white counterparts, for instance, plus-sized performers too are underpaid, and male performers can be blacklisted based on rumors of their having had same-sex sexual encounters" (163–94). Attorney Charlotte Alexander (2016) explains in an article on misclassification and discrimination that "employers are free to reject workers for jobs, fire them, and otherwise discriminate on the basis of sex, religion, or disability, for example, and to be absolutely explicit about their reasons for doing so, as long as those workers are classified as independent contractors" (908). She further analyzes the relationship between misclassified employees and their gender and race to show that misclassified independent contractors are often overrepresented with women and/or people of color. Of the cases Alexander includes in her study, misclassified workers are less likely to win cases of discrimination filed under Title 7 of the Civil Rights Act of 1964, which prohibits workplace discrimination. As of this writing, UFC fighters haven't filed gendered or racial discrimination lawsuits against the UFC, but cases in other professions suggest that reclassifying UFC fighters as employees will likely benefit those who are statistically more likely to be discriminated against in the workplace: women, people of color, and/or minoritized sexual identities.

FINANCIAL TRANSPARENCY AND REVENUE SHARE

As I discussed in the introduction, fighters earn a small percentage (10–20 percent) of the UFC's revenue. After removing the stars from the equation and deducting the associated costs of training for and participating in UFC events, most fighters take home a very modest amount of pay compared to the estimated worth of the company. When considering the median, women earn 68 percent of what male athletes make per fight and tend to fight less frequently. The promotion justifies these inequalities by arguing that the NFL, NBA, or MLB are an unfair comparison because the UFC has greater overhead costs in the production of its events. The UFC claims these production costs limit its ability to compensate fighters to a greater degree. As former UFC owner Lorenzo Fertitta explained,

> First and foremost, we absorb 100 percent of all production and marketing costs associated with the event. The NFL gets a license fee from Fox. Even boxing gets a licensing fee from HBO. Those media entities then roll in and operate the entire production. They do all of the marketing. So those expenses are not borne upon the actual league or entity. In our case, we televise the entire card. There's over a thousand people who get paychecks when we do these events. It's a massive, massive undertaking. . . . In addition to that, we're building a sport. We've had to open up offices in various countries around the world, work to get laws passed in states all over the U.S. and Canada. When you actually take into account those costs that we bear, and other leagues don't, we actually compare very favorably on an apples-for-apples basis. (Quoted in Snowden 2013)

Fertitta's description of the various costs associated with marketing, producing, and distributing globally broadcast UFC events seems logical in comparison to professional sports leagues. However, unlike the NFL, NBA, and MLB, the promotion isn't obligated to show its balance sheets in order to prove its assertion that its fighters are fairly paid.

Kajan Johnson, the vice president of Project Spearhead, finds the overhead costs defense difficult to swallow for a company valued at $7 billion (Reinsmith 2018a). He asks, "What are these exorbitant overhead costs that they incur that the NFL and the NBA doesn't have?" Johnson admits that the UFC has a huge in-house production team to produce UFC live and pay-per-view events, but he also adds that the UFC has become much more efficient at its media production since Zuffa originally took over the UFC: "I think they've got it down to a science and I think it would probably be more expensive to outsource [production at this point]." Johnson remembers a recent conversation with Ari Emanuel, the CEO of Endeavor—the company that purchased the UFC in 2016. Johnson recalls Emanuel promising to increase fighter pay if the UFC was able to increase its profits. Johnson remains doubtful:

> First of all, that's a lie, otherwise we'd be getting paid more money already. Second of all, that's just saying that your piece of the pie is not going to change. That you're not willing to pay us more until the entire pie grows, which I believe to be wrong because your cut is more than enough already.

Despite Johnson's skepticism about the UFC's primary justification for current fighter pay inadequacies, he urges that the biggest issue is the lack of budgetary transparency. He adds, "How am I going to negotiate a fair wage if I don't know what your profit is?" This is precisely the type of budgetary transparency Johnson, Smith, and Middlebrook advocate for through Project Spearhead. Smith believes that the lack of transparency enables the UFC to dodge the question of fair pay. The UFC claims that not all fighter pay is disclosed to the public, which is a way to deflect the criticism that it is failing to pay its athletes enough because the fighters and the broader public cannot confirm these claims. In effect, Project Spearhead is advocating for fighters to have access to UFC financials in order to ensure that fighters indeed receive a fair share of the revenue.

A collective bargaining agreement facilitated by a union would provide the fighters the means to negotiate the pay structure with the UFC and would better ensure that those currently most disadvantaged—that is, female fighters, and even more specifically Black female fighters—were fairly compensated. For example, between 2015 and 2018, the confirmed data on UFC payouts show that the promotion paid Black women a median of $16,000 per fight compared to a $30,000 median for other female athletes (see appendix B). Without a union, Black female athletes have little chance of advocating for improved pay. According to the Economic Policy Institute, almost half of all workers with union contractors are women and 35.8 percent are people of color (Bivens et al. 2017). Historically women and/or people of color make less than White men across a wide variety of sectors; yet, studies show that unions elevate the wages of these minoritized groups to a greater degree than nonunionized minoritized workers. Unionized women have 9.2 percent higher salaries than nonunionized women and unionized Black workers make 14.7 percent more than nonunionized Black workers (Bivens et al. 2017). Black women make 65 cents on every dollar that White men make; yet, union membership reduces the gap so that Black women make 94.9 percent of what their White male counterparts make (McNicholas and Jones 2018). These statistics suggest that the unionization of UFC fighters would likely increase transparency so that fighters could better negotiate fair wages and benefits across gendered and racial difference.

HEALTH AND DISABILITY INSURANCE

A third major issue for Project Spearhead is the current lack of comprehensive health and disability insurance for UFC fighters. The UFC provides health insurance when a fighter is injured while training for a contracted fight or if they are injured in the fight itself. Covered expenses include doctors' visits, laboratory tests, and surgeries due to that injury but has a maximum benefit of $50,000 per year (Marrocco et al. 2011). When an athlete is not under contract for a fight, then routine doctors' visits, injuries that occur outside of a contract, and other healthcare needs are the responsibility of the fighter. Smith cites health and disability insurance as her number one concern personally:

> The fighters aren't seventeen-year-old kids that appear out of nowhere to fight and disappear afterward. They're real-life adults with families they need to support and mortgages they have to pay off. Being hurt and having extended medical issues is a big problem.

Smith says the level of risk fighters take to their long-term health in order to compete in the UFC necessitates comprehensive healthcare before, during, and after fights. Even if a fighter is able to get the UFC insurance to cover their injury at 100 percent, it doesn't cover the fighter's loss of income while recovering.

The UFC's level of health coverage fails to take into account ongoing health-care needs of a group of athletes in an extreme sport such as MMA. According to data released by the UFC's Performance Institute, an average of 31.9 percent of fights end in a knockout (KO) or a technical knockout (TKO), which medical professionals classify as "concussive symptoms" indicating brain injury (UFC Performance Institute 2018). For the largest weight class, the heavyweights, 60.1 percent of fights end with a KO or TKO. Additionally, neuroscience re-search suggests that female athletes take longer to recover from concussions and experience more post-concussion symptoms than their male counterparts, thereby suggesting the concussion crisis in contact sports may leverage a higher cost for female athletes (Broshek et al. 2005; Covassin and Elbin 2011). While the UFC has committed resources to studying the impacts of head injuries on the long-term health of the fighters at the Performance Institute, the promotion has no obligation to the ongoing comprehensive healthcare of current or former fighters impacted by these injuries when classifying fighters as independent contractors. NFL players, on the other hand, have full insurance benefits while they are active in the league and for five years after they retire. These players receive additional compensation should they develop neurological conditions that have been linked with repetitive brain injuries (NFL Play Smart n.d.). As more research studying head trauma comes to light, it is clear that repetitive brain injury, even if each single injury is considered minor, may have severe long-term health consequences. Fighters place themselves at risk without the promise of ongoing healthcare provisions by the UFC. The lack of comprehensive healthcare may impact female fighters to a greater degree over time if women take longer to recover from concussions.

Fighters are statistically likely to experience some sort of injury or need assistance with recovery even if they avoid head injuries in a fight. For example, of the twenty-four fighters on the UFC Phoenix Fight Night card in February 2019, UFC doctors placed sixteen fighters on medical suspension after their bouts, which indicates a significant injury preventing further fighting by that athlete until they can be medically cleared. Most medical suspensions ranged from 30 to 180 days depending on the severity of the injury (Reinsmith 2019a) and while the UFC will cover some portion of a fighter's medical bills during the suspension, the athlete cannot earn an income from fighting until they are cleared. The causes for suspension for most events usually range from fractured bones to face lacerations to concussive symptoms. At UFC Phoenix, Cain Velasquez got a 180-day suspension for a knee injury, while Paul Felder was suspended indefinitely after he suffered a collapsed lung and needed emergency surgery (Helwani 2019). UFC doctors evaluate fighters immediately post-match and fighters must receive any additional procedures within thirty days of the fight in order for the UFC's insurance to cover that injury (Dundas 2018). However, once the fighters return home after a fight, much of their recovery work begins. A staff doctor for Jackson-Winkeljohn MMA, the fight team of UFC stars Michelle Waterson and Holly Holm, says standard recovery efforts include massage and manipulation, compression to combat swelling, and monitoring kidneys to ensure they aren't overworked processing increased waste in the bloodstream from bruising and swelling (Dundas 2018). UFC health insurance does not cover these sorts of ongoing therapies.

A VOICE IN DECISION-MAKING

Project Spearhead advocates for a collective voice for fighters as the UFC makes decisions that have direct consequences for its athletes. In the promotion's current structure, fighters have no formalized channels for advocating for their interests when it comes to UFC rules, policies, and procedures. As a result, Smith and Johnson both contend that an essential advantage of a union is a collective voice for fighters. Johnson says a union is necessary so "we can all speak with one collective voice to the company so they're not able to divide and conquer as they have been doing." The UFC is under no legal or contractual obligation to consult the people who would be most impacted by UFC policies and business decisions, namely the fighters themselves or their representatives.

For example, if the UFC had been required to consult with a fighter's union prior to the promotion's unilateral agreement to make Reebok the official apparel sponsor of the UFC, then the fighters could have negotiated to prevent a significant negative impact on their livelihoods. Prior to 2015, a major source of compensation for UFC fighters came through individually brokered sponsorship deals to wear the sponsor's logo during their fights. Fight fans who joined the UFC's viewership prior to 2015 might well remember the brand logos of Muscle Milk, Dynamic Fastener, or Affliction plastered across an athlete's fight shorts, indicating sponsorship with that brand. Each fighter negotiated a range of sponsorships to support their professional fight careers and frequently wore several logos during a fight at once. Yet, in 2015, the UFC signed a deal with Reebok for the apparel company to become the exclusive sponsor of UFC outfitting and banned athletes from wearing other sponsors in the ring (Raimondi 2018). The promotion also began requiring its athletes to wear Reebok apparel at all UFC-sponsored events. Reebok itself compensates fighters using a system that rewards the athletes for longevity; UFC fighters with one fight under their belt receive $3,500 in sponsorship pay, fighters with more than twenty-one fights receive $20,000, and champions pocket $40,000 (Reinsmith 2019b). The move didn't just significantly reduce the amount of sponsorship pay athletes could secure, it also limited fighter agency, which is an indication of employee-level control. Furthermore, in 2018 the UFC altered how fighters would be compensated through Reebok by rolling the pay from the apparel company into a set of "fight week incentive payments" with a few of its own additional stipulations for the fighters. Fighters must also abide by a "code of conduct" that subjects athletes to penalties, reductions in pay, or removal from a fight for criminal conduct or for what the UFC deems to be derogatory or offensive conduct. The restrictions that the Reebok partnership and the code of conduct places on fighters further demonstrates how much control the UFC has over its "independent contractors," which give merit to the claim that the UFC should either revert agency back to its fighters, such as the right to wear their own sponsors, or reclassify them as employees.

The Reebok deal fundamentally shifted a major source of income for all fighters, with compounded effects on women outside of straight White feminine normativity. The sponsorship tier fails to reconcile the fact that women were prohibited from fighting in the UFC until recently, even though they fought in other promotions. Fighters such as Miesha Tate have argued that the Reebok tier system is discriminatory against women because female fighters have only been in the organization since 2013. Their exclusion meant they had no possibility of acquiring the same number of fights as men who had been fighting profes-sionally the same number of years but were fighting in the UFC before women were permitted. Even when Tate received the $40,000 for being champion of her division, she claims that the payout was about 20 percent less than she could make from the sponsors she had acquired for herself prior to the Reebok deal (Brennan 2016).

It's important to note that Tate performs the athletic labor of femininity suc-cessfully, while other female fighters seeking sponsorships may find themselves lower within the UFC's hierarchies of visibility. Women who are racial minori-ties, who are non-heteronormative, and who perform female masculinity are at a particular disadvantage in the UFC when considering that fighters historically relied on sponsorship money for a large portion of their income. Just as Paige VanZant receives more visibility and sponsorship on Instagram than Angela Hill, apparel companies have long privileged heterosexy White women in advertis-ing, and the UFC's formal business relationships support that status quo. The Reebok deal is another strong example of this type of disparity. In addition to the tiered pay system for fights, the apparel company also awarded additional sponsorships for a few UFC athletes. Each of the women initially awarded these additional contracts—Ronda Rousey, Miesha Tate, Joanna Jedrzejczyk, and Paige VanZant—were White women. Rousey and Jedrzejczyk were both champions of their divisions and Tate would later become champion, so one might surmise that Reebok courted only the most successful athletes. VanZant, however, was a curi-ous addition to the other women in the group. At the time of writing, VanZant was ranked outside the top 15 in her division, but she secured one of these additional Reebok contracts before she was even ranked. The strawweight fighter is young, White, blonde, and conventionally attractive. She was also a contestant on ABC's *Dancing with the Stars* reality competition show in 2016, signaling her mainstream appeal to audiences outside the sport. Compare VanZant to Cris Cyborg, who was one of the most dominant fighters in the UFC. Even though Cyborg was a feath-erweight champion and held a near-perfect record in MMA, she never secured an individual Reebok contract while working for the UFC. Cyborg is Brazilian, very muscular, and fails to perform the athletic labor of femininity as well as VanZant does. The fact that beauty conventions in advertising impact female fighters outside the White feminine norm is further compounded by the realities that the majority of fighters are underpaid and that women already receive less than their male counterparts on average.

The prospect of being reclassified as employees, of having a greater share of the promotion's revenue, of gaining comprehensive health and disability insurance, and of having a voice in UFC decision-making each suggest tangible ways the UFC fighters' lives might be improved if they unionize, and in this sense Project Spearhead is on the right track. The challenge that remains is convincing the UFC, and even its parent company Endeavor, that the fighters deserve to be classified as employees and treated as such.

The WGA vs. Endeavor

In an era when precarious work like independent contracting and gig labor is increasingly common, companies have little internal incentive to make workers' lives better when they can deny responsibility for contracted workers. As Chuck Kleinhans (2011) cautions us to remember,

> [Precarity] is a deliberate policy and aspect of neoliberalism in its relation to the labor force. Such a policy aims to make the situation of owners, of capitalists, of employers . . . more flexible. Rather than full-time, continuous work, of indefinite duration, protected by labor unions and government regulations, with standard hours, social benefits, and a social wage (that is one that allows you to support a family), precarious work goes in the other direction.

Labor research agrees, on the contrary, that on average unionized workers experience increased wages, greater safety at work, more complete healthcare, and a greater rate of retirement benefits when they are represented as a collective (Bivens et al. 2017; Banks and Hesmondhalgh 2016; Curtin and Sanson 2016). As Miranda Banks and David Hesmondhalgh (2016) surmise, "trade unions have played a major role in efforts by workers to improve their conditions, defend their rights, and promote social justice in people's working lives" (267). The fact that the UFC blocks efforts to bring the case of its independent contracting practices before the NLRB suggests that the promotion understands the financial implications for changing the classification of their workers. The UFC's entire business model might have to drastically shift should it make fighters employees. As Jason Cruz (2020) notes, "the added overhead would sink many small-time [MMA] organizations as many could not finance the additional costs" (59). Cruz's point is astute and suggests far-reaching implications for the future of the sport. But then again, perhaps exploitative business models *should* sink. Companies *should* drastically adapt in order to establish more just working conditions for the individuals who form the base of their business and risk their health and welfare for that company to make its billions. Unions and the labor laws that support them are one avenue to incentivize the adaptation or, if change proves untenable, the extinction of businesses that exploit droves of independent contractors and gig workers.[7]

Consider the Writers Guild of America's (WGA) approach to challenging the UFC's parent company, Endeavor, for business practices that benefit a company with numerous media holdings at the expense of individual clients. Since 2010, Endeavor, which has holdings in sports, talent agencies, and event management, among others, has been buying entities at various levels of the entertainment media supply chain, including its acquisition of the UFC in 2016. As Endeavor prepared to go public on Wall Street in 2019, it met opposition from the WGA, one of the largest entertainment unions in the business. The WGA claims that Endeavor's vertical integration of its various business holdings is a conflict of interest that cannot effectively represent the interests of its clients. For example, Michelle Waterson is represented by WME (a talent agency) and is a fighter in the UFC, both of which Endeavor owns. Since her representation and her employer are intertwined, their fiscal relationship inherently raises suspicions about WME's ability to fairly represent her in business dealings in the sport. As one of the WGA's representatives argues of Endeavor's efforts to become publicly traded, "It is impossible to reconcile the fundamental purpose of an agency—to serve the best interests of its clients—with the business of maximizing returns for Wall Street. Writers will not be leveraged by their own representatives into assets for investors" (Faughnder 2019). Effectively, the WGA is concerned that Endeavor's business practices will benefit the agency and its investors at the expense of the clients it represents. Another key issue the WGA has cited is Endeavor's practice of negotiating "packaging fees" with studios who employ talent represented by the agency. In a letter citing their opposition to Endeavor becoming public on the stock exchange, the WGA charges that

> Endeavor leverages representation of its clients—primarily writers—to negotiate its own compensation, which includes upfront fees, paid out of the production budget of each episode, and a percentage of the TV series' profits, rather than the traditional 10% commission on clients' earnings. (Writers Guild of America West 2019)

Talent agencies have traditionally gained their income from taking a commission from its clients' earnings on a job; however, Endeavor now negotiates deals that produce additional revenue streams for the company, but not for the writers or the other talent it represents. The WGA charges that this approach of working with studios gives Endeavor less incentive to negotiate individual deals that will benefit its clients. As a result, the union has created a code of conduct that prohibits agents from brokering packaging fees, and 1,400 union members have terminated their representation with Endeavor (Writers Guild of America West 2019). At the time of writing, the WGA and Endeavor are in court debating the holding company's right to represent talent, buy talent, or profit on related talent business transactions all at the same time.

The lessons from WGA's public fight with Endeavor offer two main takeaways. First, the business of MMA is increasingly tied to larger trends of conglomeration that give powerful companies the ability to leverage their clout to make decisions that benefit the company above individual workers—be they television writers or UFC fighters. The concentration of media firms and the vertical and horizontal integration of their related businesses all combine to further push workers' rights to the wayside. It is an all too common neoliberal practice to grant businesses personhood status and consider it a company's right to pursue their own American dream while amassing wealth. Meanwhile, the workers who make these dreams possible toil away at their own livelihoods without reciprocal support from those who contract them. A second, more optimistic, takeaway is that labor unionizing provides an infrastructure for disseminating information to make interested parties aware of how corporate organizational trends might impact individual workers and provides a legal arm for challenging companies like Endeavor in court. Political visibility remains one of the greatest assets of labor unions.

Visibility as a Political Tool

> MMA fighters are naturally courageous people. It takes a lot of courage to step into the ring on national television and fight. Now we need to follow the courageous examples of factory workers, UPS drivers, teachers, and all the other workers across the country who have fought for a union and stood up for their rights. Fighters can draw a lot of strength, support, and inspiration from other workers who are fighting for a better future for themselves.
>
> —Leslie "The Peacemaker" Smith (quoted in Brooks 2018)

The efforts of Leslie Smith and Project Spearhead have kept discussion about labor inequality alive on various digital and legacy platforms when many fighters had previously only whispered about the topic behind closed doors. Raising awareness and galvanizing support through making social justice causes visible

Leslie Smith victorious. YouTube. UFC. UFC 198: Leslie Smith—Ready to Destroy Cyborg.

holds potential for challenging the power structures discussed in this book. I argue that visibility is precarious and can be co-opted by powerful entities, but this chapter posits that visibility can still be a political tool for the disenfranchised. In spite of losing the chance to compete on MMA's largest stage, the Peacemaker believes in the work to bring the fighters' plight into the light. She has given dozens of interviews about her organizing efforts through channels that range from niche MMA podcasts to a short segment on the satirical news show, *Full Frontal with Samantha Bee*, on the TBS television network. She also began campaigning for Andrew Yang, a 2020 democratic candidate for the U.S. presidency who included MMA labor rights on his campaign platform. Smith now fights in the MMA promotion Bellator and is also pursuing her bachelor's degree at the School of Labor and Employment Relations at Rutgers University. She plans to attend law school to study labor and employment law, with the ultimate goal of passing legislation that will protect fighters from unfair labor practices such as those she's experienced in the UFC.

Leslie Smith is just one social justice warrior, and she needs fellow fighters to believe collective action is a viable method for improving their working conditions. Men's professional sports have longer histories with organizing on behalf of players to improve pay and to give athletes a voice, but the more recent success of athletes organizing in other women's sports sends a very clear message for the future of women (and men) in the UFC: collective organizing works. In recent years, various organized groups of female athletes have taken action through unions and other affiliations to improve the conditions of play and pay around the globe. These players' associations in women's sports have made the fight for pay equity and working conditions in sports more visible, including the USWNT's and the U.S. Women's National Hockey Team's successful bids to increase higher wages and improve travel and insurance benefits, and the Australian women's cricket players organized efforts to increase their top athletes' salaries by nearly $100,000 (Pierik 2017; Langone 2018). The WNBA's players' association also recently signed a new collective bargaining agreement that included unilateral salary increases and greater maternity and childcare support ("WNBA and WNBPA" 2020). Compared to an individual sport like MMA, team sports boast the distinct advantage of already working as a collective unit on the field and off.

Individual sports like MMA lack the advantage of already having a pre-constituted group of athletes within a team. Nevertheless, the Committee on Equity in Women's Surfing (CEWS) is one example of how individual athletes still have the capacity to impact change through collective organizing even in an individual sport that showcases male and female competitors at the same events. Several female surfers and a local California politician formed the committee in 2016 to address unequal treatment of female athletes at California surf competitions and beyond ("About CEWS" n.d.). In just three years of advocacy work, CEWS successfully lobbied the World Surf League (WSL) to ensure that female surfers had equal access to its events. In 2018, the WSL announced that male and female surfers would begin receiving the same prize money after the CEWS sent a letter arguing the California-based league's inequitable pay violated California civil rights laws (Duane 2019). CEWS has since advocated for women in professional cycling to receive equal treatment in competitions by lobbying the California Department of Transportation not to issue road permits due to the unequal treatment of women in cycling races (Almond 2019). Thus, organizing individual athletes to collectively speak as a group for their rights can be fruitful in a variety of sporting contexts, including individual sports such as surfing where men and women compete in separate divisions during the same event.

In order for Project Spearhead to successfully organize fighters, they will need to overcome the primary organizational conditions that prevent athletes from joining unionization efforts: fear of retaliation, lack of support from UFC stars, individualism, and isolation. Despite the distinct challenges of organizing in MMA, it is clear that unions can and do improve the working conditions for all their athletes, but specifically for women. If Project Spearhead or another union effort succeeds, it will also offer the rare example in professional sports where a players' union works to the benefit of male and female athletes alike. Women don't have to go it alone even though female athletes stand poised to benefit most from a union's ability to advocate for the fair distribution of resources across all fighters. An individual athlete is expendable within the organization, but hundreds of athletes at once are not—especially if UFC stars assist in making the fight visible. The vast majority of UFC athletes are disenfranchised, but they also remain central to the UFC's business model because the promotion cannot exist without them. The only way for Project Spearhead or other advocacy efforts to take flight is to reconfigure the perception of the fighter as being an island unto themselves and instead leverage their political visibility into a collective front fighting for all.

Coda

On Love and Violence

> Some people watch two people fight and they see violence,
> but I look at it and see a labor of love. Two people that care
> about something so much that they will fight each other
> for it and love each other for the challenge.
>
> —Ronda Rousey ("Breaking Barriers" 2019)

Throughout *Fighting Visibility* I argue against a blanket embrace of visibility as a tool for equity for sportswomen in the media. In the process of writing this book, I have held a tension in the back of my mind that I explore here to further interrogate visibility in the UFC. My own subjectivities as a martial artist, as a consumer of the sport, and as a researcher who interviewed female fighters for this project are all factors in the ways I punctuate the close of this book. While writing, I have silently meditated on the contradictory relationship between love and violence embedded in MMA and its largest promoter. To an outsider looking in, MMA might seem like an inherently violent endeavor that produces both morally questionable entertainment content for the masses and traumatic injuries for its athletes. MMA is often dramatized as a modern Roman arena filled with gladiators in a barbaric fight to the death. The mass of fans cheering for the destruction of an athlete appear as depraved and uncivilized as the hoards in Rome who callously turned their thumbs down to call for the death of a fallen gladiator. Yet, these descriptions are too myopic in their consideration of the sport for one simple reason: love. MMA fighters love their sport, they love their teams, they love their trainers, and they even love their opponents. To love something that produces such pain and strife may seem foreign

Rousey consoles Zingano after their fight at UFC 184. Photo by Amy Kaplan.

to many readers, but MMA athletes love putting their bodies and minds to the test in a controlled environment. Fighting, as a sport, is thrilling for the very reason that it provides a relatively safe space for people to overcome their fears and the stresses of modern life. To step into the cage is to face something that scares or intimidates them, and that feels exhilarating. The fighters' love of MMA is what drives them to compete and to withstand precarity in order to do the job they love. Thus, here at the close of *Fighting Visibility*, I examine the tensions between violence and love in MMA and the millennial sports media brand that promotes it.

Many of the fighters I spoke with used the word "love" to describe their participation in MMA. I directly asked Barbie Beeman why so many fighters would continue to work for the UFC, considering all the hardship they faced financially, physically, and emotionally. She responded with laughter, more lighthearted than much of the rest of the interview:

> Because we're all stupid! No, people get into the sport for the love of it. Fighting is fun and it's one of the basic things all animals do. MMA is one of the places you're allowed to fight and not get in trouble. Humans are animals, and there are three things that all animals know how to do without anybody telling them. Reproducing, eating, and fighting or defending themselves. It's survival of the fittest. It's three things that allow us to survive or not survive. So it's something

that's ingrained in people. And once somebody gets a taste of fighting, it's fun. You know that from jiu jitsu. It's fun!

For Beeman, part of the joy of MMA is the sheer fun of the game and the ways that fighting allows a form of expression that doesn't exist elsewhere. Cynthia Calvillo teared up as she described how she began training MMA. Married as a teenager, she had just gone through a difficult divorce when she walked into a MMA gym for the first time. She says, "MMA was so liberating. I felt like so much got lifted off of me. I get choked up about it because if I hadn't found MMA, I honestly don't know where I'd be." Calvillo remembers feeling so much more confident in who she was as a woman once she began training, and she fell in love with the sport instantly.

> I love fighting so much. Even when I was working [other jobs,] I always made sure I was making enough money that I could always put training first. And even when I knew I couldn't fight. I'm obsessed with being the best athlete in the world. This is my full-time job.

The sheer love these athletes have for the sport shines through in the interviews with them. The fighters' expressions of love make it more evident why the sparkling discourses of overcoming obstacles to win in the Octagon are so appealing and why fighters continue to toil in less than desirable working conditions.

So far this book has focused not on fighters' love for the sport but on fighters struggling in a system that enacts violence against them. I don't mean violence in the traditional way that the sport has been stereotyped—as a barbaric form of entertainment that celebrates unbridled violence in a cage. I agree that we as a society have moral questions to answer about a wide range of sports that perpetuate head injuries, from youth soccer to the NFL to the UFC. In each of these instances, athletes are risking their long-term health for a short-term gain. However, I want to bracket these well-founded concerns for the moment and consider the ways the sport of MMA is not actually perpetuating a spectacle of violence to the degree that it has often been criticized.

Combat sport scholars Alex Channon and Christopher Matthews developed a campaign called Love Fighting Hate Violence to contrast the definitions of violence and sport fighting. For them, the key differences between violence and combat sports revolve around consent, respect, and violation. When two people enter a sparring session in combat sports, they are agreeing to abide by certain rules and norms. Channon and Matthews (n.d.) write that combat sport practitioners "should enter into such exchanges in a spirit of respect for one another's boundaries, as laid out by the rules or norms of their discipline, and with a view to fair competition or mutually beneficial learning" (2). Violence, on the contrary, exists within the absence of consent and fails to abide by rules or norms (Channon and Matthews n.d.).

Channon once explained the concepts of consent, respect, and violation to me through Brazilian jiu jitsu. As a grappling martial art, the goal of jiu jitsu is to control your opponent by achieving a dominant position or physically threatening a choke or joint lock, for example. When performing joint locks, chokes, or other "submissions," the aim is to execute the position just to the point that you could actually break a bone or choke your partner unconscious, but not complete that action if they signal to stop, which is the preferred result. If your training partner lightly "taps" the ground or your body with their hand or says the word "tap," then they concede to the submission and you release the attack. After the tap, then you and your training partner would likely continue without any verbal conversation about the attempted submission because it stays within the boundaries of the sport's rules of engagement. However, in jiu jitsu, if you accidentally elbow someone in the face—an act prohibited in the sport—you would likely stop training momentarily, apologize, and confirm that your partner was unhurt. The inadvertent elbow was a violation of the rules the practitioners agreed to when they begin training together. To respect one's partner is to communicate with them verbally and nonverbally to ensure both of you stay within the boundaries of the rules.

Of course, there are MMA fighters who violate the rules of consent and commit acts of violence in the sport and beyond. Just the same, many others train MMA in supportive environments that attend to the well-being of their training partners and opponents. Cortney Casey explains:

> You have to walk into the gym knowing this guy could break my arm if he wanted to. If he doesn't let go when I tap, he could break my arm. I have to give so much respect to everyone in the room, and that makes me feel, in a weird way, safe.

For Casey, part of her love of the sport developed within an environment of consent and respect that makes her feel safe. She practices a dangerous sport where physical injuries can and do happen, but ultimately she does so in a way that respects her as a person. These distinctions between fighting as consent versus violence is instructive as we consider the UFC specifically.

This book evaluates the relationship between the UFC and its fighters in terms of the principles of consent and mutual respect. It may seem brash to declare that the UFC perpetuates violence against fighters who willingly sign contracts with the promotion; however, I contend that neoliberal business practices that place organizational growth and the accumulation of wealth above human interests are inherently violent. The violence that primarily concerns me has less to do with two fighters entering a ring to compete against one another; rather, the violence of exploitation is the focus of my critique. If violence "is forced upon a person and carried out with no regard for their wishes," (Channon and Matthews n.d., 3), then fighters enter into an unequal relationship wherein the rules, norms, and expectations are frequently broken. The fact that the UFC may terminate a fighter's contract at any point even if the fighter is on a win streak and has remaining bouts left on their contract is a violation of trust. The fact that the fighter doesn't have the same rights within their agreements to break a contract indicates a lack of mutual respect. Thus, the violence *Fighting Visibility* discusses has less to do with bruises and broken bones and is more concerned with a promotion that refuses to take adequate responsibility for its athletes or to build mutually beneficial relationships outside of the promotion's superstars.

Central to the issues in this book are the ways in which visibility can be used as a tool of violence. For many female fighters in the UFC or athletes aspiring to join the promotion, visibility promises a potential path to competing in the sport they love as a career. Discourses of women's empowerment and the American dream sparkle in the bright lights of the Octagon because economies of visibility make female fighters luminous. The sheer spectacle of the UFC and women's place within it seem to suggest new possibilities for women in combat sports. Branded difference continues to insist that "representation matters," "if she can see it, she can be it," and "if you just work hard enough . . .," which are discourses that contribute to aspirational labor online, in the gym, and in the ring so that these fighters can express their love for MMA in the sport's brightest spotlight. Yet, this book asserts that the visibility of diverse female fighters in the UFC actually facilitates the exploitation of female fighters, thereby challenging the notion that representation is a strategy for equity in women's sports. Fighters understand they must adopt much of the risk when they enter into an agreement with the UFC, but many of them do so with the aspiration that their UFC dreams can become a reality. Athletes in the promotion maintain a sense of cruel optimism as they sacrifice their health, time, energy, and personal finances for the hope that their visibility in the Octagon will yield desirable results in the end. Thus, my greatest concern about violence in the UFC is the brutality of athlete exploitation as fighters strive to do what they love.

We live in a society where people frequently choose professions in which few will actually achieve the American dream, so I want to be clear that fighters are not alone in this quest, nor are they dupes to the system. Many of them understand how the UFC makes its profits, but they feel they lack the agency to shift business operations. Similarly, aspiring actors, filmmakers, and artists all make sacrifices in their personal lives and careers even though they learn along the way that few actually make a livable wage just doing what they love. Academia is another field where many sacrifice years of a full-time income to pursue a PhD and incur deep educational debt, only to struggle to find gainful employment at a college or university upon graduation. People from all walks of life understand the risks and choose their path anyway because it is important to them or they believe the system is too powerful to change. Despite the fact that precarity is a common condition across multiple sectors, its banality shouldn't absolve institutions from responsibility for their workers. Just because the UFC has grown its global brand on the backs of a contract labor force doesn't mean that the promotion has carte blanche to continue to do so with impunity. If the current organizational structure cannot fathom a path toward offering more guaranteed income, health insurance, and other ways to meet its athletes' basic human needs, then that structure must adapt or sink—especially in a profession where all fighters risk injury and long-term health complications from working for the UFC.

A collective fighter's voice is an essential path forward for fighters generally and for women in MMA in particular (see chapter 5). The UFC's business practices certainly impact both male and female fighters; however, White women and women of color struggle the most within the promotion due to long-standing gendered roadblocks in sports media and culture. The lack of transparency in the UFC's revenue model and decision-making means that fighters have few avenues for arguing for a more equitable share. The UFC classifies its workers as independent contractors while exercising control over them that mimics more formalized employment relationships, such as preventing fighters from working for other promotions while under contract. Yet, the history of unions in sports and other sectors affirms that collective bargaining and collective action works. Not only that, but the fighters who stand to benefit the most from the organizing efforts in the UFC are White women and women of color, since they experience the greatest pay gap when they enter the Octagon. For women to thrive in the UFC, they must join the efforts to organize into a collective voice.

Those of us invested in women's sports have long advocated for more meaningful representations of female athletes in the media as a centerpiece of our activism. We readily deconstruct *Sports Illustrated*'s persistent underrepresentation and sexualization of women on the magazine's covers, chastise the lack of media attention afforded the WNBA compared to their NBA counterparts, and identify sexism when Olympic broadcasters focus on the husbands of women athletes more than on the athletes themselves. While these issues maintain their relevance, we should also begin analyzing what happens when the logics of branded difference cause representations of sportswomen to proliferate, to become more meaningful, and to begin to include women who have traditionally been excluded or misrepresented, such as women of color, lesbians, and women who cannot or refuse to perform the pretty imperative on Instagram. This case study on the growing visibility of women in the UFC shows scholars, activists, and fans of women's sports that we must expand our understanding of visibility as a tool for social justice and understand that it can also be a tool of violence. Even if the UFC achieved representational parity and scheduled its events to include 50 percent women with an equal amount of promotion as their male fighters, would female athletes actually be better off? Perhaps one could posit that a few women at the top might have more opportunity, but would the scales really be tipped for the vast majority of athletes fighting for the promotion? I instead urge caution when considering what visibility can offer sportswomen in a cultural moment when gendered, racial, and sexual difference has become profitable. The fact that diverse female fighters now also have the opportunity to agree to unfair contracts and exploitative working conditions in the UFC is no cause for celebration in women's sports.

Rather than celebrate, we must instead reconcile love and violence as more women become visible in sports media. Seeing women represented as powerful athletes at the pinnacle of their crafts is exhilarating; yet, we cannot turn a blind eye to the violence of capitalistic institutions that make their profits on that visibility without fairly distributing that wealth to the athletes themselves. We cannot clamor for more visibility of women's collegiate sports unless we also critique how the structure of the NCAA makes a billion dollars a year while refusing to pay student athletes or allowing them to make money through sponsorships. We cannot celebrate NBC's broadcasting of more women's Olympic events without questioning the way the International Olympic Committee exploits host nations through unethical and corrupt business relationships. Julie Kedzie, a former UFC fighter, relayed her own meditations on love and violence in the UFC when I spoke with her. Kedzie competed in the first live women's MMA fight ever broadcast in the United States and has since been front and center watching female fighters enter the sport in her role as a matchmaker and commentator for Invicta FC, the women's professional MMA promotion. Kedzie summarizes her thoughts with keen clarity:

> Fighting in the UFC had been my dream. It had been my dream because the UFC was the pinnacle of the sport. But as James Baldwin says, "I love America more than any other country in this world, and, exactly for this reason, I insist on the

right to criticize her perpetually." I love MMA. I love some people in the UFC, but I don't know that I love the UFC itself. Because I love the sport, it needs to be critiqued, it needs to grow, and people need to be better taken care of. That's what I owe to it. I owe my voice.

Love and violence coexist in the NCAA, in the Olympics, in the UFC, and in numerous other neoliberal cultural institutions. We as a society must continue to grapple with those tensions and seriously consider paths for the eradication of violence in the sports we love. Fighting the exploitation of visibility is just one such path forward.

Publicly Available UFC Fighter Payouts, 2015–2018

The following table represents information collected from state athletic commissions that require combat sports promotions to disclose how much they pay fighters for bouts. These include the commissions in Arizona, California, Florida, Georgia, Massachusetts, Nevada, Oklahoma, Virginia, and Wisconsin. My research assistant, Jeff Luebbe, and I also queried Ohio, but that state retains payout records for only two weeks after a fight card, and we had requested the information after that deadline. The Ohio pay information on UFC 203: Miocic vs. Overeem (September 10, 2016) is therefore from MMA websites reporting on pay (their source was the Ohio Athletic Commission).

Date	Location	Event	Commission	Payout Total
1/3/15	Las Vegas, NV	UFC 182 Jones vs. Cormier	NSAC	$1.5 million
1/18/15	Boston, MA	UFC Fight Night: McGregor vs. Siver	MSAC	$1.045 million
1/31/15	Las Vegas, NV	UFC 183: Silva vs. Diaz	NSAC	$2.334 million
2/28/15	Los Angeles, CA	UFC 184: Rousey vs. Zingano	CSAC	$1.063 million
4/4/15	Fairfax, VA	UFC Fight Night: Mendes vs. Lamas	VBMWAB	$891,000
5/23/15	Las Vegas, NV	UFC 187: Johnson vs. Cormier	NSAC	$2.592 million
6/27/15	Hollywood, FL	UFC Fight Night: Machida vs. Romeo	FSBC	$801,000
7/11/15	Las Vegas, NV	UFC 189: Mendes vs. McGregor	NSAC	$2.342 million
7/12/15	Las Vegas, NV	The Ultimate Fighter: 21 Finale	NSAC	$873,000
7/15/15	San Diego, CA	UFC Fight Night: Mir vs. Duffee	CSAC	$1.214 million

Date	Location	Event	Commission	Payout Total
9/5/15	Las Vegas, NV	UFC 191: Johnson vs. Dodson 2	NSAC	$1.751 million
12/10/15	Las Vegas, NV	UFC Fight Night: Namajunas vs. VanZant	NSAC	$983,000
12/11/15	Las Vegas, NV	The Ultimate Fighter: 22 Finale	NSAC	$1.381 million
12/12/15	Las Vegas, NV	UFC 194: Aldo vs. McGregor	NSAC	$3.113 million
12/19/15	Orlando, FL	UFC on FOX: dos Anjos vs. Cerrone 2	FDBPR	$2.461 million
1/2/16	Las Vegas, NV	UFC 195: Lawler vs. Condit	NSAC	$2.098 million
1/17/16	Boston, MA	UFC Fight Night: Dillashaw vs. Cruz	MSAC	$1.622 million
2/6/16	Las Vegas, NV	UFC Fight Night: Hendricks vs. Thompson	NSAC	$1.447 million
3/5/16	Las Vegas, NV	UFC 196: McGregor vs. Diaz	NSAC	$3.329 million
4/16/16	Tampa, FL	UFC on FOX: Teixeira vs. Evans	FSBC	$1.259 million
4/23/16	Las Vegas, NV	UFC 197: Jones vs. Saint Preux	NSAC	$1.908 million
5/29/16	Las Vegas, NV	UFC Fight Night: Almeida vs. Garbrandt	NSAC	$1.323 million
6/4/16	Inglewood, CA	UFC 199: Rockhold vs. Bisping 2	CSAC	$3.184 million
7/7/16	Las Vegas, NV	UFC Fight Night: dos Anjos vs Alvarez	NSAC	$1.508 million
7/8/16	Las Vegas, NV	The Ultimate Fighter: Team Joanna vs. Team Claudia Finale	NSAC	$1.395 million
7/9/16	Las Vegas, NV	UFC 200: Tate vs. Nunes	NSAC	$7.509 million
7/30/16	Atlanta, GA	UFC 201: Lawler vs. Woodley	GAEC	$1.999 million
8/20/16	Las Vegas, NV	UFC 202: Diaz vs. McGregor 2	NSAC	$6.509 million
9/10/16	Cleveland, OH	UFC 203: Miocic vs. Overeem	OAC	$3.389 million
10/1/16	Portland, OR	UFC Fight Night: Lineker vs. Dodson	OAC	$1.053 million
12/3/16	Las Vegas, NV	The Ultimate Fighter: Tournament of Champions Finale	NSAC	$1.659 million
12/17/16	Sacramento, CA	UFC on FOX: VanZant vs. Waterson	CSAC	$1.442 million
12/30/16	Las Vegas, NV	UFC 207: Nunes vs. Rousey	NSAC	$5.134 million
1/15/17	Phoenix, AZ	UFC Fight Night: Rodriguez vs. Penn	ADG	$1.166 million
3/4/17	Las Vegas, NV	UFC 209: Woodley vs Thompson 2	NSAC	$3.435 million
6/25/17	Oklahoma City, OK	UFC Fight Night: Chiesa vs. Lee	OSAC	$1.613 million
7/7/17	Las Vegas, NV	The Ultimate Fighter: Redemption Finale	NSAC	$1.553 million
7/8/17	Las Vegas, NV	UFC 213: Romero vs. Whitaker	NSAC	$2.984 million
7/29/17	Anaheim, CA	UFC 214: Cormier vs. Jones 2	CSAC	$4.174 million
10/7/17	Las Vegas, NV	UFC 216: Ferguson vs. Lee	NSAC	$2.583 million
11/11/17	Norfolk, VA	UFC Fight Night: Poirier vs. Pettis	VDPOR	$2.283 million
12/1/17	Las Vegas, NV	The Ultimate Fighter: A New World Champion Finale	NSAC	$811,000
12/9/17	Fresno, CA	UFC Fight Night: Swanson vs. Ortega	CSAC	$1.189 million
12/30/17	Las Vegas, NV	UFC 219: Cyborg vs. Holm	NSAC	$2.165 million
1/20/18	Boston, MA	UFC 220 Miocic vs. Ngannou	MSAC	$2.999 million
2/24/18	Orlando, FL	UFC on FOX: Emmett vs. Stephens	FSBC	$1.561 million

Date	Location	Event	Commission	Payout Total
3/3/18	Las Vegas, NV	UFC 222: Cyborg vs. Kunitskaya	NSAC	$2.544 million
4/14/18	Glendale, AZ	UFC on FOX: Poirier vs. Gaethje	ADG	$1.878 million
7/6/18	Las Vegas, NV	The Ultimate Fighter: Undefeated Finale	NSAC	$991,000
7/7/18	Las Vegas, NV	UFC 226: Miocic vs. Cormier	NSAC	$3.142 million
8/4/18	Los Angeles, CA	UFC 227: Dillashaw vs. Garbrandt 2	CSAC	$1.664 million
10/6/18	Las Vegas, NV	UFC 229: Khabib vs. McGregor	NSAC	$7.082 million
11/30/18	Las Vegas, NV	The Ultimate Fighter: Heavy Hitters Finale	NSAC	$1.357 million
12/5/18	Milwaukee, WI	UFC on FOX: Lee vs. Iaquinta 2	WUCPD	$1.593 million
12/29/18	Inglewood, CA	UFC 232 Jones vs. Gustafsson 2	CSAC	$4.028 million

Publicly Available UFC Fighter Payouts by Gender and Race, 2015–2018

The following table breaks down the 2015–18 state commission confirmed payouts per fight according to gender and race of the fighters. Gender was determined by the division the fighter competed in (e.g., women's bantamweight or men's bantamweight). I determined racial background based on how fighters self-identified racially, or, in the absence of that, on visual racial signifiers (e.g., skin color) and markers of ethnicity (e.g., surname)—therefore, racial identity should be considered within these constraints. Dollar figures include "show" money (for participating in a bout), "win" money, pay from the apparel sponsor Reebok, and any additional disclosed performance bonuses. Dollar figures do not include any bonuses the UFC doesn't publicly disclose. In addition, from the payout amount, fighters are contractually obligated to pay an estimated 15 percent to managers, 10 percent to trainers, and up to 37 percent in income taxes. Fighters are also responsible for paying health insurance premiums and any other benefits normally afforded full-time employees. This table also doesn't reflect how often fighters fight. In 2018, for example, male athletes fought a median of twice each year, while female athletes fought a median of once per year. Despite the limitations in the data, this snapshot can provide the closest approximation to how fighters are paid outside the UFC publicly disclosing their financial information.

Gender and Race of Athletes	Gross Average	Gross Median
All Athletes (1,281)*	$97,869	$41,000
All male athletes (1,120)	$99,493	$43,750
All female athletes (161)	$86,571	$30,000
White male athletes (561)	$100,056	$43,000
Black male athletes (204)	$123,244	$50,500
Latino athletes (266)	$84,639	$43,000
Asian/Pacific Islander male athletes (88)	$86,693	$40,500
White female athletes (96)	$88,922	$30,000
Black female athletes (9)	$21,167	$16,000
Latina athletes (40)	$112,975	$61,000
Asian/Pacific Islander female athletes (16)	$43,250	$23,250

* Numbers in parentheses represent instances of fights rather than the number of fighters. For example, "Latina athletes (40)" means that Latina athletes fought 40 times under these state commissions, not that there were 40 Latina fighters.

Notes

Introduction. Visibility and Difference in the UFC

1. The word "female" can connote a biological definition rather than a gendered one; however, I have also written about how the UFC has deliberately excluded transgender athletes in the promotion thereby forestalling any inclusion of nonnormative gender identities (see McClearen 2015a and Fischer and McClearen 2020). Thus, "female athletes" is a more representative term of how the UFC categorizes its athletes between male and female divisions that are primarily sexed delineations that exclude transgender athletes. Since my focus is specifically on cisgender women who have been included in the UFC, the term "female athlete" seems more precise even though I occasionally use "sportswomen" as well.

2. A "card" is a series of scheduled fights on the same night in the same venue. The UFC schedules roughly fifteen fights per card.

3. The winner of UFC 1 Royce Gracie, a Brazilian jiu jitsu expert, greatly benefited from the long tradition of Gracie Challenges, a standing call to any martial artist of another style to challenge a Gracie family member to a no-holds-barred fight, or *vale tudo*. The Gracies began competing against other styles in the 1920s, and the knowledge of what worked against other arts was advantageous.

4. While rumors of women's fights in Japanese promotions date back to the mid-1990s, the first documented women's MMA fights took place in December 2000 with the Japanese Remix World Cup tournament, which featured twelve female fighters from around the world (Green and Svinth 2010).

5. A renewed cultural interest in the capitalization of Black and White when referring to the racial identity surfaced as I was finishing my edits on this book in summer

2020. General consensus prevailed that Black should be capitalized while White is still debated because this had been the problematic practice of White supremacists for some time (Perlman 2015). Capitalizing Black has been used as a method for signalizing the racial and ethnic identities of people whose ancestors originated from Africa while the lowercase "white" refers to skin color but not necessarily an ethnicity. Although I imagine this debate will wage on long after this book goes to print, I have decided to capitalize both Black and White in this book. As Eve Ewing (2020) convincingly writes, leaving "white" as lowercase "runs the risk of reinforcing the dangerous myth that White people in America do not have a racial identity." This point resonates with me, because when I teach a university course on race and media, students are sometimes surprised that we discuss Whiteness because the word "race" connotes people of color to many while *whiteness* is presumed to be the absence of race. In my own writing, when I type out "Black, Latinx, Asian, and white," the last word seems to stick out, ignoring the racialization of Whiteness. Thus, I capitalize White and Whiteness in this book to recognize White identity as "a specific social category that confers identifiable and measurable social benefits" (Ewing 2020). While that identity may not be monolithic, it assumes a position of power in society that affords it racialized benefits in media culture.

6. National Basketball Association (NBA), Women's National Basketball Association (WNBA), National Women's Soccer League (NWSL), Major League Soccer (MLS), and Major League Baseball (MLB).

7. The cage in which MMA fights are conducted, the Octagon is described more fully in chapter 1.

8. R. W Connell coined the term "emphasized femininity," which functions as hegemonic masculinity's feminine counterpart in the dominant gendered order (Connell and Messerschmidt 2005).

9. If a UFC fighter wins a championship title, then they have to defend it in order to retain the status of current champion. If the athlete loses the defense, then they become a "former" champion. If the UFC determines a fighter has taken too long to defend the title, it can "strip" the athlete of the current title and that athlete becomes a former champion.

10. At the time of writing, the UFC's parent company Endeavor is preparing to go public, which may result in greater access to the UFC's financial information in the near future.

11. The structure of a league and a fight promotion are different in a few ways. Leagues are groups of teams that play one another. Teams are financially independent and governed in some arenas, as well as dependent on the league in others. For example, the NFL is a trade association financially supported by its thirty-two teams, governed by elected officials, and responsible for negotiating television contracts, sponsorships, and other league-wide deals. A fight promotion, on the other hand, typically contracts fighters and negotiates its own broadcast and sponsorship deals without any sort of relationship to other promotions. Decision-making power is much more centralized in a fight promotion than a league.

12. This number was determined by adding up the number of fights each UFC fighter on the roster had during the 2018 calendar year and determining a median number of fights for men and women.

13. Interestingly, female athletes of color have a median pay of $32,000, largely bolstered by Latinx female fighters from Brazil who are ranked high in the UFC. Latinx female fighters made $113,000 on average, with Amanda Nunes, Claudia Gadelha, and Cris Cyborg each significantly elevating those averages.

14. As previously stated, the snapshot of fighter pay I describe is limited to the fifty-five events from 2015 to 2018 with disclosed payouts from athletic commissions compared to a total of 474 events. Several MMA websites estimate fighter payouts by using the disclosed amounts from the commissions they are able to obtain and calculating that fighters make an equivalent amount the next time they fight, which is typically consistent with fighter contracts. The median payout for UFC fighters in 2018 was $44,000 per year for men and $32,000 for women based on their estimates. Jeff Fox (2019) at MMA Manifesto approximates that UFC stars drove the average up to $138,000, with nine fighters making above $1 million for the year in show and win pay, performance bonuses, and Reebok pay. Fox suggests that Brazilian champions Cris Cyborg and Amanda Nunes were the highest paid women in 2018, at $1,080,000 and $700,000, respectively. Finally, of the 570 fighters who competed in the UFC in 2018, 32 percent made more than $100,000 (Fox 2019). These numbers do not include any sponsorships these athletes secure outside their earnings from the UFC and Reebok, so UFC stars likely make significantly more from sponsors each year.

15. The additional tax burden is because independent contractors pay 100 percent of their Social Security and Medicare contributions instead of sharing those costs with their employer. In addition, if a fight takes place outside the United States, then fighters are often obligated to pay taxes and fees associated with competing in that country. This means sometimes the fighters bear a higher or lower tax burden, depending on where they fight.

16. I examine the exclusion of Fallon Fox at length in an article that considered the ways sexism and cissexism intertwine to inform MMA discourses about her (McClearen 2015a). In a follow-up article, Mia Fischer and I interview Fox to consider how she resists these confining discourses (Fischer and McClearen 2020).

17. A "prosumer" is an amalgamation of the words "producer" and "consumer" used in media studies to describe the ways that the average person can create and share spreadable content through social media platforms (García-Galera and Valdivia 2014; Ritzer and Jurgenson 2010). For example, a UFC fan can create a compellation video of their favorite athlete's best fights and share that on YouTube. That fan is both consuming UFC content and producing it.

Chapter 1. Developing a Millennial Sports Media Brand

Sections of this chapter appeared in the article "'We Are All Fighters:' The Transmedia Marketing of Difference in the Ultimate Fighting Championship" in the *International Journal of Communication* (McClearen 2017).

1. As I argue in "We Are All Fighters" (2017), the UFC first used the reality show to allow audiences to become familiar with fighters that the UFC could build as stars, then to attempt to reach new racial demographics when it featured a YouTube famous Black fighter named Kimbo Slice on the show, and ultimately to promote the women's divisions as well. *The Ultimate Fighter* proved to be a transmedia venture that could drive traffic from the reality show to pay-per-view UFC events, all while featuring difference prominently. These efforts to use branded difference on the reality show worked simultaneously alongside the others I analyze in the next section of this chapter, "We Are All Fighters."

2. The UFC's 2019 distribution deal with ESPN shifted the promotion's relationship with pay-per-view. Fans may buy pay-per-view only through ESPN+ instead of through other Internet and cable providers. Additionally, ESPN+ now pays the UFC a license fee for the rights to air the promotion's pay-per-view events on the streaming platform (Raimondi 2019).

3. Certainly, international expansion promised economic gain in local markets around the globe, but since the UFC primarily drew millennial audiences in the United States, the orientation toward the global would appeal to its U.S. fan base as well.

4. The description of the T-shirt is from "UFC Women's We Are All Fighters Tank," n.d.

Chapter 2. Affect and the Rousey Effect

A portion of the "Revolution" section of the chapter originally appeared as "'Don't Be a Do-Nothing-Bitch: Popular Feminist and Women's Physical Empowerment in the UFC," in *New Sporting Femininities: Embodied Politics in Postfeminist Times*, edited by Kim Toffoletti, Jessica Francombe-Web, and Holly Thorpe (New York: Springer Berlin Heidelberg, 2018). Thanks to the publisher for permission to reprint.

1. The promotion had been using the same strategy for several years to court Black and Latinx boxing fans but has yet to reach the same saturation in those demographics as boxing. A Washington Post and University of Massachusetts Lowell random national sampling poll in 2017 determined that 52 percent of Black adult respondents and 61 percent of Hispanic adult respondents identified as boxing fans compared to 38 percent of Black respondents and 31 percent of Hispanic respondents labeled themselves as MMA fans (Maese and Clement 2017).

2. A walkout is a ritual of boxing, professional wrestling, and MMA events in which one fighter enters the arena while a song they have chosen to represent them plays over the loudspeakers. The fighter they will face in the match performs the same ritual.

3. Velasquez was born in the United States but refers to himself as the "first Mexican champion" (Cole 2010).

4. See McClearen (2017) for further discussion of the UFC's development of marketing the racial and ethnic difference of men on the fight roster.

5. To date, Rousey and the UFC have not used the word "feminist" to describe her, so I'm not suggesting that she or the UFC brand claim this identity. Rather, I follow the tradition in feminist media scholarship of identifying and analyzing moments in popular culture when feminist sensibilities surface in popular discourse. I am interested in the discursive deployment of feminist ideas, not in labeling particular celebrities as feminist or not.

6. UFC Gyms are franchised MMA and fitness facilities located across the United States.

Chapter 3. Gendering the American Dream

1. For the audience, combat sports are a metaphor for overcoming obstacles; for fighters they are an aspirational path to achieve the American dream. Combat sports in particular have long been the domain of the downtrodden who work their way out of real-life hardship. Boxers, for example, historically come from lower socioeconomic and ethnically diverse communities who see fighting as a means to pull themselves out of poverty to achieve fame, fortune, and stability (Heiskanen 2012; Runstedtler 2013). Jeffery T. Sammons (1990) adds that "the desire for fame, money, escape, and status in part accounts for why young men box, [but] the desperation and delusion that often drive the disadvantaged on a narrow and obstacle-ridden adventure towards the distant American dream cannot be overlooked" (251). Some of the UFC athletes I spoke with agreed that fighters as a demographic frequently come from hardship. Former UFC fighter Kajan Johnson says that "Historically the majority of the greatest fighters come from impoverished backgrounds. Fighting has always been a way for poor people to level up and bring riches and abundance to their whole family. Because of that [mentality] people are willing to fight for nothing just to get into the UFC." Thus, struggle is embedded in the very ethos of the fighter's experience, now including women.

2. The term "female masculinity" comes from theorist Jack Halberstam (2019), who dissociates masculinity from maleness to understand that some women also embrace appearances, traits, behaviors, and attitudes that society deems as masculine. The concept comes from the scholarly field of gender and women studies, which views gender as a continuum and not restricted by biological sex. This theory is useful for women in sports because some women, like Rousey, walk a duality between traditionally feminine in their self-representation out of the ring or off the field while embracing traits often considered masculine on the pitch or on the court, such as aggression, speed, and physical prowess. Other women, like Liz Carmouche, read as masculine both within their sport and when they present themselves for social and mainstream media outside of the sporting arena. As discussed in the introduction, female athletes who can perform pretty and powerful (i.e., vacillating between feminine and masculine in different contexts) are more marketable than women who perform female masculinity consistently even though they may find niche audiences through social

media. The degree of marketability is all a matter of scale within hierarchies of visibility.

Chapter 4. The Labor of Visibility on Social Media

1. Moya Bailey and Trudy (2018) coined the term "misogynoir" in 2008 to describe the intersections of misogyny and anti-Black racism leveraged against Black women.

2. For example, Andrea N. Geurin (2017) examines elite female athletes at the 2016 Rio Olympics and finds that most consider social media a key form of self-promotion for gaining sponsorships.

Chapter 5. The Fight for Labor Equity

1. The USWNT has won four FIFA World Cups, including the 2019 tournament, while the men's team failed to even qualify for the 2018 Men's World Cup. The final 2015 Women's World Cup match was the most watched soccer game in U.S. history, and the team went on to bring in more revenue for U.S. soccer in the next three years than the men's team (Bachman 2019). In 2016 alone, the women's team generated $1.9 million more than the men's team. Despite the USWNT's ability to bring in viewership and revenue, the pay disparity between the women's and men's teams remains stark. Between 2015 and 2018, the USWNT players' maximum wage was $4,950 per game, while the men's maximum was $13,166 (Young 2019). In 2017, one of the ways the USWNT has been able to improve pay disparities, including a 30 percent increase in base pay, a doubling of bonuses, and increased per diem rates has been by leveraging their negotiating power via a collective bargaining agreement (CBA) with U.S. Soccer (Das 2017). Yet, these gains are still slim compared to the U.S. Men's National Team. The USWNT is continuing their fight.

2. Jason Cruz (2020) analyzes in-depth the antitrust lawsuit filed against the UFC in 2014 that addresses the issue of the UFC's propensity for buying rival promotions and therefore limiting competition for elite fighters in other promotions. Several former fighters named as plaintiffs in the suit claim that the UFC engaged in "predatory practices" and that "the UFC held a monopsony and monopoly over the relevant markets for fighters," allowing the further suppression of wages of UFC independent contractors because the UFC had allegedly stomped out competition (120). As of this writing the case is still pending. The UFC's major defense is that they are not violating antitrust laws, claiming that the promotion was able to buy rival MMA promotions because of its "superior business acumen" (120).

3. Most of the labor laws the NLRB can enforce, including the right to form a union in the first place, apply to workers classified as employees and not as independent contractors, such as UFC fighters. None of these provisions apply to independent contractors; instead, UFC fighters must pay their own health insurance premiums, pay for healthcare costs apart from fight-related injuries, pay higher tax rates, and save for retirement on their own. By bringing the retaliation case to the NLRB, Smith

and Middlebrook believed that they had sufficient justification to force the NLRB to determine if the UFC has misclassified fighters as independent contractors while treating them like employees and pave the way for fighters to form a union.

4. Various law review articles indicate that there are several other criteria beyond those discussed here that could also be used to argue that UFC fighters are treated as employees while being misclassified as independent contractors (see Salminen 2017 for more examples).

5. In 2018, male fighters had an average of two fights per year, while female fighters averaged one fight per year.

6. Most rideshares only count "work" as the time the driver spends driving to the customer and driving them to their destination. The time the driver is waiting for someone to request a ride is not considered "working," so many drivers can keep two or more apps open while they wait for customer on Uber or Lyft, for example (Weed 2019).

7. For example, California passed a 2019 state law that provides strict criteria for classifying workers as independent contractors, causing businesses like ridesharing and freelance journalism to fall outside the boundaries of what counts as independent contracting since these workers are central to those business models (McNicholas and Poydock 2019). It remains to be seen how the law will impact the UFC's ability to hire contracted fighters for events in California. One analyst suggests that the WWE, for example, may be able to work around these laws in California by grounding its contracts in the legal jurisdiction of Connecticut, where the WWE is based (Greene 2019).

References

Personal Phone Interviews

Beeman, Barbie (pseudonym). October 16, 2018 (Skype); September 8–12, 2019 (Web messaging).

Brown, Laura (pseudonym). April 20, 2016.

Calvillo, Cynthia. July 18, 2019.

Casey, Cortney. July 18, 2019.

Clark, Jessica-Rose. July 31, 2019.

Hartling, Doug. March 18, 2016.

Hill, Angela. October 26, 2018.

Huxley, Neil, and Aaron Shact. February 29, 2016 (Skype).

Johnson, Kajan. October 26, 2018.

Kartzmark, Chris. April 22, 2016.

Kedzie, Julie. October 21, 2018.

Middlebrook, Lucas. October 19, 2018.

Modafferi, Roxanne. August 1, 2019.

Sholler, Dave. May 13, 2016.

Smith, Leslie. October 25, 2018.

Rangel, Fabiola. February 12, 2016.

Other Sources

"About CEWS." N.d. Committee for Equity in Women's Surfing. Accessed October 4, 2019. http://surfequity.org/about-cews.

Adichie, Chimamanda Ngozi. 2009. *The Danger of a Single Story*. https://www.ted.com/talks/chimamanda_adichie_the_danger_of_a_single_story?language=en.

Ahmed, Sara. 2004. "Affective Economies." *Social Text* 22 (2): 117–39.

Alexander, Charlotte S. 2016. "Misclassification and Antidiscrimination: An Empirical Analysis." *Minnesota Law Review* 101 (3): 907–62.

Almond, Elliott. 2019. "Amgen Tour of California: Fighting for Equality for Women Cyclists." Mercury News. May 9, 2019. https://www.mercurynews.com/2019/05/09/the-amgen-tour-fighting-for-equality-for-women-cyclists/.

Andrejevic, Mark. 2009. "Visceral Literacy: Reality TV, Savvy Viewers, and Auto-Spies." In *Reality TV: Remaking Television Culture*, edited by Susan Murray and Laurie Ouellette, 321–42. New York: New York University Press.

Andrew, Scottie. 2019. "UFC Fighter Paige VanZant Says She Makes More on Instagram than She Does in Fights." CNN.com, August 28, 2019. https://www.cnn.com/2019/08/28/us/ufc-paige-vanzant-instagram-pay-trnd/index.html.

Andrews, David L. 1999. "Whither the NBA, Whither America?" *Peace Review* 11 (4): 505–10.

Antunovic, Dunja, and Erin Whiteside. 2018. "Feminist Sports Media Studies: State of the Field." In *Feminist Approaches to Media Theory and Research*, edited by Dustin Harp, Jaime Loke, and Ingrid Bachmann, 111–30. Cham, Switzerland: Springer International.

Anyangwe, Eliza. 2015. "Misogynoir: Where Racism and Sexism Meet." *Guardian*, October 5, 2015. https://www.theguardian.com/lifeandstyle/2015/oct/05/what-is-misogynoir.

Aronczyk, Melissa. 2013. *Branding the Nation: The Global Business of National Identity*. New York: Oxford University Press.

Aronczyk, Melissa, and Devon Powers. 2010. *Blowing Up the Brand: Critical Perspectives on Promotional Culture*. New York: Peter Lang.

Arsenault, Amelia, and Alisa Perren. 2016. *Media Industries: Perspectives on an Evolving Field*. Seattle: CreateSpace Independent Publishing Platform.

Associated Press. 2017. "Cheers! Modelo Inks Multimillion-Dollar Ad Deal with UFC." Associated Press, October 9, 2017. https://www.apnews.com/63fdec80c29b42d79903c5fa5241aad2.

Bachman, Rachel. 2019. "U.S. Women's Soccer Games out-Earned Men's Games." *Wall Street Journal Online*, June 17, 2019. https://www.wsj.com/articles/u-s-womens-soccer-games-out-earned-mens-games-11560765600.

Badenhausen, Kurt. 2019. "Social Media's Most Valuable Athletes: Ronaldo, McGregor and LeBron Score Big." *Forbes*, August 3, 2019. https://www.forbes.com/sites/kurtbadenhausen/2019/08/03/social-medias-most-valuable-athletes-ronaldo-mcgregor-and-lebron-score/.

Bailey, Moya, and Trudy. 2018. "On Misogynoir: Citation, Erasure, and Plagiarism." *Feminist Media Studies* 18 (4): 762–68.

Baker, Aaron. 2003. *Contesting Identities: Sports in American Film*. Urbana: University of Illinois Press.

Banet-Weiser, Sarah. 2012. *Authentic TM: The Politics and Ambivalence in a Brand Culture*. New York: New York University Press.

———. 2015. "Keynote Address: Media, Markets, Gender: Economies of Visibility in a Neoliberal Moment." *Communication Review* 18 (1): 53–70.

———. 2018. *Empowered: Popular Feminism and Popular Misogyny*. Durham, NC: Duke University Press.

Banks, Miranda, and David Hesmondhalgh. 2016. "Internationalizing Labor Activism: Building Solidarity among Writers' Guilds." In Curtin and Sanson, *Precarious Creativity*, 267–80.

Barakat, Christie. 2014. "Emotional Branding and the Emotionally Intelligent Consumer." *Adweek*, January 12, 2014. http://www.adweek.com/digital/emotional-branding-emotionally-intelligent-consumer/#/.

Barnes, Katie. 2017. "To Build Her Star Power, Michelle Waterson Needs to Win." ESPN.com, April 11, 2017. https://www.espn.com/espnw/story/_/id/19136294/michelle-waterson-ufc-star-power-just-needs-keep-winning.

Beck, Ulrich. 2000. *The Brave New World of Work*. Translated by Patrick Camiller. Cambridge, UK: Polity.

Beltrán, Mary. 2010. "Meaningful Diversity: Exploring Questions of Equitable Representation on Diverse Ensemble Cast Shows." *Flow: A Critical Forum on Television and Media Culture*, August 27, 2010. https://www.flowjournal.org/2010/08/meaningful-diversity/.

Berg, Heather, and Constance Penley. 2016. "Creative Precarity in the Adult Film Industry." In Curtin and Sanson, *Precarious Creativity*, 159–71.

Berlant, Lauren. 2008. *The Female Complaint: The Unfinished Business of Sentimentality in American Culture*. Durham, NC: Duke University Press.

———. 2011. *Cruel Optimism*. Durham, NC: Duke University Press.

Billings, Andrew C., Michael L. Butterworth, and Paul D. Turman. 2014. *Communication and Sport: Surveying the Field*. New York: Sage.

Birren, Genevieve F. E., and Tyler J. Schmitt. 2017. "Mixed Martial Artists: Challenges to Unionization." *Marquette Sports Law Review* 28 (1): 85–106.

Bivens, Josh, Lora Engdahl, Elise Gould, Teresa Kroeger, Celine McNicholas, Lawrence Mishel, Zane Mokhiber, Heidi Shierholz, Marni von Wilpert, Valerie Wilson, and Ben Zipperer. 2017. "How Today's Unions Help Working People: Giving Workers the Power to Improve Their Jobs and Unrig the Economy." Economic Policy Institute, August 24, 2017. https://www.epi.org/publication/how-todays-unions-help-working-people-giving-workers-the-power-to-improve-their-jobs-and-unrig-the-economy/.

Bohn, Mike. 2015. "Henry Cejudo: UFC's Immigrant Son Fights for the American Dream." *Rolling Stone*, November 20, 2015. https://www.rollingstone.com/culture/

culture-sports/henry-cejudo-ufcs-immigrant-son-fights-for-the-american
-dream-51458/.

——. 2017. "Leslie Smith Asks Kobe Bryant about 'Extremely Important' Union at
UFC Athlete Retreat." MMA Junkie, May 23, 2017. Accessed July 14, 2020. https://
mmajunkie.usatoday.com/2017/05/leslie-smith-kobe-bryant-unions-ufc-athlete
-retreat-lakers-mma.

Borden, Sam. 2019. "USWNT Lawsuit in the News, but Pay Equality a Global Fight at
Women's World Cup." ESPN.com, June 24, 2019. https://www.espn.com/soccer/fifa
-womens-world-cup/story/3884422/uswnt-lawsuit-in-newsbut-pay-equality
-a-global-fight-at-womens-world-cup.

Botter, Jeremy. 2017. "Why Isn't Cris Cyborg the Huge Star She Should Be?" Bleacher
Report, December 29, 2017. https://bleacherreport.com/articles/2751449-why-isnt
-cris-cyborg-the-huge-star-she-should-be.

"Breaking Barriers: The Story of Ronda Rousey and the Rise of Women's MMA." 2019.
UFC. YouTube, June 17, 2019. https://www.youtube.com/watch?v=PAzgG57J05k.

Brennan, Andrew. 2016. "Which Sports Have the Largest and Smallest Pay Gaps?"
Forbes, May 5, 2016. https://www.forbes.com/sites/andrewbrennan/2016/05/05/
the-pay-discrimination-in-sports-we-wish-didnt-exist-will-only-dissipate-with
-womens-leadership/.

Brooks, Chris. 2018. "Boss Fight." *Jacobin*, September 1, 2018. https://www.jacobinmag
.com/2018/09/mixed-martial-arts-ufc-union-contractors.

Broshek, Donna K., Tanya Kaushik, Jason R. Freeman, David Erlanger, Frank Webbe,
and Jeffrey T. Barth. 2005. "Sex Differences in Outcome Following Sports-Related
Concussion." *Journal of Neurosurgery* 102 (5): 856–63.

Bruce, Toni. 2016. "New Rules for New Times: Sportswomen and Media Representation in the Third Wave." *Sex Roles* 74 (7): 361–76.

Bruce, Toni, Jorid Hovden, and Pirkko Markula. 2010. *Sportswomen at the Olympics: A
Global Content Analysis of Newspaper Coverage.* Leiden, Switzerland: Brill.

"Brutal Beginnings of the UFC." 2013. FOX Sports. YouTube, November 6, 2013. https://
www.youtube.com/watch?v=zuzImQo7cdg.

Butterworth, Michael L. 2007. "Race in 'The Race': Mark McGwire, Sammy Sosa,
and Heroic Constructions of Whiteness." *Critical Studies in Media Communication* 24
(3): 228–44.

Butterworth, Michael L., and Stormi D. Moskal. 2009. "American Football, Flags,
and 'Fun': The Bell Helicopter Armed Forces Bowl and the Rhetorical Production
of Militarism." *Communication, Culture and Critique* 2 (4): 411–33.

Buzinski, Jim. 2011. "Dana White Says He Wishes Gay UFC Fighters Would Come
out." Outsports, October 31, 2011. https://www.outsports.com/2011/10/31/4052052/
dana-white-says-he-wishes-gay-ufc-fighters-would-come-out.

——. 2018. "Majority of MLS, NWSL Teams to Hold LGBT Pride Games." Outsports, May
21, 2018. https://www.outsports.com/2018/5/21/17366998/mls-nwsl-2018-lgbt
-pride-nights.

Carah, Nicholas, and Michelle Shaul. 2016. "Brands and Instagram: Point, Tap, Swipe, Glance." *Mobile Media & Communication* 4 (1): 69–84.

Chandran, Nyshka. 2014. "Asia Is Grappling with This Billion-Dollar Industry." CNBC, July 16, 2014. https://www.cnbc.com/2014/07/16/asia-is-grappling-with-this -billion-dollar-industry.html.

Channon, Alex, and Christopher Matthews. N.d. "Manifesto." Love Fighting Hate Violence. http://lfhv.org/wp-content/uploads/lfhv-manifesto.pdf.

Chappell, Bill. 2015. "U.S. Women Shatter TV Ratings Record For Soccer With World Cup Win." NPR, July 6, 2015. https://www.npr.org/sections/thetwo-way/ 2015/07/06/420514899/what-people-are-saying-about-the-u-s-women-s-world -cup-win.

Chin, Jessica W., and David L. Andrews. 2016. "Mixed Martial Arts, Caged Oriental-ism, and Female Asian American Bodies." In *Asian American Sporting Cultures*, edited by Stanley I. Thangaraj, Constancio R. Arnaldo Jr., and Christina B. Chin, 152–79. New York: New York University Press.

Clarke, Liz. "Double-Earners: The U.S. Women's Soccer Team Is Fighting for Greater Equity while Playing for a Fourth World Cup Title." *Washington Post*, June 11, 2019. https://www.washingtonpost.com/graphics/2019/sports/uswnt-equal-pay-fight/.

Cole, Ross. 2010. "Cain Velasquez UFC 121 Post-Fight Reaction." MMA Insight, Octo-ber 24, 2010. https://mmainsight.com/featured/cain-velasquez-ufc-121-post-fight -reaction.

"The Complete Guide to Instagram Influencer Rates in 2019." 2019. Hootsuite So-cial Media Management, March 4, 2019. https://blog.hootsuite.com/instagram -influencer-rates/.

Connell, R. W., and James W. Messerschmidt. 2005. "Hegemonic Masculinity: Re-thinking the Concept." *Gender & Society: Official Publication of Sociologists for Women in Society* 19 (6): 829–59.

Connolly, Matt. 2017. "'The Karate Hottie' Michelle Waterson Talks UFC Rise, WME Deal, Acting Future And More." *Forbes*, February 15, 2017. https://www.forbes.com/ sites/mattconnolly/2017/02/15/michelle-waterson-exclusive-karate-hottie-talks -ufc-rise-wme-deal-acting-future-and-more/.

Cooky, Cheryl, and Dunja Antunovic. 2020. "'This Isn't Just about Us': Articulations of Feminism in Media Narratives of Athlete Activism." *Communication & Sport* 8 (4–5): 692–711.

Cooky, Cheryl, and Nicole M. Lavoi. 2012. "Playing but Losing: Women's Sports after Title IX." *Contexts* 11 (1): 42–46.

Cooky, Cheryl, Michael A. Messner, and Michela Musto. 2015. "'It's Dude Time!' A Quarter Century of Excluding Women's Sports in Televised News and Highlight Shows." *Communication & Sport* 3 (3): 261–87.

Cooky, Cheryl, Michael Messner, and Robin Hextrum. 2013. "Women Play Sport, but Not on TV: A Longitudinal Study of Televised News Media." *Communication and Sport* 1 (3): 203–30.

Cooper, James. 2014. "How the World's Top Sports Marketers Learned to Love Mobile, Social and Female Fans." *Adweek*, July 15, 2014. http://www.adweek.com/news/ advertising-branding/how-ronda-rousey-convinced-ufc-head-dana-white-use -women-fighters-158884.

Costume Works. N.d. "UFC Ronda Rousey—Halloween Costume Contest at Costume." Pinterest. Accessed August 20, 2019. https://www.pinterest.com/ pin/521010250621779487/.

Covassin, Tracey, and R. J. Elbin. 2011. "The Female Athlete: The Role of Gender in the Assessment and Management of Sport-Related Concussion." *Clinics in Sports Medicine* 30 (1): 125–31.

Crenshaw, Kimberlé. 1991. "Mapping the Margins: Intersectionality, Identity Politics, and Violence against Women of Color." *Stanford Law Review* 43 (6): 1241–99. https:// doi.org/10.2307/1229039.

Cruz, Jason J. 2020. *Mixed Martial Arts and the Law: Disputes, Suits and Legal Issues*. Jefferson, NC: McFarland.

Curtin, Michael, and Kevin Sanson. 2016. "Precarious Creativity: Global Media, Local Labor." In Curtin and Sanson, *Precarious Creativity*. https://doi.org/10.1525/ 9780520964808–003.

Curtin, Michael, and Kevin Sanson, eds. 2016. *Precarious Creativity: Global Media, Local Labor*. Oakland: University of California Press. https://doi.org/10.1525/ 9780520964808–022.

"Dana White: Women's MMA Is 'Like a (Expletive) Rocket Ship Right Now.'" 2017. MMA Weekly, October 19, 2017. https://sports.yahoo.com/dana-white-women -mma-expletive-rocket-ship-now-182114321-mma.html.

"Dana White—Women Will Never Fight in the UFC." 2011. TMZ. YouTube, January 19, 2011. https://www.youtube.com/watch?v=I4X6cUOQv6w.

"Dana White on Conor McGregor Being P4P, Rousey's Return, Donald Trump." 2016. The Fight Life, YouTube. 2016. https://www.youtube.com/watch?v=QaQiwPbVYiQ (dead).

Das, Andrew. 2017. "Long Days, Google Docs and Anonymous Surveys: How the U.S. Soccer Team Forged a Deal." *New York Times*, April 5, 2017. https://www.nytimes .com/2017/04/05/sports/soccer/uswnt-us-soccer-labor-deal-contract.html.

Dawson, Alan. 2019. "Another Popular UFC Fighter Says Company President Dana White Is a Bully." *Business Insider*, July 29, 2019. https://www.businessinsider.com/ ufc-boss-dana-white-is-a-bully-cris-cyborg-says-2019–7.

Dawson, Steve. 2016. "What Happened to Kimbo Slice? What's He Doing Now? Gazette Review." Gazette Review, May 10, 2016. http://gazettereview.com/2016/05/ where-is-kimbo-slice-now-what-happened-to-him/.

Deleuze, Gilles. 1988. *Foucault*. Translated and edited by Seán Hand. Minneapolis: University of Minnesota Press.

"Dern: 'I Was Always against Doing MMA.'" 2016. Fight Sports, October 15, 2016. https://www.fightsports.tv/dern-i-was-always-against-doing-mma/.

Desmond-Harris, Jenée. 2018. "Despite Decades of Racist and Sexist Attacks, Serena Williams Keeps Winning." Vox. https://www.vox.com/2017/1/28/14424624/serena-williams-wins-australian-open-venus-record-racist-sexist-attacks.

Dhrodia, Azmina. 2017. "Unsocial Media: The Real Toll of Online Abuse against Women." Amnesty Global Insights. Medium, November 20, 2017. https://medium.com/amnesty-insights/unsocial-media-the-real-toll-of-online-abuse-against-women-37134ddab3f4.

Douban, Gigi. 2016. "How Cage-Match Fights Became a $4B Business." Marketplace.org. July 11, 2016. http://www.marketplace.org/2016/07/11/world/how-cage-match-fights-became-4b-business.

Duane, Daniel. 2019. "The Fight for Gender Equality in One of the Most Dangerous Sports on Earth." *New York Times*, February 7, 2019. https://www.nytimes.com/interactive/2019/02/07/magazine/women-surf-big-wave.html.

Dubrofsky, Rachel E., and Antoine Hardy. 2008. "Performing Race in *Flavor of Love* and *The Bachelor*." *Critical Studies in Media Communication* 25 (4): 373–92.

Dubrofsky, Rachel E., and Megan M. Wood. 2014. "Posting Racism and Sexism: Authenticity, Agency and Self-Reflexivity in Social Media." *Communication and Critical/Cultural Studies* 11 (3): 282–87.

Duffy, Brooke Erin. 2017. *(Not) Getting Paid to Do What You Love.* New Haven, CT: Yale University Press. https://doi.org/10.12987/yale/9780300218176.001.0001.

Dugan, Lauren. 2011. "UFC to Pay Its Fighters $240,000 to Tweet." *Adweek*, May 12, 2011. https://www.adweek.com/digital/ufc-to-pay-its-fighters-240000-to-tweet/.

Du Gay, Paul, Stuart Hall, Linda Janes, Anders Koed Madsen, Hugh Mackay, and Keith Negus. 2013. *Doing Cultural Studies: The Story of the Sony Walkman.* New York: Sage.

Duggan, Maeve. 2017. "Online Harassment 2017." Internet & Technology, Pew Research Center. July 11. https://www.pewinternet.org/2017/07/11/online-harassment-2017/.

Dundas, Chad. 2018. "MMA the Morning After: The Reality of Recovering from Fight Night." Bleacher Report, September 21, 2018. https://bleacherreport.com/articles/2776401-mma-the-morning-after-the-reality-of-recovering-from-fight-night.

Dyer, Richard. 1997. *White: Essays on Race and Culture.* London: Routledge.

Ennis, Dawn. 2019a. "Play Ball! All but 2 MLB Teams Are Hosting Pride Events This Season." Outsports, March 28, 2019. https://www.outsports.com/2019/3/28/18285393/baseball-mlb-opening-day-hosting-pride-events.

———. 2019b. "LGBT Lakers Fans: Pucker Up for 2nd Annual Pride Night." Outsports, September 25, 2019. https://www.outsports.com/2019/9/25/20883042/nba-lakers-second-lgbt-pride-night-los-angeles.

Epstein, Lawrence. 2018. "Ultimate Fighting Championship (UFC) Board Packet." UFC. Uploaded by the Nevada Governor's Office of Economic Development and available at http://www.diversifynevada.com/wp-content/uploads/2018/10/6-H.-Zuffa-LLC-dba-Ultimate-Fighting-Championship-UFC-Board-Packet.pdf.

Erickson, Matt, Nolan King, John Morgan, Simon Samano, Farah Hannoun, Simon Head, MMA Junkie Staff, Farah Hannoun, The Blue Corner, Christian Stein, and Mike Bohn. 2018. "Nicco Montano's Coach: UFC 228 Weigh-In Situation, Title Stripping 'a Freaking Nightmare.'" *USA Today*, September 10, 2018. https://mma junkie.usatoday.com/2018/09/nicco-montano-coach-ufc-228-weigh-ins-title -stripping-freaking-nightmare-valentina-shevchenko-dana-white.

ESPN. 2019. "The Increasing Popularity of Women's MMA." ESPN, March 22, 2019. https://www.espn.com/video/clip/_/id/26334343.

Ewing, Eve L. 2020. "I'm a Black Scholar Who Studies Race. Here's Why I Capitalize 'White.'" *Zora*, July 2, 2020. Accessed July 15, 2020. https://zora.medium.com/im-a -black-scholar-who-studies-race-here-s-why-i-capitalize-white-f94883aa2dd3.

Faughnder, Ryan. 2019. "Writers Guild Blasts Plans by Endeavor for an IPO Later This Year." *Los Angeles Times*, March 29, 2019. https://www.latimes.com/business/ hollywood/la-fi-ct-endeavor-ipo-20190329-story.html.

"Female Fighter's Panel." 2015. Public Panel. UFC International Fight Week Fan Exposition, July 10, 2015. Las Vegas, Nevada.

Ferenstein, Gregory. 2011. "UFC and Its Gang of 4.6 Million Facebook Friends Body Slam Sports Broadcasting." *Fast Company*, February 4, 2011. https://www.fastcompany .com/1723897/ufc-and-its-gang-46-million-facebook-friends-body-slam-sports -broadcasting.

Fey, Tina. 2016. "Ronda Rousey." *Time*, April 20, 2016. https://time.com/collection-post/ 4298235/ronda-rousey-2016-time-100/.

"Fighting Spirit with Dana White." 2018. Modelo USA. YouTube, January 17, 2018. https://www.youtube.com/watch?v=AMAt2dvaezU.

Fischer, Mia. 2014. "Commemorating 9/11 NFL-Style: Insights into America's Culture of Militarism." *Journal of Sport & Social Issues* 38 (3): 199–221.

———. 2019. *Terrorizing Gender: Transgender Visibility and the Surveillance Practices of the U.S. Security State*. Lincoln: University of Nebraska Press.

Fischer, Mia, and Jennifer McClearen. 2020. "Transgender Athletes and the Queer Art of Athletic Failure." *Communication & Sport* 8 (2): 147–67.

Fox, Jeff. 2019. "2018 UFC Fighter Salaries—Complete List." MMA Manifesto, January 13, 2019. https://thesportsdaily.com/2019/01/13/2018-ufc-fighter-salaries -complete-list-fox11/.

Frye, Andy. 2019. "MMA Fighter Michelle Waterson Talks Combat Sports, Holly Holm and Ronda Rousey." *Forbes*, February 20, 2019. https://www.forbes.com/sites/ andyfrye/2019/02/20/mma-fighter-michelle-waterson-talks-combat-sports-holly -holm-and-ronda-rousey/.

García, Justin D. 2013. "Boxing, Masculinity, and Latinidad: Oscar De La Hoya, Fernando Vargas, and Raza Representations." *Journal of American Culture* 36 (4): 323–41.

García-Galera, María-Carmen, and Angharad Valdivia. 2014. "Media Prosumers: Participatory Culture of Audiences and Media Responsibility." *Comunicar* 22 (43): 10–13.

Garrison, Olivia. 2016. "The Ultimate Brand Loyalty: A Look Into Sports Team Mania." Creative Click Media, October 6, 2016. https://creativeclickmedia.com/ultimate-brand-loyalty-sports-team-mania/.

Gaul, Carl J., IV. 2016. "The Ultimate Fighting Championship and Zuffa: From Human Cock-Fighting to Market Power." *American University Business Law Review* 6 (3): 647–83.

Gentry, Clyde. 2011. *No Holds Barred: The Complete History of Mixed Martial Arts in America*. Chicago: Triumph Books.

Gerbasi, Thomas. 2013. "Warning: Jessica Eye Is Tougher than You." UFC, October 15, 2013. https://www.ufc.com/news/warning-jessica-eye-tougher-you.

———. 2017. "Parental Inspiration Pushes Calvillo to Fight on." UFC, April 7, 2017. https://www.ufc.com/news/parental-inspiration-pushes-calvillo-fight.

———. 2019a. "Rich Franklin Embodied the 'We Are All Fighters' Mantra." UFC, April 16, 2019. https://www.ufc.com/news/ufc-rich-franklin-embodied-we-are-all-fighters-mantra-hall-of-fame.

———. 2019b. "Drakkar Klose Is a Different Breed." UFC, August 16, 2019. https://www.ufc.com/news/drakkar-klose-different-breed.

Geurin, Andrea N. 2017. "Elite Female Athletes' Perceptions of New Media Use Relating to Their Careers: A Qualitative Analysis." *Journal of Sport Management* 31 (4): 345–59.

Gibbs, Anna. 2002. "Disaffected." *Continuum: Journal of Media & Cultural Studies* 16 (3): 335–41.

Gift, Paul. 2019. "UFC Lawsuit: Select Promoter Financials Finally Released, Including The Big One." *Forbes*, July 16, 2019. https://www.forbes.com/sites/paulgift/2019/07/16/ufc-lawsuit-select-promoter-financials-finally-released-including-the-big-one/.

Gill, Rosalind. 2017. "The Affective, Cultural and Psychic Life of Postfeminism: A Postfeminist Sensibility 10 Years On." *European Journal of Cultural Studies* 20 (6): 606–26.

Giroux, Henry A. 2000. *Impure Acts: The Practical Politics of Cultural Studies*. New York: Routledge.

Golden State Warriors. 2019. "Warriors to Celebrate Women's Empowerment Throughout March." NBA.com, March 1, 2019. https://www.nba.com/warriors/news/wem-march-2019.

Gordon, Grant. 2012. "Glendale Fighting Club's Ronda Rousey Signs with UFC." *Los Angeles Times*, November 17, 2012. https://www.latimes.com/socal/glendale-news-press/sports/tn-gnp-glendale-fighting-clubs-ronda-rousey-signs-with-ufc-20121116-story.html.

Gough, Christina. 2018. "World's Most Valuable Sports Business Brands 2017." Statista, December 18, 2018. https://www.statista.com/statistics/253349/brand-value-of-sports-businesses-worldwide/.

Gray, Herman. 2013a. "Race, Media, and the Cultivation of Concern." *Communication and Critical/Cultural Studies* 10 (2–3): 253–58. https://doi.org/10.1080/14791420.2013.821641.

———. 2013b. "Subject(ed) to Recognition." *American Quarterly* 65 (4): 771–98.

———. 2016. "Precarious Diversity: Representation and Demography." In Curtin and Sanson, *Precarious Creativity*, 241–53.

Gray, Jonathan. 2010. "Texts That Sell: The Culture in Promotional Culture." In *Blowing Up the Brand: Critical Perspectives on Promotional Culture*, edited by Melissa Aronczyk and Devon Powers, 307–26. New York: P. Lang.

Green, Thomas A., and Joseph R. Svinth. 2010. *Martial Arts of the World: An Encyclopedia of History and Innovation*. Santa Barbara, CA: ABC-CLIO.

Greene, Dan. 2019. "How Does New CA Independent Contractor Law Impact WWE?" *Sports Illustrated*, September 19, 2019. https://www.si.com/wrestling/2019/09/19/wwe-labor-independent-contractors-california-law.

Gregg, Melissa, and Gregory J. Seigworth. 2010. *The Affect Theory Reader*. Durham, NC: Duke University Press.

Griffin, Hollis F. 2016. *Feeling Normal: Sexuality and Media Criticism in the Digital Age*. Bloomington: Indiana University Press.

Grossberg, Lawrence. 2015. "Learning from Stuart Hall, Following the Path with Heart." *Cultural Studies of Science Education* 29 (1): 3–11.

Guillen, Adam, Jr. 2018. "Robert Whittaker: UFC Giving Title Shots to Fighters Who Miss Weight Isn't Fair." MMAmania.com, August 27, 2018. https://www.mmamania.com/2018/8/27/17789220/ufc-robert-whittaker-giving-title-shots-fighters-miss-weight-isnt-fair-mma.

Halberstam, Jack. 2019. *Female Masculinity*. 20th anniv. ed. Durham, NC: Duke University Press.

Hall, Stuart. 1997. "The Work of Representation." In *Representation: Cultural Representations and Signifying Practices*, edited by Stuart Hall, 13–69. Thousand Oaks, CA: Sage, in association with the Open University.

Hall, Stuart, and Doreen Massey. 2010. "Interpreting the Crisis." *Soundings* 44 (44): 57–71.

Hampton, Liz. 2017. "Women Comprise Nearly Half of NFL Audience, but More Wanted." *Reuters*, February 4, 2017. https://www.reuters.com/article/us-nfl-superbowl-women-idUSKBN15J0UY.

Haraway, Donna. 1997. *Modest_Witness@Second_Millenium. FemaleMan©_Meets_Onco-Mouse™: Feminism and Technoscience*. New York: Routledge.

Harkness, Ryan. 2016. "Ronda Rousey Credits Gina Carano with Inspiring Her to Fight." UPROXX, September 29, 2016. https://uproxx.com/mma/ronda-rousey-gina-carano-inspired-fight/.

Harris, Scott. 2017. "For Love, Not Money: How Low Fighter Pay Is Undermining MMA." Bleacher Report, January 11, 2017. https://bleacherreport.com/articles/2685605-for-love-not-money-how-low-fighter-pay-is-undermining-mma.

Hartman, Mitchell. 2018. "What Makes Gig Economy Workers Anxious? Marketplace." Marketplace, March 8, 2018. https://www.marketplace.org/2018/03/08/economy/anxiety-index/gig-workers-and-economically-anxious-lifestyle.

Hearn, Alison. 2008. "Meat, Mask, Burden: Probing the Contours of the Branded 'Self.'" *Journal of Consumer Culture* 8 (2): 197–217.

———. 2012. "Brand Me 'Activist.'" *Commodity Activism: Cultural Resistance in Neoliberal Times*, 23–38.

Hedges, Josh. 2002. "UFC Too Broadcast Fights on WOWOW-TV in Japan, Globosat in Brazil Starting in March, April." Full Contact Fighter, March 2, 2002. http://fcfighter .com/ufc-to-broadcast-fights-on-wowow-tv-in-japan-globosat-in-brazil-starting -in-march-april/.

Heiskanen, Benita. 2012. *The Urban Geography of Boxing: Race, Class, and Gender in the Ring*. New York: Routledge.

Helwani, Ariel. 2019. "Felder Undergoes Surgery on Collapsed Lung." ESPN, February 20, 2019. https://www.espn.com/mma/story/_/id/26041950/paul-felder -undergoes-surgery-collapsed-lung.

Heywood, Leslie. 2018. "Third-Wave Feminism and Representation." In *The Palgrave Handbook of Feminism and Sport, Leisure and Physical Education*, edited by Louise Mansfield, Jayne Caudwell, Belinda Wheaton, and Beccy Watson, 463–77. London: Palgrave Macmillan UK.

Heywood, Leslie, and Shari L. Dworkin. 2003. *Built to Win: The Female Athlete as Cultural Icon*. Minneapolis: University of Minnesota Press.

Himberg, Julia. 2018. *The New Gay for Pay: The Sexual Politics of American Television Production*. Austin: University of Texas Press.

Holt, Jennifer, and Alisa Perren. 2009. "Introduction: Does the World Really Need One More Field of Study?" In *Media Industries: History, Theory, and Method*, edited by Jennifer Holt and Alisa Perren, 1–16. Malden, MA: Wiley-Blackwell.

Hubbard, Phil, and Eleanor Wilkinson. 2015. "Welcoming the World? Hospitality, Homonationalism, and the London 2012 Olympics." *Antipode*. https://doi.org/10.1111/ anti.12082.

Hui, Ray. 2012. "UFC Twitter Bonuses: Silva, Dos Santos, Schaub, Le Are Most Followed." MMA Fighting, February 8, 2012. https://www.mmafighting.com/ufc/ 2012/2/8/2785539/ufc-twitter-bonuses-silva-dos-santos-schaub-le-are-most -followed.

Hunt, Loretta. 2012. "Loretta Hunt: The Long Road to Saturday's Women's-Only MMA Card." SI.com, April 27, 2012. https://www.si.com/more-sports/2012/04/27/invicta.

Hutchins, Brett. 2011. "The Acceleration of Media Sport Culture: Twitter, Telepresence and Online Messaging." *Information, Communication and Society* 14 (2): 237–57.

Hutchins, Brett, and David Rowe. 2012. *Sport beyond Television: The Internet, Digital Media and the Rise of Networked Media Sport*. New York: Routledge.

Huxley, Neil. 2015. *"Revolution"—UFC 193 Rousey v. Holm Promo*. Vimeo, October 15, 2015. https://vimeo.com/142580820.

Ismail, Kaya. 2018. "Social Media Influencers: Mega, Macro, Micro or Nano." *CMS Wire*, December 10. https://www.cmswire.com/digital-marketing/social-media -influencers-mega-macro-micro-or-nano/.

Jenkins, Henry. 2008. *Convergence Culture: Where Old and New Media Collide*. New York: New York University Press.

Jenkins, Henry, Sam Ford, and Joshua Green. 2013. *Spreadable Media: Creating Value and Meaning in a Networked Culture*. New York: New York University Press.

Jennings, L. A. 2014. *She's a Knockout! A History of Women in Fighting Sports*. Lanham, MD: Rowman & Littlefield.

Johnson, Victoria E. 2009. "Everything New Is Old Again: Sport Television, Innovation, and Tradition for a Multi-Platform Era." In *Beyond Prime Time: Television Programming in the Post-Network Era*, edited by Amanda D. Lotz, 114–37. New York: Routledge.

———. 2016. "'Together, We Make Football': The NFL's 'Feminine' Discourses." *Popular Communication* 14 (1): 12–20.

———. 2019. "More than a Game: LeBron James and the Affective Economy of Place." In *Racism Postrace*, edited by Roopali Mukherjee, Sarah Banet-Weiser, and Herman Gray, 154–77. Durham, NC: Duke University Press.

Joseph, Ralina L. 2009. "'Tyra Banks Is Fat': Reading (Post-)Racism and (Post-)Feminism in the New Millennium." *Critical Studies in Media Communication* 26: 237–54.

———. 2017. "What's the Difference with 'Difference'? Equity, Communication, and the Politics of Difference." *International Journal of Communication* 11: 3306–26.

———. 2018. *Postracial Resistance: Black Women, Media, and the Uses of Strategic Ambiguity*. New York: New York University Press.

Kane, Mary Jo. 1988. "Media Coverage of the Female Athlete Before, During, and after Title IX: Sports Illustrated Revisited." *Journal of Sport Management* 2 (2): 87–99.

Kane, Mary Jo, and Heather D. Maxwell. 2011. "Expanding the Boundaries of Sport Media Research: Using Critical Theory to Explore Consumer Responses to Representations of Women's Sports." *Journal of Sport Management* 25 (3): 202–16.

Klein, Naomi. 2009. *No Logo: No Space, No Choice, No Jobs*. London: Picador.

Kleinhans, Chuck. 2011. "'Creative Industries,' Neoliberal Fantasies, and the Cold, Hard Facts of Global Recession: Some Basic Lessons." *Jump Cut: A Review of Contemporary Media* 53. https://www.ejumpcut.org/archive/jc53.2011/kleinhans-creat Indus/.

Kohnen, Melanie. 2015. "Cultural Diversity as Brand Management in Cable Television." *Media Industries Journal* 2 (2). https://doi.org/10.3998/mij.15031809.0002.205.

Kurchak, Sarah. 2016. "Stop Talking about Cyborg's One Positive Steroid Test." Fightland, May 20, 2016. http://fightland.vice.com/blog/stop-talking-about-cyborgs -one-positive-steroid-test.

———. 2017. "Meet the MMA Fighters Who Are Proof that Women Throw Down in the Ring." *Teen Vogue*, June 30, 2017. https://www.teenvogue.com/story/amanda -nunes-nina-ansaroff-interview.

Langone, Alix. 2018. "Before Team USA Women's Hockey Won Olympic Gold, They Won Equality Off the Ice." *Money*, February 22, 2018. http://money.com/ money/5170726/usa-olympics-womens-hockey-boycott-gold/.

Lee, Alexander K. 2018. "Nicco Montano Releases Statement on UFC Title Stripping, 'Lying Bully' Valentina Shevchenko." MMA Fighting, September 9, 2018. https://www.mmafighting.com/2018/9/9/17836892/nicco-montano-releases-statement-on-ufc-title-stripping-lying-bully-valentina-shevchenko.

———. 2019. "Max Holloway and Frankie Edgar Successfully Make Weight for UFC 240 Championship Main Event." MMA Fighting, July 26, 2019. https://www.mmafighting.com/2019/7/26/8931353/max-holloway-makes-weight-for-ufc-240-title-defense-vs-frankie-edgar.

Lieber, Chavie. 2018. "How and Why Do Influencers Make So Much Money? The Head of an Influencer Agency Explains." Vox, November 28, 2018. https://www.vox.com/the-goods/2018/11/28/18116875/influencer-marketing-social-media-engagement-instagram-youtube.

Littler, Jo. 2017. *Against Meritocracy: Culture, Power and Myths of Mobility.* New York: Routledge. https://www.oapen.org/download?type=document&docid=1004179.

Lole, Kevin. 2017. "Fox, FS1 Ratings Show that Women's Fights Are Exceptionally Popular with UFC Fans." Yahoo! Sports, January 27, 2017. https://sports.yahoo.com/news/fox-fs1-ratings-show-that-womens-fights-are-exceptionally-popular-with-ufc-fans-183134436.html.

Lotz, Amanda D. 2015. "Assembling a Toolkit." *Media Industries* 1 (3): 18–21.

Luther, Jessica. 2015. "Ronda Rousey: Pioneer, Megastar, Badass." Bleacher Report, July 29, 2015. https://bleacherreport.com/articles/2529961-ronda-rousey-pioneer-megastar-badass.

Macur, Juliet. 2014. "Coast Cleared by Others, W.N.B.A. Finally Finds Its Gay Pride." *New York Times*, June 11, 2014. https://www.nytimes.com/2014/06/11/sports/wnba-finally-advertises-its-gay-pride.html.

Maese, Rick. 2018. "NBA Twitter: A Sports Bar That Doesn't Close, Where the Stars Pull up a Seat Next to You." *Washington Post*, May 31, 2018. https://www.washingtonpost.com/news/sports/wp/2018/05/31/nba-twitter-a-sports-bar-that-doesnt-close-where-the-stars-pull-up-a-seat-next-to-you/.

Maese, Rick, and Scott Clement. 2017. "Before Mayweather-McGregor, Poll Shows MMA Isn't Stealing Boxing's Popularity." *Washington Post*, August 25, 2017. https://www.washingtonpost.com/sports/boxing/before-mayweather-mcgregor-poll-shows-mma-isnt-stealing-boxings-popularity/2017/08/25/f9b3f47a-892f-11e7-a50f-e0d4e6ec070a_story.html.

Main, Sami. 2017. "Micro-Influencers Are More Effective with Marketing Campaigns than Highly Popular Accounts." *Adweek*. https://www.adweek.com/digital/micro-influencers-are-more-effective-with-marketing-campaigns-than-highly-popular-accounts/.

Marrocco, Steven, MMA Junkie Staff, Matt Erickson, Farah Hannoun, John Morgan, and Blue Corner. 2011. "A Closer Look at the Benefits of UFC's New Accident-Insurance Policy for Fighters." *USA Today*, May 9, 2011. https://mmajunkie.usatoday

.com/2011/05/a-closer-look-at-the-benefits-of-ufcs-new-accident-insurance
-policy-for-fighters.

Martin, Damon. 2015a. "Ronda Rousey: 'I'm the Highest Paid Fighter in the UFC.'"
FOX Sports, September 14, 2015. https://www.foxsports.com/ufc/story/ufc-ronda
-rousey-ellen-degeneres-i-m-the-highest-paid-fighter-in-the-ufc-091415.

———. 2015b. "Revolution Will Be Televised: How the Rousey-Holm Promo Was Built
from Script to Screen." FOX Sports, November 9, 2015. http://www.foxsports.com/
ufc/story/ufc-ronda-rousey-holly-holm-promo-video-commercial-revolution
-neil-huxley-script-to-screen-110915.

———. 2016. "GSP, Cerrone and Others Take Aim at UFC with New Fighter's Association."
FOX Sports, November 30, 2016. https://www.foxsports.com/ufc/story/georges
-st-pierre-cowboy-cerrone-and-others-take-aim-at-ufc-with-new-fighters
-association-113016.

Mason, Corinne Lysandra. 2016. "Tinder and Humanitarian Hook-Ups: The Erotics
of Social Media Racism." *Feminist Media Studies* 16 (5): 822–37.

Mazique, Brian. 2017. "The UFC Needs to Make an Example of Colby Covington." *Forbes*,
November 20, 2017. https://www.forbes.com/sites/brianmazique/2017/11/20/the
-ufc-needs-to-make-an-example-of-colby-covington/.

McClearen, Jennifer. 2015a. "The Paradox of Fallon's Fight: Interlocking Discourses
of Sexism and Cissexism in Mixed Martial Arts Fighting." *New Formations* 86 (86):
74–88.

———. 2015b. "Unbelievable Bodies: Audience Readings of Action Heroines as a Post-
Feminist Visual Metaphor." *Continuum: Journal of Media & Cultural Studies* 29 (6):
833–46. https://doi.org/10.1080/10304312.2015.1073683.

———. 2017. "'We Are All Fighters': The Transmedia Marketing of Difference in the
Ultimate Fighting Championship (UFC)." *International Journal of Communication Systems* 11 (0): 18.

———. 2018. "Don't Be a Do-Nothing-Bitch: Popular Feminism and Women's Physical
Empowerment in the UFC." In *New Sporting Femininities: Embodied Politics in Postfeminist
Times*, 43–62. New York: Springer.

McNicholas, Celine, and Janelle Jones. 2018. "Black Women Will Be Most Affected by Ja-
nus." Economic Policy Institute, February 13, 2018. https://www.epi.org/publication/
black-women-will-be-most-affected-by-janus/.

McNicholas, Celine, and Margaret Poydock. 2019. "How California's AB5 Protects
Workers from Misclassification." Economic Policy Institute, November 19, 2019.
https://www.epi.org/publication/how-californias-ab5-protects-workers-from
-misclassification/.

McRobbie, Angela. 2009. *The Aftermath of Feminism: Gender, Culture and Social Change.*
Los Angeles: Sage.

Meltzer, Dave. 2015. "What the UFC Pay-per-View Turnaround Does and Doesn't
Mean for Popularity Overall." MMA Fighting, September 4, 2015. https://www

.mmafighting.com/2015/9/4/9163513/what-the-ufc-pay-per-view-turnaround-does
-and-doesnt-mean-for.

Mindenhall, Chuck. 2017. "Cat Zingano on 'Awkward' UFC Athlete Retreat: 'I Don't
Think They Considered Our Positions.'" MMA Fighting, May 27, 2017. https://www
.mmafighting.com/2017/5/27/15698148/cat-zingano-talks-awkward-ufc-fighter
-retreat-the-infamous-reebok-coupon-and-insulting-nature-of-it.

Modafferi, Roxanne. 2019. "I Just Realized I Have 50,000 Followers! Thank You so Much,
Everyone! I Don't Even Post Bikini Pictures. So Nice to Know 50K Ppl like My Heart
and Soul. ☺ Lol Nothing against Those Who Do, of Course! #bestfansever #happy
#HappyWarrior #thankful #nobikinipics #geek #nerd #otaku #bjj #anime #school-
teacher #ufc #mma." Instagram, September 2, 2019. https://www.instagram.com/p/
B155lXIgket/.

"Modelo Fighting Spirit Stories." N.d. Effie.org. Accessed September 19, 2019. https://
www.effie.org/case_database/case/NA_2018_E-2910–928.

"Modelo TV Commercial, 'Fighting to Uphold Heritage with Stipe Miocic.'" N.d. iSpot
.tv. Accessed September 20, 2019. https://www.ispot.tv/ad/d6Dx/modelo-fighting
-to-uphold-heritage-with-stipe-miocic.

Mukherjee, Roopali, and Sarah Banet-Weiser. 2012. *Commodity Activism: Cultural Resistance in Neoliberal Times*. New York: New York University Press.

Nash, John S. 2016. "Why Do Boxers Make More than MMA Fighters?" Bloody Elbow, August 23, 2016. https://www.bloodyelbow.com/2016/8/23/12512178/why-do
-boxers-make-more-than-mma-fighters.

Neff, Gina. 2012. *Venture Labor: Work and the Burden of Risk in Innovative Industries*. Cambridge, MA: Massachusetts Institute of Technology Press.

Negra, Diane, and Yvonne Tasker. 2014. *Gendering the Recession: Media and Culture in an
Age of Austerity*. Durham, NC: Duke University Press.

Neisser, Drew. 2012. "Want a Branding Challenge? Try Marketing an NFL Team." *Fast
Company*, July 23, 2012. https://www.fastcompany.com/1843230/want-branding
-challenge-try-marketing-nfl-team.

NFL Play Smart, Play Safe. N.d. "Overview of NFL Player Benefits." NFL Play Smart,
Play Safe. Accessed September 23, 2019. https://www.playsmartplaysafe.com/
resource/nfl-benefits/.

"Nicco Montaño Found Out on Instagram She Was Stripped of UFC Title." 2018. The
MMA Hour, MMA Fighting. YouTube, September 10, 2018. https://www.youtube
.com/watch?v=N4Cneob5dkQ.

Nishime, Leilani. 2014. *Undercover Asian: Multiracial Asian Americans in Visual Culture*.
Urbana: University of Illinois Press.

Nittle, Nadra. 2018. "The Serena Williams Catsuit Ban Shows that Tennis Can't Get Past
Its Elitist Roots." Vox, August 28, 2018. https://www.vox.com/2018/8/28/17791518/
serena-williams-catsuit-ban-french-open-tennis-racist-sexist-country-club
-sport.

Noll, Roger G. 2007. "Broadcasting and Team Sports." *Scottish Journal of Political Economy* 54 (3): 400–421.

Okamoto, Brett. 2016. "UFC Fighters Form Mixed Martial Arts Athletes Association." ABC7 San Francisco, December 1, 2016. https://abc7news.com/sports/ufc-fighters -form-mixed-martial-arts-athletes-association/1634278/.

Ortiz, Maria. 2013. "Social Media: Inside the UFC, Dana White." ESPN.com, March 1, 2013. https://www.espn.com/blog/playbook/trending/post/_/id/14717/social -media-inside-the-ufc-dana-white.

Osborne, Anne Cunningham, and Danielle Sarver Coombs. 2015. *Female Fans of the NFL: Taking Their Place in the Stands*. New York: Routledge.

Ouellette, Laurie. 2016. *Lifestyle TV*. New York: Routledge.

Papacharissi, Zizi. 2015. *Affective Publics: Sentiment, Technology, and Politics*. New York: Oxford University Press.

Papenfuss, Mary. 2018. "'Progressive' Nike and Workers Donated 3 Times More Money to GOP than Democrats." HuffPost, September 25, 2018. https://www.huffpost.com/ entry/nike-and-workers-donate-three-times-more-money-to-gop-than-dems_n _5ba999e1e4b0375f8f9fe4dd.

Perlman, Merrill. 2015. "Black and White: Why Capitalization Matters." *Columbia Journalism Review*, June 23, 2015. Accessed July 15, 2020. https://www.cjr.org/analysis/ language_corner_1.php.

Pew Research Center. 2018. "The Generation Gap in American Politics." Pew Research Center for the People and the Press, March 1, 2018. https://www.people-press.org/ 2018/03/01/the-generation-gap-in-american-politics/.

Pham, Minh-Ha T. 2015. *Asians Wear Clothes on the Internet: Race, Gender, and the Work of Personal Style Blogging*. Durham, NC: Duke University Press.

Pierik, Jon. 2017. "Women, Test Stars Big Winners in Cricket Australia Pay Offer." *Sydney Morning Herald*, March 21, 2017. https://www.smh.com.au/sport/cricket/women -test-stars-big-winners-in-cricket-australia-pay-offer-20170321-gv2sly.html.

Piligian, Craig, Frank Fertitta II, Lorenzo Fertitta, and Dana White. 2017. *The Ultimate Fighter: A New World Champion*. Season 26, episode 7, aired October 18, 2017, on Fox Sports 1.

Pitcher, Laura. 2019. "How Female Athletes Are Becoming Social Media's Newest 'Influencers.'" I-D, May 29, 2019. https://i-d.vice.com/en_us/article/a3xnkj/how -female-athletes-are-becoming-social-medias-newest-influencers.

"Project Spearhead Home." N.d. Project Spearhead. Accessed September 23, 2019. http://www.projectspearhead.com/.

Puar, Jasbir K. 2007. *Terrorist Assemblages: Homonationalism in Queer Times*. 1st ed. Durham, NC: Duke University Press.

——. 2013. "Rethinking Homonationalism." *International Journal of Middle East Studies* 45 (2): 336–39.

Raimondi, Marc. 2015. "Invicta Phenom Alexa Grasso Inspired by Ronda Rousey: 'I Want to Be Like Her.'" MMA Fighting, February 26, 2015. https://www.mmafighting

.com/2015/2/26/8112693/invicta-phenom-alexa-grasso-inspired-by-ronda-rousey
-i-want-to-be.

———. 2018. "Click Debate: 'Reebok Pay' Now a Thing of the Past, and Was Never
Really a Thing in the First Place." MMA Fighting, February 25, 2018. https://www
.mmafighting.com/2018/2/25/17049852/click-debate-reebok-pay-now-a-thing
-of-the-past-and-was-never-really-a-thing-in-the-first-place.

———. 2019. "UFC's New Exclusive Pay-per-View Deal with ESPN+, Explained." MMA
Fighting, March 19, 2019. https://www.mmafighting.com/2019/3/19/18272292/
ufcs-new-exclusive-pay-per-view-deal-with-espn-explained.

Reams, Lamar, and Stephen Shapiro. 2017. "Who's the Main Attraction? Star Power
as a Determinant of Ultimate Fighting Championship Pay-per-View Demand."
European Sport Management Quarterly 17 (2): 132–51.

Reid, Tony. 2017. "Q&A: Leslie Smith Fights to Promote Peace." Fighters Only, July
18, 2017. https://www.fightersonlymag.com/interviews/qa-leslie-smith-fights
-promote-peace/.

Reinsmith, Trent. 2018a. "With Dana White's Claim That the UFC Is Worth $7 Billion,
It's Time to Revisit Fighter Pay." *Forbes Magazine*, August 21, 2018. https://www.forbes
.com/sites/trentreinsmith/2018/08/21/with-dana-whites-claim-that-the-ufc-is
-worth-7-billion-its-time-to-revisit-fighter-pay/.

———. 2018b. "Nicco Montano Answers 'Lying Bully' Valentina Shevchenko After Being Stripped of Her UFC Title." *Forbes*, September 9, 2018. https://www.forbes.com/
sites/trentreinsmith/2018/09/09/nicco-montano-answers-lying-bully-valentina
-shevchenko-after-being-stripped-of-her-ufc-title/.

———. 2019a. "UFC on ESPN 1 Medical Suspensions: Paul Felder Out Indefinitely
with Collapsed Lung." *Forbes*, February 21, 2019. https://www.forbes.com/sites/
trentreinsmith/2019/02/20/ufc-on-espn-1-medical-suspensions-paul-felder-out
-indefinitely-with-collapsed-lung/.

———. 2019b. "UFC 235's Ben Askren on Reebok Outfitting Program Pay: 'It's Pretty
Terrible.'" *Forbes*, March 1, 2019. https://www.forbes.com/sites/trentreinsmith/
2019/03/01/ufc-235s-ben-askren-on-reebok-outfitting-program-pay-its-pretty
-terrible/.

Rentschler, Carrie A. 2017. "Affect." In *Keywords for Media Studies*, edited by Laurie
Ouellette and Jonathan Gray, 12–14. New York: New York University Press.

Rezende, Lucas. 2016. "Correia Details Online Harassment: 'Guys Send Me Videos
of Them Masturbating' to My Pictures." Bloody Elbow, July 6, 2016. https://www
.bloodyelbow.com/2016/7/6/12102566/bethe-correia-claudia-gadelha-constant
-online-sexual-harassment-ufc-news.

Ritzer, George, and Nathan Jurgenson. 2010. "Production, Consumption, Prosump-
tion: The Nature of Capitalism in the Age of the Digital 'Prosumer.'" *Journal of Consumer Culture* 10 (1): 13–36.

Roberts, Daniel. 2015. "Was Ronda Rousey's Loss Also a Loss for UFC?" *Fortune*, November 16, 2015. https://fortune.com/2015/11/16/ronda-rousey-loss-disaster-ufc/.

Rothstein, Mike. 2019. "How Colby Covington Became the UFC's Biggest Villain." ESPN.com, August 2, 2019. https://www.espn.com/mma/story/_/id/27295062/how-colby-covington-became-ufc-biggest-villain.

Rousey, Ronda, with Maria Burns Ortiz. 2015. *My Fight Your Fight: The Official Ronda Rousey Autobiography*. New York: Regan Arts.

Rovel, Darren, and Brett Okamoto. 2016. "Dana White on $4 Billion UFC Sale: 'Sport Is Going to the Next Level.'" ESPN.com, July 11, 2016. https://www.espn.com/mma/story/_/id/16970360/ufc-sold-unprecedented-4-billion-dana-white-confirms.

Runstedtler, Theresa. 2013. *Jack Johnson, Rebel Sojourner: Boxing in the Shadow of the Global Color Line*. Berkeley: University of California Press.

Sager, Jessica. 2019. "WWE Slams John Oliver for 'Last Week Tonight' Segment on Wrestlers' Health, Says He 'Ignored the Facts.'" Fox News, April 1, 2019. https://www.foxnews.com/entertainment/john-oliver-slams-wwe-for-allegedly-not-taking-care-of-wrestlers-health-on-last-week-tonight.

Salminen, Vincent. 2017. "UFC Fighters Are Taking a Beating Because They Are Misclassified as Independent Contractors. An Employee Classification Would Change the Fight Game for the UFC, Its Fighters, and MMA." *Pace Intellectual Property, Sports & Entertainment Law Forum* 7 (1).

Same, Jeffrey B. 2012. "Breaking the Chokehold: An Analysis of Potential Defenses against Coercive Contracts in Mixed Martial Arts." *Michigan State Law Review*, 1057 (3).

Sammons, Jeffrey T. 1990. *Beyond the Ring: The Role of Boxing in American Society*. Urbana: University of Illinois Press.

Sashittal, Hemant C., Monica Hodis, and Rajendran Sriramachandramurthy. 2015. "Entifying Your Brand among Twitter-Using Millennials." *Business Horizons* 58 (3): 325–33.

Schrager, P. 2012. "UFC Blazing a Social Media Trail." Fox Sports, August 2, 2012. https://www.foxsports.com/ufc/story/ufc-social-media-twitter-facebook-communicating-with-fans-dana-white-080212.

Schultz, Jaime. 2005. "Reading the Catsuit: Serena Williams and the Production of Blackness at the 2002 U.S. Open." *Journal of Sport and Social Issues* 29 (3): 338–57.

Scott, Patrick. 2017. "Revealed: The Full Extent of Elite Sport's Yawning Gender Pay Gap." *Daily Telegraph*, June 20, 2017. https://www.telegraph.co.uk/sport/2017/06/20/revealed-full-extent-elite-sports-yawning-gender-pay-gap/.

Segura, Melissa. 2013. "Melissa Segura: Invicta's Michelle Waterson Rediscovered Martial Arts in Thailand." *Sports Illustrated*, March 27, 2013. https://www.si.com/mma/2013/03/27/michelle-waterson-invicta.

"SheBelieves." N.d. US Soccer. Accessed July 14, 2020. https://www.ussoccer.com/shebelieves.

"SheBelieves Cup." N.d. US Soccer. Accessed July 14, 2020. https://www.ussoccer.com/shebelieves/cup.

Sheppard, Samantha N. 2018. "The Exception That Proves the Rule: Race, Place, and Meritocracy in Rand University." *Black Camera* 10 (1): 162–76.

Silva, Kristian. 2019. "Study Finds Female Athletes Cop Brunt of Online Abuse." New Daily, April 24, 2019. https://thenewdaily.com.au/sport/2019/04/24/female-athletes-online-abuse/.

Singer, Dan. 2017. "We Are Wrong about Millennial Sports Fans." McKinsey & Company, October 2, 2017. https://www.mckinsey.com/industries/technology-media-and-telecommunications/our-insights/we-are-wrong-about-millennial-sports-fans.

Smith, Christie, and Stephanie Turner. 2015. "The Radical Transformation of Diversity and Inclusion: The Millennial Influence." N.p.: Deloitte University and Billie Jean King Leadership Initiative. http://www.bjkli.org/wp-content/uploads/2015/05/report.pdf.

Smith, Katherine Taken. 2012. "Longitudinal Study of Digital Marketing Strategies Targeting Millennials." *Journal of Consumer Marketing* 29 (2). DOI: 10.1108/07363761211206339

Smith, Lauren Reichart, and Jimmy Sanderson. 2015. "I'm Going to Instagram It! An Analysis of Athlete Self-Presentation on Instagram." *Journal of Broadcasting & Electronic Media* 59 (2): 342–58. https://doi.org/10.1080/08838151.2015.1029125.

Smith, Valerie. 1998. *Not Just Race, Not Just Gender*. New York: Routledge.

Snel, Alan. 2013. "UFC Plots Aggressive Path to Expand Global Empire." *Las Vegas Review-Journal*, August 12, 2013. http://www.reviewjournal.com/sports/mma-ufc/ufc-plots-aggressive-path-expand-global-empire Accessed March 1, 2016.

Snowden, Jonathan. 2010. *Total MMA: Inside Ultimate Fighting*. Toronto: ECW Press.

———. 2013. "The Business of Fighting: A Look Inside the UFC's Top-Secret Fighter Contract." Bleacher Report, May 14, 2013. https://bleacherreport.com/articles/1516575-the-business-of-fighting-a-look-inside-the-ufcs-top-secret-fighter-contract.

Stainer, Jon, and Stephan Master. 2018. *Year in Sports Media Report: U.S. 2017*. Nielsen Sports. http://nielsensports.com/wp-content/uploads/2014/09/Nielsen-Year-in-Sports-Media-2017-2.pdf.

Stern, Mark Joseph. 2017. "Donald Trump's Union-Busting Appointees Just Incinerated Obama's Labor Legacy." Slate, December 19, 2017. https://slate.com/news-and-politics/2017/12/donald-trumps-union-busting-appointees-just-incinerated-obamas-labor-legacy.html.

Sykes, Heather. 2016. *The Sexual and Gender Politics of Sport Mega-Events: Roving Colonialism*. New York: Routledge.

Tainsky, Scott, Steven Salaga, and Carla Almeida Santos. 2013. "Determinants of Pay-Per-View Broadcast Viewership in Sports: The Case of the Ultimate Fighting Championship." *Journal of Sport Management* 27 (1): 43–58.

Thorpe, Holly, Kim Toffoletti, and Toni Bruce. 2017. "Sportswomen and Social Media: Bringing Third-Wave Feminism, Postfeminism, and Neoliberal Feminism Into Conversation." *Journal of Sport & Social Issues* 41 (5): 359–83.

Toffoletti, Kim. 2016. "Analyzing Media Representations of Sportswomen—Expanding the Conceptual Boundaries Using a Postfeminist Sensibility." *Sociology of Sport Journal* 33 (3): 199–207.

———. 2017. *Women Sport Fans: Identification, Participation, Representation.* New York: Routledge. https://doi.org/10.4324/9781315641690.

Toffoletti, Kim, and Holly Thorpe. 2018. "The Athletic Labor of Femininity: The Branding and Consumption of Global Celebrity Sportswomen on Instagram." *Journal of Consumer Culture* 18 (2): 298–316.

Torres, Aaron. 2016. "Dana White Discusses the Most Important Fight in UFC History." FOX Sports, July 8, 2016. http://www.foxsports.com/ufc/story/dana-white-ufc-200-preview-and-picks-jon-jones-most-important-fight-ufc-history-070816.

Trackalytics. N.d. "Missjessyjess" Trackalytics. Accessed September 11, 2019. https://www.trackalytics.com/instagram/profile/missjessyjess/.

Travers, Ann, and Mary Shearman. 2017. "The Sochi Olympics, Celebration Capitalism, and Homonationalist Pride." *Journal of Sport and Social Issues* 41 (1): 42–69. https://doi.org/10.1177/0193723516685273.

"Troll Watch: Online Harassment Toward Women" 2019. NPR, January 6, 2019. https://www.npr.org/2019/01/06/682714973/troll-watch-online-harassment-toward-women.

"2 UFC 127 Bouts on Facebook." 2011. UFC, February 22, 2011. Accessed July 14, 2020. https://www.ufc.com/news/2-ufc-127-bouts-facebook.

UFC. 2010. "Dana White Reaches 1 M Twitter Followers." UFC, February 11, 2010. https://www.ufc.com/news/dana-white-reaches-1-m-twitter-followers.

———. 2011a. "Introducing UFCLatino.com." UFC, April 25, 2011. https://us.ufcespanol.com/news/introducing-ufclatinocom.

———. 2011b. "UFC Names Twitter Bonus Winners." UFC, November 7, 2011. https://www.ufc.com/news/ufc-names-twitter-bonus-winners.

———. 2019. "UFC + Miracle Flights." UFC, February 20, 2019. https://ru.ufc.com/news/ufc-miracle-flights.

———. N.d. "About UFC." UFC. Accessed October 9, 2019. https://www.ufc.com/about.

"UFC 157 Countdown: Rousey vs. Carmouche." 2013. UFC Espanol. YouTube, February 20, 2013. https://www.youtube.com/watch?v=hTYB_-L8Xj8.

"UFC on Fox 8: Jessica Andrade Emerges." 2013. UFC. YouTube, July 26, 2013. https://www.youtube.com/watch?v=Xj0-1NtaeAw.

UFC Performance Institute. 2018. "A Cross-Sectional Performance Analysis and Projection of the UFC Athlete." http://media.ufc.tv/ufcpi/UFCPI_Book_2018.pdf.

"UFC President Dana White and Fighter Liz Carmouche." 2018. Larry King. YouTube, May 30, 2018. https://www.youtube.com/watch?v=U7OXtAxdJxE.

"UFC's White Says He's Sorry for Anti-Gay Slur." 2009. ESPN.com, April 3, 2009. https://www.espn.com/extra/mma/news/story?id=4038944.

"UFC 228: Nicco Montano—Fighting Spirit." 2018. UFC. YouTube, August 27, 2018. https://www.youtube.com/watch?v=Mhq4CVy6uH8.

UFC—Ultimate Fighting Championship. 2019. "Making of the Mom Champ—Michelle Waterson." YouTube, October 7, 2019. https://www.youtube.com/watch?v=rPHiTI-5H5Q.

"UFC Women's We Are All Fighters Tank." N.d. UFC Store. Accessed October 2, 2019. https://ufcstore.com/collections/we-are-all-fighters/products/ufcglt0063-ufc -womens-we-are-all-fighters-tank.

Vahey, David, Ian Bolyard, and John Vahey. 2012. "Fighting Politics." Fighting Politics. 2012. https://sellfy.com/p/OYbm/ (dead).

VanZant, Paige. 2019. "'To Be a Successful Person . . . '" Instagram, April 24, 2019. https://www.instagram.com/p/BwpQk54AyQW/.

Wallender, Andrew, and Hassan A. Kanu. 2019. "Trump's Labor Board Has Unions Shelving Complaints." Bloomberg Law, May 20, 2019. https://news.bloomberglaw .com/daily-labor-report/do-not-publish-trumps-labor-board-scaring-away-union -complaints-9–10.

Warner, Kristen. 2016. "Strategies for Success?: Navigating Hollywood's 'Postracial' Labor Practices." In Curtin and Sanson, *Precarious Creativity*, 172–84.

———. 2017. "In the Time of Plastic Representation." *Film Quarterly* 71 (2): 32–37.

Weaving, Charlene. 2014. "Cage Fighting Like a Girl: Exploring Gender Constructions in the Ultimate Fighting Championship (UFC)." *Journal of the Philosophy of Sport* 41 (1): 129–42.

———. 2015. "'Chicks Fighting in a Cage': A Philosophical Critique of Gender Con- structions in the Ultimate Fighting Championship." In *Global Perspectives on Women in Combat Sports: Women Warriors around the World*, edited by Alex Channon and Chris- topher R. Matthews, 57–72. New York: Palgrave Macmillan.

Weed, Julie. 2019. "These Apps Are an Uber Driver's Co-Pilot." *New York Times*, October 17, 2019. Accessed July 14, 2020. https://www.nytimes.com/2019/10/17/business/ apps-uber-lyft-drivers.html.

Wernick, Andrew. 1991. *Promotional Culture: Advertising, Ideology and Symbolic Expression*. Thousand Oaks, CA: Sage.

Wilks, Lauren. 2020. "The Serena Show: Mapping Tensions between Masculinized and Feminized Media Portrayals of Serena Williams and the Black Female Sporting Body." *Feminist Media Histories* 6 (3): 52-78.

Willis, George. 2008. "Diversity in the Cage." ESPN.com, December 26, 2008. https:// www.espn.com/extra/mma/news/story?id=3792904.

"WNBA and WNBPA Reach Tentative Agreement on Groundbreaking Eight-Year Collective Bargaining Agreement." 2020. WNBA.com, January 14, 2020. https:// www.wnba.com/news/wnba-and-wnbpa-reach-tentative-agreement-on-ground breaking-eight-year-collective-bargaining-agreement/.

Wood, Rachel, and Benjamin Litherland. 2018. "Critical Feminist Hope: The Encounter of Neoliberalism and Popular Feminism in WWE 24: Women's Evolution." *Feminist Media Studies* 18 (5): 905–22.

Woodward, Kath. 2006. *Boxing, Masculinity and Identity: The 'I' of the Tiger*. New York: Routledge.

Writers Guild of America West. 2019. "The Risks of Investing in Endeavor." Writers Guild of America West, July 25, 2019. https://www.wga.org/uploadedfiles/new s_and_events/press_room/2019/the_risks_of_investing_in_endeavor.pdf.

Young, Jared. 2019. "Breaking down the Actual Cost of Equal Pay for the US Women." Stars and Stripes FC, May 15, 2019. https://www.starsandstripesfc .com/2019/5/15/18564612/breaking-down-cost-equal-pay-ussf-women-uswnt.

Zeisler, Andi. 2016. *We Were Feminists Once: From Riot Grrrl to CoverGirl®, the Buying and Selling of a Political Movement*. New York: BBS and Public Affairs.

Zidan, Karim. 2019. "Islamophobia and the UFC: How Conor McGregor Uses Ethnic and Religious Tension to Sell Fights." Bloody Elbow, April 4, 2019. https://www .bloodyelbow.com/2019/4/4/18295311/islamophobia-ufc-conor-mcgregor-ethnic -religious-tension-fight-promotion-khabib-crime-mma.

——. 2020. "McGregor Madness: How the UFC PR Machine Protects Its Most Volatile Asset." Bloody Elbow, January 16, 2020. https://www.bloodyelbow.com/ 2020/1/16/21068608/conor-mcgregor-ufc-sexual-assault-allegations-crime-mma -feature-news.

Index

Endeavor, 21, 135, 150, 155–57, 176n10

ESPN, 5, 28, 37–38; ESPN+, 47, 178n2

ethnicity, 15, 62–65, 89, 92–93, 175–76n5. *See also* race

Evans-Smith, Ashlee, *2, 3*

Ewing, Eve, 175–76n5

Eye, Jessica, 97, 139

Facebook, 10–11, 29, 43, 45, 51, 128. *See also* social media; social media engagement

Felder, Paul, 152

female masculinity, 92, 94, 154, 179–80n2. *See also* femininity; masculinity

femininity, 28–29; athletic labor of, 115–16, 133; emphasized femininity, 17, 29, 74, 93, 115–17, 176n8; online harassment and, 128–32; racialized labor and, 117–22; White, 70, 72, 117, 127. *See also* masculinity

feminism, 30–31, 66, 179n5; popular, 67, 69, 71–74, 80–81, 94, 117; scholarship and, 3, 12, 15, 20, 34

Fertitta, Frank, 40, 41, 50, 103

Fertitta, Lorenzo, 40, 41, 50, 103, 149

fight cards, 1–2, 175n2; UFC 1, 4, 35, *36*, 38, 175n3; UFC 40, 41; UFC 157, *8*, *9*, 10–12, 60, 79; UFC 180, 139; UFC 184, *64*; UFC 189, 70; UFC 190, 57–58; UFC 194, 87; UFC 239, 22

fighters' associations, 136, 139, 140–41, 146. *See also* unionization efforts

fighter's mindset, 96–98, 99, 103

fight promotion: marketing, 42–43, 86, 98; organization, 21, 25, 176n11

financial model, 20–25. *See also* contract labor; labor; labor model; payout

financial transparency, 149–51, 166, 176n10

Fox, Fallon, 27, 177n16

Franklin, Rich, 52

Gadelha, Claudia, 75, *130*, 130, 177n13

gender discrimination, 18, 81; *Revolution* (promotional video), 69, 71, 73, 74; US-WNT lawsuit, 138–39

gender identity, 175n1. *See also* femininity; masculinity

gig economy, 22–25, 148, 155, 156, 181n6.

See also contract labor; financial model; labor practices

global audiences, 34, 36–38, 47–51, 53–54, 95

Golden State Warriors, 10

Gordeau, Gerard, 35, *36*

graduate student labor, 24

Grasso, Alexa, 78, *78*

Gray, Herman, 13–14, 19, 59

harassment, online, 128–36. *See also* bigotry; social media engagement

heel, 106, 113

Herrig, Felice, 87

heterosexiness, 95, 115, 116, 154. *See also* femininity, emphasized

Hill, Angela, *118*, 118–19, 125, 131; personal brand, 122–24, 127, 132

Hispanic identities, 48, 50, 88–89, 178n1 (ch2). *See also* Latinx identities

Holloway, Max, 101–2

Holm, Holly, 1, 22, 74, 81, 94; *Revolution* (promotional video), 29, 69–74, *72, 73*

homonationalism, 95. *See also* LGBTQ identities

homophobia, 14, 26–27, 31, 94. *See also* bigotry

Hook-n-Shoot, 5–6

hypermasculinity, 1, 4, 68, 70. *See also* femininity; masculinity

immigrants, 26, 89, 97. *See also* American dream

independent contractors. *See* contract labor

individualism, 89–90, 95–96, 159. *See also* contract labor

injuries, 97–101, 133, 152; brain injuries, 35, 151–52

Instagram, 38, 46, 48; femininity and, 115–117, 121, 154, 167; harassment and, 129; influencers, 124–28, 132; personal brands and, 122–24. *See also* social media; social media engagement

insurance, 23–25, 98, 111, 133–34, 151–52, 180n3

International Fight Week, 51, 64, 105

internationalization, 49; international audiences, 49–51; international events, 95

JENNIFER McCLEAREN is an assistant professor in the Department of Radio-Television-Film at the University of Texas at Austin.

STUDIES IN SPORTS MEDIA

The University of Illinois Press
is a founding member of the
Association of University Presses.

University of Illinois Press
1325 South Oak Street
Champaign, IL 61820-6903
www.press.uillinois.edu